MIDLIFE MYTHS

SAGE SOURCEBOOKS FOR THE HUMAN SERVICES SERIES

Series Editors: ARMAND LAUFFER and CHARLES GARVIN

A source is a starting point, a place of origin, information, or payoff. The volumes in this series reflect these themes. For readers they will serve as starting points for new programs, as the place of origin of advanced skills, or as a source for information that can be used in the pursuit of professional and organizational goals.

Sage Sourcebooks are written to provide multiple benefits for both professionals and advanced students. Authors and contributors are recognized authorities in their fields or at the cutting edge of new knowledge and technique. Sourcebooks deal with new and emerging practice tools and current and anticipated policy issues, transforming knowledge from allied professions and the social sciences into information applicable to the human services.

THE TRAPPED WOMAN: Catch-22 in Deviance and Control
edited by JOSEFINA FIGUEIRA-McDONOUGH & ROSEMARY SARRI

FAMILY THERAPY WITH ETHNIC MINORITIES
by MAN KEUNG HO

**WORKING IN SOCIAL WORK: Growing and Thriving in
Human Services Practice**
by ARMAND LAUFFER

**MIDLIFE MYTHS: Issues, Findings, and
Practice Implications**
edited by SKI HUNTER & MARTIN SUNDEL

MIDLIFE MYTHS
Issues, Findings, and Practice Implications

EDITED BY

Ski Hunter
Martin Sundel

SAGE SOURCEBOOKS FOR THE HUMAN SERVICES   7

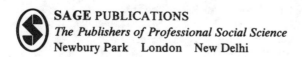

SAGE PUBLICATIONS
The Publishers of Professional Social Science
Newbury Park   London   New Delhi

To my close friends for the times of
intellectual and emotional challenge.

—S. H.

To Selma and Louis Kitzman,
whose friendship over the years
has enriched my life.

—M. S.

For information address:

SAGE Publications, Inc.
2111 West Hillcrest Drive
Newbury Park, California 91320

SAGE Publications Ltd.
28 Banner Street
London EC1Y 8QE
England

SAGE Publications India Pvt. Ltd.
M-32 Market
Greater Kailash I
New Delhi 110 048 India

Printed in the United States of America

Library of Congress Cataloging-in-Publication Data
Main entry under title:

Midlife myths: issues, findings, and practice implications / edited
     by Ski Hunter and Martin Sundel.
          p. cm.—(Sage sourcebooks for the human services series ;
     v. 7)
     Bibliography: p.
     ISBN 0-8039-2964-1. — ISBN 0-8039-2965-X (pbk.)
     1. Middle age—United States   I. Hunter, Ski.   II. Sundel,
Martin, 1940- .   III. Series.
HQ1059.5.U5M534 1989
305.2′44—dc19   88-37601
                                                        CIP

FIRST PRINTING 1989

Contents

Preface

Helping professionals concerned with people at all periods of life are looking for accurate and useful knowledge about the life course to use in their practice. This book attempts to fill in the knowledge gap about midlife and draw implications for practice. A number of widely held beliefs about midlife are examined in the context of research findings that demythologize, dispel, or challenge them with alternative perspectives. Together, these beliefs constitute what we call the midlife mythology.

This book is directed to a wide audience of both graduate and undergraduate students in the social and behavioral sciences. The content is relevant to both beginning and experienced social workers, psychologists, psychiatrists, family doctors, and other physicians, nurses, marriage and family counselors and therapists, pastoral counselors, and employment and vocational counselors. We will often refer to this audience collectively throughout the volume as "helping professionals" or "professional helpers" and in some places we will use the term *counselors and therapists* to include the full range of personnel functioning in those roles. Individuals in the "general public" either approaching or already at middle age are also likely to be interested in the book.

To obtain contributors to this volume we identified researchers and scholars who were on the forefront of adding to or revising the knowledge about midlife. We asked them to present research evidence, wherever possible, that could demythologize or dispel erroneous beliefs surrounding their topics.

We were saddened that Dr. Nancy Datan was unable to complete her chapter for the volume because of her untimely death. She was a pioneer in the study of midlife and encouraged us to pursue our goals for the book.

Terry Hendrix, our editor at Sage, believed in this book from the outset and provided many helpful suggestions. Charles Garvin, coeditor of the Sage Sourcebooks in the Human Services, also provided support. Special thanks go to Sandra Stone Sundel for her review of the entire manuscript and helpful comments. We are also grateful to Joy Crow, who typed numerous versions of the manuscript in her typically enthusiastic and competent manner.

—*Ski Hunter*
—*Martin Sundel*
Arlington, Texas

7

Introduction:
An Examination of
Key Issues Concerning Midlife

Ski Hunter
Martin Sundel

Research on the midlife period is only about 15 years old. Social workers, psychologists, and other helping professionals have attempted to access this literature to serve their clients better. What they often discover, however, are contradictory findings, which makes it difficult, if not impossible, to apply such knowledge clearly or confidently in service provision.

This introduction provides an overview of the volume and identifies several of the important contradictions in the midlife literature. The major emphasis of the book is positive and challenges some of the most prevalent negative images of midlife in American society. We recognize that in reality there is a mixture of both positive and negative events associated with midlife. Our emphasis on positive findings, however, is intended to dissuade the helping person from stereotyping midlife clients or arriving at limiting, self-fulfilling prophecies, and to promote a more accurate and fuller realization of the potential at midlife for change and personal growth.

This chapter will discuss definitions of the boundaries of midlife; research status of the adult development field, including midlife; the midlife crisis image and counterimages; and the concept of midlife mythology. An overview of the book also will be given.

Midlife Entrance and Exit

During the twentieth century, life expectancy, or the average number of years one is likely to live, has dramatically increased. In 1900 it was around 50 years for both males and females. By 1980 it increased to around 70 years for males and 78 years for females (Riley, 1984). As the stretch of time between birth and death increased, so did the division of the life course into more stages.

The midlife period is a contemporary development, due in large part to increased life expectancy. Another major change that led to the inclusion of a midlife period in the life course was the "empty nest" or the time after one's children leave home. "The average couple," according to Schaie and Willis (1986, p. 256), "can now expect to live almost twenty years alone after the last child has left home." Because of the gender difference in life expectancy, women are likely to have more postparental years of life than are men (Block, Davidson, & Grambs, 1981).

Midlife, then, is viewed as a typical stage most people will experience. So, when does it start and end? This is not an easy question to answer because of shifting perceptions.

Researchers and scholars tend to use chronological age boundaries for life stages, those for midlife often following Levinson's (1978) designated midlife era from 35-40 to 60-65. But chronological age as a definer of developmental periods has limitations. For example, chronological markers of middle age change as people live longer. Remember when reaching 30 signified being "over the hill" or not being young any more? This age-related perception of reaching midlife is already outdated because, as the life course lengthens, the perceived time of movement from youth to the middle of life advances.

Although midlife is often viewed as if it begins at some certain chronological age, there actually is no agreement about the exact age at which it begins. It varies: 30, 40, 50, or 60 (Schlossberg, 1986). There are individuals in their thirties, for example, who do not think they have begun midlife because they are in school or have not yet married, had any children, or bought a house, and so on. Other reasons may be job change or retraining, or separation or divorce (Brooks-Gunn & Kirsh, 1984). In terms of even later ages, as posed by Fiske (1979, p. 23): "Does a 45 or 50-year-old man who marries a 30-year-old and starts a family (or a new family) think of himself as middle aged?" A woman may also postpone "being at midlife" if she still has children and/or adolescents at home in her forties and fifties (Brooks-Gunn & Kirsh, 1984).

Perhaps many adults do not view the idea of life stages, especially as connected to specific chronological ages, to be pertinent to them (Fiske, 1979, 1980). Fiske (1979, p. 23) proclaimed that "middle age is a state of mind." It is more that than a fixed number of years. Instead of a chronological definition of middle age, Cohler and Boxer (1984, p. 149) "focused on the middle adult years as those during which individuals create highly complex and demanding role portfolios when compared to other points in the life cycle."

In addition to increased life expectancy and the fuzziness of chronological age numbers, other factors influence the varied perceptions of when one is middle-aged. As summarized by Clausen (1986, p. 152): "How one views oneself will depend on social-class background, on the degree to which physical strength and appearance are highly valued attributes, on actual physical condition and health, and on one's future prospects as compared with one's past accomplishments." Working-class men, for example, who are likely to value physical strength and vigor, tend to see middle age as beginning at 35 and old age at 60, whereas middle-class individuals tend to see middle age beginning at 45 and old age at 70 (Neugarten, 1968a). There are also cultural differences in health status and longevity that are likely to influence perception of an earlier beginning of midlife. According to Spurlock (1984), Black women, for example, are likely to age more quickly due to disproportionate poverty and poor health and poor nutrition. On the other hand, the health of middle-class women is generally good. If the physical aches and pains associated with midlife do not fit one's experience, one may not think one has reached midlife yet (Brooks-Gunn & Kirsh, 1984). In terms of appearance, both men and women view women as being middle-aged earlier than men. For example, gray hair for women is considered a sign of aging but for men it is distinguished (Schlossberg, 1986).

Individuals generally feel ambivalent about any perceived movement away from youth. The adult world "is often seen as equivalent to the end of exploration and growth" and "as muted rather than vivid, dead rather than passionate and alive" (Brooks-Gunn & Kirsh, 1984, p. 27). Consequently, even the perception "not yet old but not young either" is not easily welcomed. On the other hand, middle age is preferable to old age because of the anticipation of even greater negative attributes. So, the exit of midlife is pushed upward. A study that included middle-class males over 80 found that about half thought of themselves as old; however, the others still saw themselves as middle-aged (Eisdorfer & Lawton, 1973). Unless one is senile, incompetent, or physically debilitated, one is not likely to perceive oneself as old (Brooks-Gunn & Kirsh, 1984).

There appear to be few, if any, general patterns in midlife. As Brim and Kagan (1980, p. 13) stated: "Persons of the same age, particularly beyond adolescence, and the same historical period are undergoing different changes; one person may show an increase in certain attributes while another shows a decline in the same aspects of behavior and personality." According to Butler (1974), chronological definitions of adult life periods result in the myth of chronological aging. A more realistic view is that the rates of aging regardless of area—physiological, psychological, social—vary greatly from one person to another and within the same person. It is not surprising, then, that the life events associated with midlife are variable, lack cohesion, and are not readily predictable. Not all individuals experience them. Individuals who do, experience them at different times or in a different sequence. Midlife is not a well-defined phase of life. Instead, it is ambiguous (Brooks-Gunn & Kirsh, 1984).

The field of study known as life-span developmental psychology accepts the ambiguity of midlife boundaries by stressing the multidimensional and multidirectional nature of change (Brim & Kagan, 1980). Accordingly, the boundaries of any life phase may be more fluid than rigid. Whether a social definition or one proposed by scientists, the age boundaries of midlife are no more set in concrete than they are for other life periods such as "old age." Consequently, no one can be easily classified in a life phase category. Although the boundaries for midlife might be fixed in people's minds, in reality they are fluid (Brooks-Gunn & Kirsh, 1984).

There are variations, then, in the perceived age boundaries of midlife, as well as how old or young any particular individual feels at different ages or is perceived to be by others. In this book, we use Levinson's (1978) estimates of the beginning and end of midlife: 40 to 60 with 5 years before and after as transition or entrance-exit periods. It is only an estimate, though. As suggested above, age alone is often not a precise indicator of life period status. There is also a difference between those who study the period versus those who experience it, or scientific versus subjective definitions. And there are different views among the individuals within each group. This volume will reflect to some extent the ambiguity of age boundaries regarding midlife.

Research Status

As suggested in Schaie and Willis's (1986) review of the research status of the adult development field, it is a relatively new area of investigation and research studies are few. In the studies that exist, there are problems with research design, nonrepresentative samples, and ambiguous measurement instruments. It is uncertain, then, what beliefs about adult development, including midlife, are correct.

Several key reasons for the relatively recent investigation of adult development include popular interest in various major life transitions such as getting married or "turning 40." Also, research participants who were children in longitudinal studies initiated in the 1920s and 1930s became adults by the 1940s and 1950s. Prominent among such investigations were the Berkeley Growth and Guidance studies (Eichorn, Clausen, Haan, Honzik, & Mussen, 1981). As pointed out by Schaie and Willis (1986), much of what we know about adult development comes from these longitudinal studies that attempt to tie events in adulthood to childhood experiences. These studies provide more meaningful data than the more common type of study—cross-sectional—which compares different age groups. In cross-sectional studies age differences between persons at midlife and at young adulthood, for example, may often result from generational differences between cohorts rather than individual development. Schaie and Willis (1986) cautioned, however, that the older longitudinal studies are also not satisfactory because they were designed to study children, not adults. Better alternatives are longitudinal studies that specifically focus on adults and their diverse social contexts, across and within groups.

As we have already seen, among other things, one's particular social contexts (for example, gender, social class, nutrition, health care, beliefs, goals, and social values) strongly influence one's perceptions as young, middle-aged, or old. According to Brandtstädter (1984), the social context is powerful because it shapes one's beliefs about aging and one's appraisal of life events. Dannefer (1984, p. 106) criticized the major models used in adult development research—stage theory, life-span developmental psychology, and dialectical life-span psychology—because they ignore "the pervasive impact of social structure as an organizer of development." As an alternative, he (1984, p. 106) proposed sociological research and theory because they provide "the basis for understanding human development as socially organized and socially produced, not only by what happens in early life but also by the effects of social structure, social interaction, and their effects on life chances throughout the life course." Even in this approach, however, generalizations about individual development will be limited to individuals with specific characteristics in a specific historical period (Clausen, 1986).

As indicated, studies of the midlife period reflect the research limitations of the adult field as a whole. As a result there are variable images of midlife. Perhaps the most notable inconsistency is reflected in the crisis versus no-crisis debate.

The Crisis Image of
Midlife and Counterimages

Positive and Negative
Images of Midlife

Conflicting images about midlife abound. We hear that it is the peak period of life. People at this stage are seen as wise and powerful—in charge of themselves and others (Neugarten, 1968b; Schlossberg, 1986; Tamir, 1982). They have "a sense of competence, self-confidence, and purpose" (Sze & Ivker, 1987, p. 82). On the other hand, a typical assumption is that "life after forty" starts a downhill slide in energy, attractiveness, occupational performance, and happiness at home (Clausen, 1986; Schlossberg, 1986). Men are often depicted as "bored with their jobs, their wives, their lives" (Schlossberg, 1986, p. 240). It is supposed that they find true happiness by leaving spouses and having face lifts—"designed to reinvigorate them after their apparent midlife crisis" (Schlossberg, 1986, p. 240).

Midlife men, then, are thought to be anxious, conflicted, and going through a crisis. The women are menopausal, fretful, and depressed (Katchadourian, 1987). The culprit of the negative psychological reactions is seen to be signs of aging or losing youth (e.g., menopause, hair loss, slowing of reaction time, a fortieth or fiftieth birthday) (Schaie & Willis, 1986). The strongest cues that affect how old one feels are most likely changes in health and appearance (Troll, 1985).

The idea that the central theme of midlife is crisis often appears in the popular press and media (Chew, 1976; Conway, 1980; Nichols, 1986; Sheehy, 1976). It also appears in the scientific literature, but the crisis image is only one model used to conceptualize development at midlife. A competing model is based on a transition image (Schaie & Willis, 1986). There is a debate in the social sciences regarding which model best describes and explains the developmental changes that occur during midlife. The crisis model assumes that normative developmental changes, including a crisis at midlife, occur within the individual at certain ages. The alternative conceptualization, or transition model, rejects the notion that a midlife crisis or any other crisis is a normative developmental event. Still, in the popular press, media, and some of the scientific literature, the crisis model appears to dominate (Schaie & Willis, 1986).

Crisis View

As described by Schaie and Willis (1986), the crisis model proposes that development for everyone moves through the same series of stages. Each individual experiences a particular type of crisis at each stage of development in a particular chronological age range. In order to advance successfully to the next stage, the crisis accompanying the current stage must be resolved (e.g., Erikson, 1963, 1968). Another implicit assumption of the crisis model is that the crisis results in significant changes in one's self-perception, life-style, or both (Schaie & Willis, 1986).

In the mid-1960s, the experience of a midlife crisis was noted in an article by Jaques (1965) on the career crises of artists. In almost every case at around age 35, he found some kind of dramatic change. In many instances the period of crisis was associated with realization of personal mortality or time left to live, rather than time since birth.

In the early 1970s, three studies described the existence of regular stages of development in adulthood, including the midlife crisis (Gould, 1978; Levinson, 1978; Vaillant, 1977). In these studies, the term *midlife crisis* was used to describe "radical changes within personality associated with the adult's reexamination of goals, priorities, and life accomplishment as the midpoint of life was passed" (Whitbourne, 1986a, p. 229). A heightened sense of aging and of time running out was common. Intensive interviews with selected and primarily male samples of adults indicated that turmoil and depression occurred during the early forties. Levinson (1978, p. 60), for example, stated that "for the great majority of men this is a period of great struggle within the self and with the external world. Their Mid-life Transition is a time of moderate or severe crisis." More recent studies of women, following the biographical interviewing methods of Levinson, suggested a progression of developmental periods similar to men's although women's dreams were more complex and difficult to achieve. Also, it was around age 30 that their lives were most likely to be characterized by emotional crisis, centered on reappraisal of their commitments to career and marriage (Adams, 1983; Droege, 1982; Furst, 1983; Roberts & Newton, 1987; Stewart, 1977).

Limits of the Crisis View

Research methods. Several limitations of the methods used in the research based on the crisis model stand out. According to Schaie and Willis (1986), two major problems in midlife crisis research are the almost total use of interview data and the use of cross-sectional design. Also, the interview data have rarely been quantified or cross-validated through standardized instruments. And, as indicated by Schaie and Willis (1986, p. 265), without longitudinal studies there are serious limitations. They stated: "It is not possible . . . to compare functioning in early or later adulthood with functioning in midlife, and determine whether midlife is indeed marked by a period of greater instability." The confounding of age and cohort raises interpretive problems as to whether patterns of change are individual maturational processes or socially produced (Dannefer, 1984).

Populations. There are issues regarding the representativeness of samples that raise questions about generalizing the findings of research studies to the adult population. For example, White, middle-class subjects are over-represented. Many of the study samples providing research findings about adults, therefore, may be representative of the White middle-class but not of the adult population in general. Similarly, some studies used "clinical" rather than "normal" samples so that resultant findings also might not be applicable to the adult population at large.

Gender is another important issue. Men are much more frequently studied than women. In fact, the debate about the midlife crisis is concerned almost entirely with middle-class males (Bray & Howard, 1983; Levinson, 1978).

As Baruch and Brooks-Gunn (1984) discussed, the male bias overemphasizes negative images about midlife that may not apply to most women. The relevance of male themes such as "anguish over mortality and over the inadequacy of one's achievements" has been questioned (Baruch & Brooks-Gunn, 1984, p. 6). Because of the difference in life expectancy between males and females (almost eight years less for males when comparing males to females of the same age), males may feel closer to death.

When women are studied, attention is often given to menopause and "the empty nest." It is supposed that these events in particular cause distress for women at midlife. For the majority of women, however, the evidence does not support this view (Lowenthal & Chiriboga, 1972; Neugarten, Wood, Kraines, & Loomis, 1968; Newman, 1982; Reinke, Ellicott, Harris, & Hancock, 1985). Instead, most women look forward to both events.

Increased attention to women will not necessarily lead to bipolar distinctions from men. As posed by Ryff (1985, p. 106), a more precise question might be: "Which parts of what theories are or are not appropriate for men and for women?" In a study of adult identity, Whitbourne (1986b, p. 12) found no "fundamental split between men and women in their orientation to self and life."

Another problem concerning populations is that, as indicated earlier, much of the research is based on the same birth cohort—individuals born at similar times. This raises questions about the generalizability of findings to other generations. As indicated by Schaie and Willis (1986, p. 264), "To the extent that the problems of midlife are related to specific societal and historical trends and events, we may expect that midlife may be experienced qualitatively differently by various generations."

Crises may be coincidental to birth cohort (Baruch, 1984). As Glenn (1975) pointed out in his study of the impact of the Great Depression, for example, men born in the 1920s and 1930s were socialized to be achievers and breadwinners. In their forties (during the 1960s and 1970s), they may have assessed the costs of their progress. Women of that era found themselves increasingly free of child-rearing responsibilities as they neared 40 and may have also seemed in crisis about what to do with approximately half of their life still left. More young women have careers now, however, and will continue them through their child-rearing years. At midlife, they are unlikely to experience the same issues as the Great Depression cohort.

Empirical and epidemiological challenges. An increasing body of empirical and epidemiological data challenge the idea of a crisis as typical at midlife. Some of the empirical challenges are found within the crisis-model studies themselves. Levinson (1978), for example, identified five patterns of development in the midlife transition; however, only two suggested a possible midlife crisis. These included serious failure or decline within a stable life structure and breaking out of a current life structure (Whitbourne, 1986a).

There are also other types of empirical challenges. The Berkeley longitudinal data described personality development from early adolescence to middle adulthood. No midlife crisis was found (Haan, 1981). In addition, direct attempts have been made to identify a crisis at the midlife transition period identified by Levinson (age 40 to 45). In a sample of 60 adult women, however, no midlife crisis in the early forties was discovered (Reinke, Holmes, & Harris, 1985). In another study, no age-related progression of Levinson's stages was found (Rush, Peacock, & Milkovich, 1980).

McCrae and Costa (1984) developed the Midlife Crisis Scale, which was based on Gould's (1978) work. The scale included issues related to the concerns of men that Gould and others claimed were pertinent at midlife. Examples of items were "sense of meaninglessness, dissatisfaction with job and family, inner turmoil and confusion, and sense of impending physical decline and death" (McCrae & Costa, 1984, pp. 103-104). Subjects were grouped as midlife, premidlife, and postmidlife. Both in this study and a later one using a shortened version of the Midlife Crisis Scale, there was no peak of distress found in any of the groups. Only a few men appeared to be in a crisis and they did not cluster at a certain age. A concurring result showed up in Farrell and Rosenberg's (1981) sample of men. Using a similar midlife crisis scale, they also found no differences among age groups. Although many of the men had difficulties in their lives, they were not heavily concentrated in a particular period of life.

Based on a large national survey of adults, Pearlin (1975) did not find a "piling up" of transitions, crises, depression, or anxiety at midlife. In fact, it was young adults, not middle-aged or other age groups, who experienced more change in a concentrated period of time. As young adults are moving away from their parents, they are developing careers, intimate relationships, families, and so on. As reported by Veroff and Feld (1970), the middle-aged considered their early adulthood to be the time of greatest emotional difficulty. These empirical studies, then, showed no support for the midlife crisis model.

Epidemiologists have also found little support for midlife being a time of excessive negative events such as career disillusionment leading to career change, diminished sexuality, divorce, death anxiety, alcoholism, neuroticism, depression, or suicide. In fact, it is often during other periods of life when these events peak, if ever.

A midlife crisis is generally assumed to include an abrupt and drastic *career change* (Schaie & Willis, 1986). It is supposed that this is due to *disillusionment over not attaining prior career aspirations*. No general midlife transition has been found, however, in terms of occupational change. In a study of midcareer change, Vaitenas and Weiner (1977) found no relationship between age and career change. In fact, people change occupations with decreasing frequency in the later years (Gottfredson, 1976).

But, do middle-aged adults still have problems with the contrast between their earlier career aspirations and current reality? The research, including intensive studies of men in middle-management jobs and studies of larger cross sections of middle-aged workers, suggests that this conceptualization fits for only a small minority of men (Bray & Howard, 1980; Sofer, 1970). The emerging picture is more one of realistic assessments of efforts, gains, and costs. Compared with those who have achieved top mobility, those who are less successful do not appear to be less happy or well adjusted. One's reflections may more often be on what has been accomplished versus what has not. Also, people constantly compare themselves with others and thereby evaluate their performances. They periodically readjust their goals rather than wait until the launch of midlife to do so (Clausen, 1986). During later midlife, most men look forward to retirement. Neither anticipation of retirement nor its actual occurrence generally result in significant dissatisfaction. The exception is unexpected retirement (Atchley, 1976).

Women currently at midlife often move from not working to entering or reentering the job market. Many begin working because of divorce or as children are leaving home. This is often a period of excitement and challenge for women. They have the opportunity to focus on their own development outside of the home (Schaie & Willis, 1986).

For most individuals there is also no predicted period of crisis or despair during midlife regarding diminished *sexual activity*. Any changes are gradual and there is individual variation in their timing (Clausen, 1986; Newman, 1982). Also regarding couples, *divorce* does not peak at midlife (England & Kunz, 1975; National Center for Health Statistics, 1984, table 2.12).

What about *death anxiety*? Because more than one-half of normal life expectancy is over by age 40, some writers emphasize awareness of mortality and of future personal death as provoking a crisis. Jaques (1965, p. 506), a psychiatrist, suggested that this awareness is "the central and crucial feature of the midlife phase." In contrast to such clinical reports, however, there is no strong evidence that fear of death is an issue at midlife resulting in a crisis. Riegel (1975) believed that middle-aged adults should be able to face the inevitability of death. On the other hand, most midlife individuals probably are aware that the amount of time left to live and to accomplish their goals is limited. As stated by Clausen (1986, p. 153), "A major illness or the death of a friend brings stark awareness that one's time of accomplishment and enjoyment may be limited."

What about *psychiatric disorders*? Claims that neuroticism, alcoholism, depression, suicide, and admissions to psychiatric hospitals result from a midlife crisis are refuted through epidemiological data. The data do not support age-specific peaks in those areas. For example, personality characteristics such as *neuroticism* are stable over much of the life course and do not surge at midlife (McCrae & Costa, 1983). Farrell and Rosenberg (1981) studied 500 men at midlife. Only a minority appeared to have a crisis, the roots of which appeared to be neurotic conflicts and problems experienced earlier in their lives.

Costa and McCrae (1978) predicted that if one is high in neurotic traits, especially anxiety and depression, one might experience midlife as a crisis. But events later in life such as poor health (Costa & McCrae, 1980) and retirement will also be frustrating and disappointing. In old age, these individuals are at risk for depression and despair as Erikson (1963) predicted (Costa & McCrae, 1984).

Middle-aged *alcoholics* are represented in mental hospitals, but most of them were drinking heavily in their early adult years or even in their high school years (Jones, 1981). Kramer and Redick (cited in Brim, 1977) found no notable clustering of alcoholism in males during midlife. *Depression* peaks among women prior to age 35, but among men, between 55 to 70 (Weissman & Myers, 1978). More *suicide* occurs among the young and elderly than at midlife (Kramer, Taube, & Redick, 1973). *Admissions to psychiatric hospitals* do not peak at age 40 (Kramer, Taube, & Redick, 1973).

According to Clausen (1986, p. 162), "If we are to talk of a midlife crisis, there should be some typical events that precipitate a crisis at a particular age or time, or some criteria that permit us to say that the crisis exists." Following this definition, although some men and women probably do experience a crisis in their middle years, most do not appear to do so.

Transition or No-Crisis View

According to the transition model, one's whole life course, for the most part, is predictable, anticipated, and orderly. Most major life events are expected according to a timetable largely linked to age such as when one is to marry, raise children, and retire. Transitions, then, are typical situations that are likely to confront most people. During the period of the transition, the individual goes through various psychological and social adaptations (Berardo, 1982).

Anticipated life events can be prepared for and are likely to be less stressful than those that are unanticipated or occur off-time. As one approaches midlife, events such as career-advancement peaks can be anticipated, prepared for, and even looked forward to, as opposed to causing a crisis. "Anticipatory socialization" for expected life events at midlife usually prevents distress of crisis proportions (Troll, 1985). Individuals are not likely to wait "for age 40" to consider the adaptations called for at the middle period (Clausen, 1986).

The transition model may be more generally applicable at midlife than the crisis model. Studies directly supporting this view include those that attempted to find crisis as predicted by Levinson and Gould, but did not (McCrae & Costa, 1984; Reinke, Holmes, & Harris, 1985; Rush, Peacock, & Milkovich, 1980), and those that did not find particular life events (for example, menopause) to be associated with trauma or crisis (Neugarten et al., 1968).

A midlife crisis, according to the transition view, is not a "normal" experience. Instead, it may be more of a socially constructed experience or a self-fulfilling prophecy supported by cultural attention particularly to the "male midlife crisis," and reinforced by "science," "media attention," and professional helpers. What appears to have cultural objectivity is a social construction (Dannefer, 1984; Kearl & Hoag, 1984).

Revised Research Approaches Needed for Crisis and No-Crisis Models

Schaie and Willis (1986) pointed out the disparities and commonalities that exist between the methods of research used for the crisis and transition models. Disparities include the heavy, although not total, reliance on clinical populations for the crisis model versus the use of nonclinical populations for the transition model. Types of measures have also varied with interview data being the primary measure used in the crisis model. Interviewers may look for "inner turmoil" and, therefore, find it. In addition to interviews, the transition model uses projective techniques and self-reports or self-ratings of life satisfaction and happiness. Commonalities of research methods of the two models include two major limitations: the overrepresentation of White, middle-class male samples and the lack of longitudinal studies. Future research, therefore, requires revision in design, samples, and data collection methods.

Conclusions

Discussions of the middle years are often gloomy. A typical focus is a growing emotional (versus intellectual) awareness of mortality and limited possibilities for achieving one's goals. As Clausen (1986, p. 161) stated: "Middle age is a period in which some hopes are blighted, some opportunities are seen as forever lost." Nevertheless, most people will not experience a crisis at midlife. A persuasive body of evidence directly challenges the midlife crisis theory. Instead, midlife for most people is likely to be a relatively calm transition. There may be reevaluation of one's accomplishments and disappointments, but this will not result in a tumult of crisis proportions. This is not to say that no one experiences a crisis at midlife.

Some individuals apparently do, but they are exceptions and are as likely to experience crisis during other life transitions (McCrae & Costa, 1984).

Individual differences in personality and coping skills are important in terms of experiencing a life transition as a positive challenge or a reason for despair. As suggested by Stevens-Long (1988, p. 242), "Not the events of midlife themselves, or age alone, or timing, can explain individual responses to the challenge of middle age. Rather, it is the perception of those events . . . that is central."

Midlife is likely to pose a variety of challenges just as other life periods do and there will also be varied resolutions (Giele, 1982). In addition, not all of the challenges will be posed to every individual at midlife, or in the same way. As viewed by Mailick (1987, p. 18), "Some challenges may have been encountered and resolved in an earlier period of life while others may wait until a later period, or not occur at all."

The popular crisis image of midlife appears to be erroneous. Along with other misconceptions of midlife, it is a myth. Myths are dangerous when they result in oversimplified stereotypes that influence personal perceptions, social interactions, and social policy (Schaie & Willis, 1986). In the human services, myths can be detrimental to the design, development, and provision of care for individuals and groups. Misinformed members of the helping professions can be guided, for example, by myths that do not apply but could be detrimental to their middle-aged clients.

Myths can be refuted or qualified with contradictory evidence based on objective sources or scientific methods. The dispelling of myths is a major purpose of science (Schaie & Willis, 1986). The chapters in this book challenge the accuracy and legitimacy of various myths about midlife. Most of the chapters are based on empirical investigations. Several are theoretical in addressing midlife stereotypes.

Our goal is to move from narrow conceptions of midlife to an enlarged view. The emerging empirical understanding of midlife is less stereotypic and less gloomy than the once-accepted view that reaching this period of life meant that "the good life" was over. In this volume, we hope to add to a more balanced view of midlife that recognizes the potential for continued growth and satisfaction.

Overview of the Volume

Five prominent areas of midlife are identified in this volume that are associated with negative images. They include (a) physical status, (b) cogni-

tive structures and intelligence, (c) mental health and personality development, (d) the social context of marriage and the family, and (e) personal
development and social responsibility. Highlights of the chapters and their
myth-dispelling focuses will be presented.

Part I: Physical Status

The first two chapters in this section are related to physical status. In
Chapter 1, Weg presents evidence on continued sexual desire, capacity, and
pleasure in midlife to counter the myth of decline in these areas. She uses the
term *sensuality/sexuality* to signify a broader concept of sexuality than is
usually considered and shows its usefulness in enhancing sexual pleasure at
midlife. In Chapter 2, Dan and Bernhard present research findings suggesting that, contrary to popular belief, menopause is not viewed by women as a
significant factor in their well-being at midlife. In fact, women who have
experienced menopause evaluate it much more positively than either
premenopausal women or men. The authors also discuss other health issues
related to women at midlife. Ways to manage menopause and the other
health issues are identified.

Part II: Cognitive Structures

In Chapter 3, Labouvie-Vief and Hakim-Larson identify two modes of
cognitive thought: child-centered and adult-centered. Recent research by the
authors and others shows that the child-centered mode is inappropriate for
evaluating adult cognitive competency. The adult-centered mode is often
more adaptive to everyday life. An integration of the two modes of thought
can occur and result in an optimally mature level of thought.

In Chapter 4, Willis shows that whereas early cross-sectional studies
indicated a marked decrease in tested intelligence over the adult years, more
recent longitudinal studies have shown a normative pattern of little or no
decrease. In fact, there may be increases in certain abilities related to
intelligence for some middle-aged individuals. Individual differences are
identified that affect intellectual functioning generally and the issue of
professional obsolescence specifically.

Part III: Mental Health and
Personality Development

The three chapters in this section cover the topics of mental health and
stress, developmental gains at midlife, and modern myths about men at

midlife. In Chapter 5, Chiriboga reports that only a slight proportion of individuals at midlife have serious mental health problems. Instead of showing deterioration in well-being, most people remain stable and some even develop further. Along this line, five theories of mental health during midlife are reviewed. In addition, Chiriboga examines the impact of various social stressors on mental health.

In Chapter 6, Haan counters the view that no significant personal development takes place in adulthood. She presents evidence showing developmental gains in the midlife period such as increased self-confidence, openness, and flexibility. Also, in the research findings she reviews, Haan did not find evidence of a universal midlife crisis.

In Chapter 7, Tamir examines myths related to men at work, in the family, and in social relationships. Instead of being obsolete at work, she shows that men are often at the height of job prestige and job satisfaction. Tamir also counters the view that men at midlife leave or want to leave their wives for younger women; in fact, marital satisfaction is usually high during this time. Social-class differences are a notable theme in her chapter.

Part IV: The Social Context:
Marriage and Family

The three chapters in this section examine marriage, dual-career couples, and intergenerational relationships at midlife. In Chapter 8, Rollins counters the myths that the quality of marriage inevitably declines during the midlife period and that divorce is common. His literature review, including his and his colleagues' research, indicates that a high-quality marriage can be maintained even through the stressful years of child rearing. This is not likely to be easy, however, and requires the price tag of considerable effort in retaining marital communication and companionship, sacrifices for children, and delayed gratification.

Chapter 9, by Gilbert and Davidson, considers the satisfactions, stressors, and myths of dual-career couples at midlife. Various ways of combining work and family are identified along with factors that influence the different types of combinations: personal, relational, and environmental. These factors are also applied to an analysis of what makes dual-career marriages work.

In Chapter 10, Troll addresses 15 general myths concerning the relationships of midlife parents and their children, as well as with their own parents. She concludes that most midlife individuals are involved with their children and parents. Women, particularly, help out when there is need. Intergenerational relationships are enjoyed, especially when there is dependence and separate households. If elderly parents become dependent, they usually receive assistance from their children, particularly a daughter.

Part V: Personal Development and Social Responsibility

The two chapters in this section focus on change and personal empowerment at midlife, and on socially responsible involvements. In Chapter 11, Weick examines how adults continually rework various growth tasks. She describes an alternate model to the popular but questionable model that assumes growth occurs in sequential, age-related stages. According to Weick's Growth Task Model, adults are continually redefining and reworking tasks such as nurturance and productivity. Adults at midlife are not expected to be perfect because they are "grownups." Instead, they are challenged to change and, through experiencing their own power in the change process, they can influence others to do the same.

In Chapter 12, Maas traces the growth of social development over the life course. He presents a schema for social development that identifies the capacities required for socially responsible involvements at midlife. Maas also identifies specific ways in which social responsibility can be expressed at midlife.

In the Conclusion, Sundel and Hunter formulate questions concerning midlife myths and answer them with the key findings presented by the contributors to the volume. They also identify several common issues that surface throughout the book. Implications of these key findings and issues are drawn both for middle-aged persons and professional helpers.

It is exciting to realize that the study of midlife is coming of age with more scholarly efforts directed toward discovering shared characteristics, perceptions, and experiences of individuals during this period of life. Although the research findings and knowledge presented in this volume may only be a modest step toward this goal, we hope that they will contribute toward a more realistic preparation of professionals and others working on behalf of individuals and couples at midlife.

References

Adams, D. (1983). *The psychosocial development of professional black women's lives and the consequences of career for their personal happiness.* Unpublished doctoral dissertation, Wright Institute, Berkeley, CA.

Atchley, R. C. (1976). *The sociology of retirement.* Cambridge, MA: Schenkman.

Baruch, G. (1984). The psychological well-being of women in the middle years. In G. Baruch & J. Brooks-Gunn (Eds.), *Women in midlife* (pp. 161-180). New York: Plenum.

Baruch, G., & Brooks-Gunn, J. (1984). The study of women in midlife. In G. Baruch & J. Brooks-Gunn (Eds.), *Women in midlife* (pp. 1-8). New York: Plenum.

Berardo, F. M. (1982). Preface. *The Annals of the American Academy of Political and Social Science, 464,* 9-10.

Block, M. R., Davidson, J. L., & Grambs, J. D. (1981). *Women over forty.* New York: Springer.

Brandtstädter, J. (1984). Personal and social control over development: Some implications of an action perspective in life-span developmental psychology. In P. B. Baltes & O. G. Brim, Jr. (Eds.), *Life-span development and behavior* (Vol. 6, pp. 1-32). New York: Academic Press.

Bray, D. W., & Howard, A. (1980). Career success and life satisfactions of middle-aged managers. In L. A. Bond & J. C. Rosen (Eds.), *Competence and coping during adulthood* (pp. 258-287). Hanover, NH: Cambridge University Press.

Bray, D. W., & Howard, A. (1983). The AT&T longitudinal studies of managers. In K. W. Schaie (Ed.), *Longitudinal studies of adult psychological development* (pp. 266-312). New York: Guilford.

Brim, O. G., Jr. (1977). Theories of the male mid-life crisis. In N. K. Schlossberg & A. D. Entine (Eds.), *Counseling adults* (pp. 1-18). Monterey, CA: Brooks/Cole.

Brim, O. G., Jr., & Kagan, J. (1980). Constancy and change: A view of the issues. In O. G. Brim & J. Kagan (Eds.), *Constancy and change in human development* (pp. 1-25). Cambridge, MA: Harvard University Press.

Brooks-Gunn, J., & Kirsh, B. (1984). Life events and the boundaries of midlife for women. In G. Baruch & J. Brooks-Gunn (Eds.), *Women in midlife* (pp. 11-30). New York: Plenum.

Butler, R. N. (1974). Successful aging. *Mental Hygiene, 58,* 6-12.

Chew, P. (1976). *The inner world of the middle-aged man.* New York: Macmillan.

Clausen, J. A. (1986). *The life course: A sociological perspective.* Englewood Cliffs, NJ: Prentice-Hall.

Cohler, B. J., & Boxer, A. M. (1984). Middle adulthood: Settling into the world—person, time, and context. In D. Offer & M. Sabshin (Eds.), *Normality and the life cycle* (pp. 145-203). New York: Basic Books.

Conway, S. (1980). *You and your husband's midlife crisis.* New York: New American Library.

Costa, P. T., Jr., & McCrae, R. R. (1978). Objective personality assessment. In M. Storandt, I. C. Siegler, & M. F. Elias (Eds.), *The clinical psychology of aging* (pp. 119-143). New York: Plenum.

Costa, P. T., Jr., & McCrae, R. R. (1980). Somatic complaints of males as a function of age and neuroticism: A longitudinal analysis. *Journal of Behavioral Medicine, 3,* 245-257.

Costa, P. T., Jr., & McCrae, R. R. (1984). Personality as a lifelong determinant of wellbeing. In C. Z. Malatesta & C. E. Izard (Eds.), *Emotion in adult development* (pp. 141-157). Beverly Hills, CA: Sage.

Dannefer, D. (1984). Adult development and social theory: A paradigmatic reappraisal. *American Sociological Review, 49,* 100-116.

Droege, R. (1982). *A psychosocial study of the formation of the middle adult life structure in women.* Unpublished doctoral dissertation, California School of Professional Psychology, Berkeley, CA.

Eichorn, D. H., Clausen, J. A., Haan, N., Honzik, M. P., & Mussen, P. H. (Eds.). (1981). *Present and past in middle life.* New York: Academic Press.

Eisdorfer, C., & Lawton, M. P. (Eds.). (1973). *The psychology of adult development and aging.* Washington, DC: American Psychological Association.

England, J. L., & Kunz, P. R. (1975). The application of age-specific rate to divorce. *Journal of Marriage and the Family, 37,* 40-48.

Erikson, E. (1963). *Childhood and society* (2nd ed.). New York: Norton.

Erikson, E. (1968). Generativity and ego integrity. In B. L. Neugarten (Ed.), *Middle age and aging.* Chicago: University of Chicago Press.

Farrell, M. P., & Rosenberg, S. (1981). *Men at midlife.* Boston: Auburn House.

Fiske, M. (1979). *Middle age: The prime of life?* New York: Harper & Row.

Fiske, M. (1980). Tasks and crises of the second half of life: The interrelationship of commitment, coping, and adaptation. In J. E. Birren & R. B. Sloane (Eds.), *Handbook of mental health and aging* (pp. 337-373). Englewood Cliffs, NJ: Prentice-Hall.

Furst, K. (1983). *Origins and evolution of women's dreams in early adulthood.* Unpublished doctoral dissertation, California School of Professional Psychology, Berkeley, CA.

Giele, J. Z. (1982). Women in adulthood: Unanswered questions. In J. Z. Giele (Ed.), *Women in the middle years* (pp. 1-35). New York: John Wiley.

Glenn, N. D. (1975). The contribution of marriage to the psychological well-being of males and females. *Journal of Marriage and the Family, 37,* 544-600.

Gottfredson, G. (1976). *Career stability and redirection in adulthood* (Report No. 219). Baltimore: Johns Hopkins University, Center for Social Organization of Schools.

Gould, R. L. (1978). *Transformation: Growth and change in adult life.* New York: Simon & Schuster.

Haan, N. (1981). Common dimensions of personality development: Early adolescence to middle life. In D. H. Eichorn, J. A. Clausen, N. Haan, M. P. Honzik, & P. H. Mussen (Eds.), *Present and past in middle life* (pp. 17-151). New York: Academic Press.

Jaques, E. (1965). Death and the mid-life crisis. *International Journal of Psychoanalysis, 46,* 502-514.

Jones, M. C. (1981). Midlife drinking patterns: Correlates and antecedents. In D. H. Eichorn, J. A. Clausen, N. Haan, M. P. Honzik, & P. H. Mussen (Eds), *Present and past in middle life* (pp. 223-242). New York: Academic Press.

Katchadourian, H. (1987). *Fifty: Midlife in perspective.* New York: Freeman.

Kearl, M. C., & Hoag, J. (1984). The social construction of the midlife crisis: A case study in the temporalities of identity. *Sociological Inquiry, 54,* 279-350.

Kramer, M., Taube, C., & Redick, R. (1973). Patterns of use of psychiatric facilities of the aged: Past, present and future. In C. Eisdorfer & M. P. Lawton (Eds.), *The psychology of adult development and aging* (pp. 428-528). Washington, DC: American Psychological Association.

Levinson, D. J. (1978). *The seasons of a man's life.* New York: Knopf.

Lowenthal, M. F., & Chiriboga, D. (1972). Transition to the empty nest: Crisis, challenge or relief? *Archives of General Psychiatry, 26,* 8-14.

Mailick, M. D. (1987). A gender balancing perspective in teaching about middle age. *Report on a Project to Integrate Scholarship on Women in the Professional Curriculum at Hunter College* (pp. 14-24). New York: Hunter College.

McCrae, R. R., & Costa, P. T., Jr. (1983). Psychological maturity and subjective well-being: Toward a new synthesis. *Developmental Psychology, 19,* 243-248.

McCrae, R. R., & Costa, P. T., Jr. (1984). *Emerging lives, enduring dispositions: Personality in adulthood.* Boston: Little, Brown.

National Center for Health Statistics. (1984). *Vital statistics of the United States, 1980* (PHS Vol. 3). Washington, DC: Government Printing Office.

Neugarten, B. L. (1968a). Adult personality: Toward a psychology of the life cycle. In B. L. Neugarten (Ed.), *Middle age and aging* (pp. 137-147). Chicago: University of Chicago Press.

Neugarten, B. L. (1968b). The awareness of middle age. In B. L. Neugarten (Ed.), *Middle age and aging* (pp. 93-98). Chicago: University of Chicago Press.

Neugarten, B. L., Wood, V., Kraines, R. J., & Loomis, B. (1968). Women's attitudes toward menopause. In B. L. Neugarten (Ed.), *Middle age and aging* (pp. 195-200). Chicago: University of Chicago Press.

Newman, B. M. (1982). Midlife development. In B. B. Wolman (Ed.), *Handbook of developmental psychology* (pp. 617-635). Englewood Cliffs, NJ: Prentice-Hall.

Nichols, M. P. (1986). *Turning forty in the eighties: Personal crisis, time for change.* New York: Norton.

Pearlin, L. (1975). Sex roles and depression. In N. Datan & L. H. Ginsberg (Eds.), *Life-span developmental psychology: Normative life crises* (pp. 191-207). New York: Academic Press.

Reinke, B. J., Ellicott, A. M., Harris, R. L., & Hancock, E. (1985). Timing of psychosocial change in women's lives. *Human Development, 28,* 259-280.

Reinke, B. J., Holmes, D. S., & Harris, R. L. (1985). The timing of psychosocial changes in women's lives: The years 25-45. *Journal of Personality and Social Psychology, 48,* 1353-1364.

Riegel, K. F. (1975). Adult life crises: A dialectical interpretation of development. In N. Datan & L. H. Ginsberg (Eds.), *Life-span developmental psychology: Normative life crises* (pp. 99-128). New York: Academic Press.

Riley, M. W. (1984). Women, men, and the lengthening life course. In A. Rossi (Ed.), *Gender and the life course* (pp. 333-347). Chicago, IL: Aldine.

Roberts, P., & Newton, P. M. (1987). Levinsonian studies of women's adult development. *Psychology and Aging. 2,* 154-163.

Rush, J. C., Peacock, A. C., & Milkovich, G. T. (1980). Career stages: A partial test of Levinson's model of life/career stages. *Journal of Vocational Behavior, 16,* 347-359.

Ryff, C. D. (1985). The subjective experience of life-span transitions. In A. S. Rossi (Ed.), *Gender and the life course* (pp. 97-113). New York: Aldine.

Schaie, K. W., & Willis, S. L. (1986). *Adult development and aging* (2nd ed.). Boston: Little, Brown.

Schlossberg, N. (1986). Mid-Life. In C. Tavris (Ed.), *Everywoman's emotional well-being* (pp. 238-257). Garden City, NY: Doubleday.

Sheehy, G. (1976). *Passages: The predictable crises of adult life.* New York: Dalton.

Sofer, C. (1970). *Men in mid-career, a study of British managers & technical specialists.* Cambridge, England: Cambridge University Press.

Spurlock, J. (1984). Black women in the middle years. In G. Baruch & J. Brooks-Gunn (Eds.), *Women in midlife* (pp. 245-260). New York: Plenum.

Stevens-Long, J. (1988). *Adult life* (3rd ed.). Mountain View, CA: Mayfield.

Stewart, W. (1977). *A psychosocial study of the formation of the early adult life structure in women.* Unpublished doctoral dissertation, Columbia University, New York.

Sze, W. C., & Ivker, B. (1987). Adulthood. In *Encyclopedia of Social Work* (18th ed., pp. 75-89). Silver Spring, MD: National Association of Social Workers.

Tamir, L. M. (1982). Men at middle age: Developmental transitions. *Annals of the American Academy of Political and Social Science, 464*, 47-56.

Troll, L. E. (1985). *Early and middle adulthood* (2nd ed.). Belmont, CA: Brooks/Cole.

Vaitenas, R., & Weiner, Y. (1977). Developmental, emotional, and interest factors in voluntary mid-career change. *Journal of Vocational Behavior, 11*, 291-304.

Vaillant, G. E. (1977). *Adaptation to life*. Boston: Little, Brown.

Veroff, J. E., & Feld, S. (1970). *Marriage and work in America: A study of motives and roles*. New York: Van Nostrand Reinhold.

Weissman, M. M., & Myers, J. K. (1978). Rates and risks of depressive symptoms in a United States urban community. *Acta Psychiatric Scandanavica, 57*, 219-231.

Whitbourne, S. K. (1986a). *Adult development* (2nd ed.). New York: Praeger.

Whitbourne, S. K. (1986b). *The me I know: A study of adult identity*. New York: Springer-Verlag.

Part I
Physical Status

The two chapters in Part I of this volume address the physical status of individuals at midlife. In Chapter 1, Weg counters the myth of declining sexual pleasure in midlife by emphasizing the minimal consequences of physiological changes for both males and females and the potential for even greater pleasure through incorporating aspects of sensuality into a couple's relationship. She uses the term *sensuality/sexuality* to broaden the concept of sexuality to include intimacy and communication, as well as genital contact. Weg describes physiological and role changes occurring in men and women and how these changes can affect their sexual performance. Factors influencing the relationships of same-sex partners are also discussed.

Social workers, psychologists, psychiatrists, and other professional helpers can use the author's findings to inform and guide their clients toward a more positive and realistic conception of sexuality at midlife. For example, Weg suggests that psychotherapy can help individuals enhance their understanding of intimacy as a part of sexuality and foster more appropriate values and goals in their relationships.

In Chapter 2, Dan and Bernhard discuss menopause and other health issues of women at midlife. The authors review multiple definitions of menopause and provide an informative description of the physiological and psychological symptoms supposedly associated with various definitions. They also present research studies indicating the actual effects of menopause on women. In particular, the findings show that most women who have experienced menopause do not regard this as a significant factor in their well-being.

Dan and Bernhard believe that conceptualizations of menopause as disease, deficiency, or decline can stereotype the menopausal woman as an unattractive person and also create anxiety in women concerned about menopause. They describe sociocultural aspects of the menopausal experience and management approaches for menopausal problems. The authors conclude that menopause for most women is neither easy nor difficult, but somewhere in between, and that in working with midlife women it is important to recognize the full range of possible experiences. Therapists and counselors can inform their clients on the menopause phenomenon, which could prove particularly beneficial for women holding erroneous conceptions that limit their functioning and personal growth. Additional health issues for women are addressed, including bleeding and hysterectomy, breast and lung cancer, osteoporosis, and weight control and fitness.

1

Sensuality/Sexuality of the Middle Years

Ruth B. Weg

The Backdrop:
More Than Genitalia

Destructive stereotypes of sexuality in the middle and later years have been nurtured from the beginning of humankind through religious tenets about proper sexual behavior, coupled with societal proscription. Current perceptions of middle age include the persistence of sexual myths—despite evidence to the contrary (Brecher, 1984; Butler & Lewis, 1986; Weg, 1982, 1983a, 1983c). For example, sexuality still connotes primarily genital intercourse. Left out is sensuality, which is rarely discussed alone or together with sexuality in articles and books. For this author, sensuality is related to whole person arousal, excitement of all the senses, and consequent behavior such as eye-to-eye exchanges, hugging, hand-holding, walking arm in arm, touching and stroking, and holding each other in and out of bed. Expressions of sensuality are not necessarily a prelude to genital activity. Rather, they reflect caring, affection, and intimacy—each of which can be enjoyed.

People begin their lives as sensual/sexual human beings and remain so at 30, 50, 70, or 100. What changes with the years are options, opportunities, and expression related to sensuality/sexuality (Adams & Turner, 1985; Butler & Lewis, 1976, 1986; Weg, 1983c). Many also arrive at midlife with ignorance and prejudices about this period of life including its sensual/sexual aspects. The myths of midlife sexuality have pointed to a continuing diminution of activity, capacity, interest, and pleasure—a dismal future—loveless, sexless, based primarily on the supposed major anatomical and physiological changes in the reproductive system (Weg, 1982, 1983c).

Through the centuries, sexuality (generally assumed to be intercourse) and potency have been goals to ensure youthful vigor and long life (Tannahill, 1980; Trimmer, 1970). Currently, though slices of bull testes and bird's nest soup are no longer consumed for rejuvenation, there are the promises of ginseng, diet, aerobics, and gerovital. From the earliest records of the human family, attempts to remain youthful have equated potency, intercourse, and orgasm with human sensuality/sexuality, suggesting that only the physical self is involved in relationships (Bullough, 1976; Tannahill, 1980; Weg, 1983b).

In the effort to legitimize the study of human sexuality for the scientific fellowship early in this century, Kinsey and his colleagues initiated inquiries into American human sexual behavior directed to quantification and so-called objective evaluation of genital sexuality (Kinsey, Pomeroy, & Martin, 1948; Kinsey, Pomeroy, Martin, & Gebhard, 1953). In their extensive inquiry, orgasms per week were counted, achieved heterosexually, bisexually, or homosexually, or through self-stimulation, intercourse, cunnilingus, fellatio, or fantasy. This "scientific," quantitative approach continues to ignore human feelings, desires, and needs, and the meaning of sexual expression; it reinforces frequency, quantity, and orgasm as the most reportable, significant sexual information. Techniques are detailed in the multitude of "how-to" books that ensure multiple orgasm, the remarkable physical results of pornographic films, and vibrators—all committed to the altar of genital sex. Are there only genitalia and orgasm to be considered? What of the person who lives a whole life—alone and in relationships? Human sensuality/sexuality encompasses much more than intercourse and orgasm—playing, caring, loving, sharing, trusting, and touching.

The majority of men and women experience growing middle-aged and older differently from each other. The myths and stereotypes of midlife sexuality will, therefore, have a number of gender-related emphases. This suggests the need for gender-related as well as universal coping strategies and interventions. First, comparisons between the midlife female and male will be presented. Later in the chapter, gender differences in coping and intervention strategies will also be discussed.

The Midlife Female

Heritage and Mythology

The American woman has made progress in educational and career opportunities, though equity still eludes her. Physiologically, the human female is born advantaged; she is sturdier (evidenced from embryonic phases throughout life), has a lower mortality rate, and suffers less severely from the major chronic-disease killers (Verbrugge, 1983, 1986). Yet, to grow up female remains for many a psychosocial challenge. She is still surrounded by the mythology that identifies her as less than healthy, competent, worthy, and sexual. Throughout ancient and contemporary history she has been largely valued as the mother of generations and her sexuality perceived in that context. As stated elsewhere by Weg (1987c, p. 127):

> Sexuality of the human family through the centuries is the primacy of marital, procreative sexuality above all other dimensions of sexual behavior. The corollary is the labeling as asexual the middle and later, barren years of the female whose womb is the incubator of the future.

The female has been largely expected to serve the sexual needs and drives of a mate—preferably a husband—without regard for her needs and wants. Societal rewards and approval have been abundant for the female who commits herself to such roles as mother, wife, housekeeper (Tannahill, 1980; Weg, 1983c, 1987a, 1987c). If she has been primarily a homemaker, mother, and compliant, accepting mate, however, she is more likely to be uneasy and depressed at midlife (British Medical Journal, 1976; Scully & Bart, 1973; Weg, 1987c). She is often disturbed about her physique; she perceives herself as increasingly wrinkled, matronly, and dull in appearance. In confronting the impending loss of birthing and primary mothering—and the expected diminution of youthful verve and traditional "femininity"—she may question her reason for being (Weg, 1982, 1983c). At the least, her identity may be at risk (Masters, Johnson, & Kolodny, 1986; Weg, 1982). Societal feedback has been a major stimulus for these stereotypes and behavior.

The Physiology

In addition to the already noted visible differences in body contour, other consequential changes occur, such as the following:

Fewer follicles responsive to stimulation by pituitary gonadotropins, an apparent modification of the hypothalamic-pituitary and gonad interaction; temporary normal or elevated estrogen results and fertility diminishes (Dilman, 1971; Sherman & Korenman, 1975; Weg, 1983c).

There are more frequent irregular menstrual cycles. Related to the lack of regular estrogen rise and fall, pituitary follicle stimulating hormone (FSH) levels begin to increase. Intermittent bleeding may take place, and can be pathologically excessive, often treated successfully by dilatation and curettage. Almost 75% of such bleeding is self-correcting, but 25% may be due to malignancy (Weg, 1983c).

The decrease in follicular responsivity and maturation, and the fall in corpora lutea (parts of the capsule that ovarian follicles leave in the ovary after an egg is expelled) lowers the secretion of female sex hormones. If pregnancy does not occur these corpora lutea degenerate, leading to the continued decrease in estrogen/progesterone concentration and activity. Premenstrual uterine proliferation and blood engorgement, typical of earlier menstrual years, decreases to a minimal level.

With the diminution of sex hormones, other estrogen-related systemic functions, such as protein synthesis, salt and water balance, bone formation, immune effectiveness, and interaction with other hormones begin decreasing in efficiency, which is not generally noticeable or measurable until well into the sixties.

There is gradual atrophy in the genital, urinary, and musculoskeletal systems, which, by the seventies and eighties, becomes more obvious, especially if hormonal replacement therapy is lacking. Skin elasticity diminishes, glandular and muscle tissue decrease, and ligaments relax. The redistribution of fatty tissue contributes to the middle-aged profile. The urethra and bladder may also atrophy slightly and exacerbate urogenital difficulties. Genital tissues undergo gradual anatomical changes. Vulvar tissue is diminished, major labia are less full, and the mons is flatter. Ovaries, fundus of the uterus, and cervix begin their reduction in size. Perhaps the most troublesome changes occur in the vagina, that organ so important to traditional sexual activity. The mucosal rugal pattern slowly becomes smooth, the canal becomes thin and decreases in length, and elasticity and capacity for expansion are decreased. Within five to ten years postmenopause, vaginitis can be a problem; dryness and friability may become barriers to comfortable and pleasurable physical, sexual expression. The clitoris may decrease in size minimally; there is no "objective evidence to date to suggest any appreciable loss in sensate focus" (Masters & Johnson, 1970, p. 337). This fact is critical in orgasmic responsivity.

After a few years of irregular cycles, a particular point in the climacteric occurs—the cessation of menses, or menopause—accompanied by a marked reduction in estrogen/progesterone. This is the recognizable close of the menstrual cycle and usually fertility as well, but not the end of libido or capacity as a sexual partner.

Various subjective and objective symptoms traditionally assigned to all premenopausal, menopausal, and postmenopausal women cover a gamut of psychological, emotional, and physical symptoms—loss of appetite, insomnia, dizziness, hot flashes, sweating, hypertension, palpitations, depression, anxiety, irritability, uncontrolled temper, and crying (Bates, 1981; Weg, 1981). Many of these signs and symptoms can be a function of non-menopausal disturbances or aberrations, especially because a number of these also are complaints of younger men and women.

Contrary to the popular stereotype, as noted by McArthur (1981, p. 148), it would appear "that no constellation of symptoms exists that is identified as a 'menopausal syndrome.' " It may be useful to note that the "hot flash," a vascular instability (dilatation and constriction of small blood vessels) was considered inevitable for generations. Although experienced by some menopausal women, many females complete the climacteric and menopause without a single "flash" (Weg, 1983c, 1987b). Women who choose to live multiple roles (mother, wife, worker, lover) generally report minimal or no symptoms (Bart & Grossman, 1978; Neugarten & Datan, 1976).

Waning procreation, either by surgery or natural hormonal, physiological alterations, is no cause for loss of libido, capacity, and pleasure in the physical expression of sexuality. More often than not, at this time, a woman is reaching a peak of desire, capacity, and pleasure in sexual activity (Kaplan, 1974; Masters, Johnson, & Kolodny, 1985; Weg, 1983c).

Females as Sexual Partners

Despite the gradual physiological changes, the middle-aged woman remains advantaged and functional as a sexual partner. More time and appropriate stimulation may be required for vaginal lubrication and orgasmic responsivity. This is similar to parallel needs of the middle-aged male for more time and touching to reach an erection. There is more time for the caressing and sharing of lovemaking rather than the short, urgent release of goal-oriented, genital sexual expression.

A survey of 160 midlife women found that the picture was generally one of improving sexuality (Rubin, 1982). These middle-aged women in a relationship (marriage or otherwise) became able to take the sexual initiative more often, and to appreciate their own sexual needs and desires rather than being primarily a participant in activity to please a partner. In another recent study, self-ratings of sexual activities and feelings among middle-aged and older men and women were included. The researchers found female sexual interest was greater than that of males. This difference was "attributed to role transitions, menopause, changing cultural standards for female sexuality and increased control over one's sexual life" (Adams & Turner, 1985, p. 126). In another study, some women reported that they could no longer continue to submit to relationships with poor communication, lack of intimacy, and perfunctory sexual intercourse (Hite, 1987).

Lesbians appear to make a relatively smooth transition into the middle years, with many in lasting, single relationships (Masters et al., 1986). Some midlife women who have been in long-term deteriorating heterosexual relationships (married or not, with or without children) seek and consummate satisfying lesbian coupling. Although still problematic in some communities, there is more acceptance of the reality of homosexual life-styles. Peplau (1981), in her study comparing homosexuals and heterosexuals, learned that gender—being a man or woman—often has a greater effect on the relationship than orientation. Goals for a woman in an intimate relationship were similar whether the partner was a woman or man.

Peplau found that 61% of a group of 50 lesbians reported being in a romantic/sexual relationship with a woman. The length of the lesbian relationship ranged from 1 month to 25 years with a median of 2.5 years; more than 95% had dated a man at some time; 84% had experienced one or more love/sexual relationships with a man.

The life course has undergone significant change in the last 10 to 15 years—especially for the middle-aged female. There is greater participation in the work force, a growing number of societally acceptable social roles, and a changing attitude toward the integration of family and work force activities (Steitz, 1981-1982; Van Dusen & Sheldon, 1976). The middle-aged woman has grown less naive, dependent, and fearful. The woman who has the option of moving away from isolation in the home, who aspires to opportunity, privilege, and power in the social arena, will continue to reach for intimacy, pleasure, and autonomy in the sexual realm. The middle years can become a time for renewal, regeneration, and discovery (Porcino, 1983; Reitz, 1977; Weg, 1982).

The Midlife Male

Recent History

During the 1960s and 1970s the concerns of men in midlife were variously noted in scientific and lay literature as male menopause, male climacteric, and midlife crisis (Levinson, Darrow, Klein, Levinson, & McKee, 1978; Masters & Johnson, 1970; Pfeiffer & Davis, 1972; Rosenberg, Farrell, & Por, 1976; Rutherford, 1956; Sheehy, 1976). The male climacteric, not unlike the female climacteric, is a period accompanied by a range of physiological, psychological, and social changes that precipitate attempts for redefinition and reexamination of accomplishments, goals, and life status. The male climacteric, like the female climacteric, is an individual experience, expressed differently depending upon physical, emotional, cognitive, and situational factors (Greenblatt, Nezhat, Roesel, & Natrajan, 1979; Parker, 1985; Weg, 1983c, 1985).

Clinical data about the male climacteric are characterized by generalized loss of well-being, fatigue, increased irritability, poor appetite, a difficulty with concentration, diminished libido, and occasional impotence. This kind of empirical evidence encourages professional acceptance of the reality of the male climacteric (Albeaux-Fernet, Bohler, & Karpas, 1978; Greenblatt et al., 1979; Henker, 1977; Weg, 1983c). There is resistance, however, to the recognition of a male climacteric because men have historically and traditionally been identified with everlasting virility, fertility, and sexual potency (Tannahill, 1980). Such standards have led to reservations in the admission to any possible sexually related concerns or dysfunctions. Nevertheless, there has been increased reporting of male sexual anxiety and/or dissatisfaction with sexual life (Featherstone & Hepworth, 1985).

Some of the concerns of males have been assigned to the social context of changing sex roles, to lowered testosterone, to the learned mythology of sexual changes with age, and anxiety over performance. Other areas of concern are the effects of chronic illness and of boredom in life-style, particularly with the patterns of longtime sexual behaviors (Stoppard, 1983; Weg, 1983c). In commenting on sexual dysfunction during midlife, Masters and Johnson (1970) noted that diminishing sexual responsivity in the middle-aged male generally had its origin in a number of psychosocial factors ranging from occupational stress to the lack of physical fitness.

It also is possible that the traditional image of male sexuality, the emergence of a strong sexual component in later life, and the debunking of the myth of the asexual menopausal and postmenopausal woman have contributed to midlife male distress by the creation of new, unrealistic myths, for example, the everlasting maintenance of youthful libido and sexual vigor (Featherstone & Hepworth, 1983, 1985; Weg, 1983c). As with the female climacteric, however, there is growing realization that middle age for the male is not necessarily a crisis and can also be perceived as a beginning or a renewal of personal growth and positive change. Furthermore, with widespread education, men could develop an understanding perspective about the gradual changes in the physical expression of their sexuality (Featherstone & Hepworth, 1985; Henker, 1977; Weg, 1983c).

The Physiology

By midlife there are minimal physiological alterations in the male sexual system such as the following:

There may or may not be lower levels of testosterone; there are fewer viable sperm.

If there is a decrease in the sex steroids, the nonreproductive, nonsexual processes that are sex-steroid-related may be affected, including salt and water balance, cardiovascular function, protein synthesis, immune surveillance, and generalized muscle strength and tone.

The testes begin to grow smaller, more flaccid.

The prostate gland enlarges slightly in many middle-aged men, its contractions grow weaker, and there are consequential changes in the ejaculate. Prostatitis (an inflammation and enlargement) may increase, though it is probably not related to changing testosterone activity. This condition can result in excessive or inhibited urination, pain in the testes and tip of the penis, and pain during intercourse (Biggs & Spitz, 1975).

The ejaculate changes in nature, with a reduction in viscosity and volume contributing to a decreased force during ejaculation.

Males as Sexual Partners

There are signs among many middle-aged men of functional changes in sexual responsivity and libido. More time and direct stimulation to the penis are needed to attain erection, and the drive for intercourse is frequently diminished. A gradual reduction in ejaculatory inevitability is noticed, which allows for longer maintenance of an erection and fits well with the longer time the middle-aged woman may require for lubrication and excitation. Many men report a decrease in frequency of intercourse and an increase in impotent encounters. Finally, there is the gradual increase in the refractory period and what was a few minutes in youth between erections and orgasms may become many minutes, hours, or a day or longer (Masters, Johnson, & Kolodny, 1982).

None of the physiological changes described is sufficient to alter significantly the interest and pleasure in a sensual/sexual life. Nevertheless, for some, a single impotent experience or partial erection can ignite a submerged pool of fear that the "end is in sight." This fear could be followed by withdrawal to avoid "failure" or periods of emotional impotence unrelated to age. If the male is in a couple relationship, this kind of emotional or physical dysfunction that can create emotional and physical distance compounds the initial difficulty (Renshaw, 1985). The man may seek a new relationship (often with a younger woman) to wake him from the doldrums that he hopes is due to boredom with a longtime mate (Weg, 1983c). Some midlife men are reported to have become anxious and preoccupied with their physical appearance, which is similar to the panicky behavior often identified with the traditional middle-aged woman. These men demonstrate increasing concerns that their needs for love, companionship, and understanding are not being met by existing heterosexual pairing (Gould, 1980).

Gay men in their middle years are frequently in a love relationship (as are lesbians) and avoid gender-based roles that earlier stereotypes have suggested (Bell & Weinberg, 1978; Peplau, 1981). Gay men (and lesbians) often note that the flexibility of roles in their relationships is an advantage. Peplau (1981) found that homosexual and heterosexual couples are similar in a number of ways, especially in their desire for a close and loving relationship with one special person. Middle-aged gays, like heterosexual men, experience body and sexual changes, and feel conflicts, satisfaction, and joy in relationships. In her sample of 128 gay men, Peplau found that the length of same-sex relationships ranged from 2 months to 11 years with a median of 15 months. "More than 92% had dated a woman at some time, two-thirds had had sexual intercourse with a woman" (1981, p. 30).

There is little doubt that the middle-aged male with no marked sexual or systemic pathology can remain a capable sexual partner. If ignorance of the minimal anatomical and functional changes is overcome, the middle-aged male is in a better position, with experience and sensitivity, to take advantage of the longer periods of intimate, tender lovemaking (Weg, 1985, 1987b).

Possible Barriers to
Sensual/Sexual Lives

As discussed, there are normative, limited physiological changes for the middle-aged that leave capacities and potentials for a rich sensual, sexual life. What, then, are the possible sources for barriers that appear to exist? Physical changes that could play a role range from mild physical and emotional illness to severe pathology. Other physical and mental assaults include drugs, surgeries, and depression. Constraints may also be found in psychosocial realities—early socialization, societal attitudes, shifting sex roles, two-career families, absent or erratic communication, and busy daily schedules that many persons in their middle years pursue.

Illness, Disease, and
Psychosocial Problems

The susceptibility and incidence of chronic disease (e.g., coronary disease, cerebrovascular accidents, hypertension, diabetes, pelvic disorders, arthritis, and cancer) increase with age. During the middle years some of these diseases become symptomatic for the first time (Weg, 1985). Circulatory dysfunction can lower the volume of blood to the penis, decrease penile engorgement, and interfere with a full erection. Coronary disease has often resulted in the termination of sexual expression for men who fear sudden coronary death during intercourse (Weg, 1985). A stroke frequently limits sexual expression because of associated physical disability or depression. Anemia and chronic or periodic physical and emotional fatigue also affect libido and physical expression for men and women.

Both males and females with long-term diabetes may experience a range of altered responsivity. It appears that more men than women are affected, and the consequences may be more dysfunctional for the male. Neuropathy (damage to pelvic nerves) and disturbed circulation are characteristic and contribute to difficulty with penile engorgement and erection resulting in partial erection or erectile failure and, less frequently, in retrograde and premature ejaculation (Melman & Henry, 1979). Despite the presence of libido, studies have found that about 50% of diabetic males fail to stimulate erection by masturbation or any other method (Kolodny, Kahn, Goldstein, & Barnett, 1974). Although libido may also remain in diabetic women, vaginal lubrication can decrease. These dysfunctions are not universal. A study of 100 female diabetics found normal libido and orgasmic capacity in 82 of the women (Ellenberg, 1977).

Depression can be both cause and effect in regard to libido and functional activity in a sexual relationship. If the middle years are perceived as threatening to self-image and sexuality, depression can develop and exacerbate any existing problem. Recognized changes in libido, potency, or sexual responsivity can lead to depression. If depression is present, interest in a sexual, loving partner can rarely be expressed. Often the depressed individual comes to be viewed as burdensome and unlovable. When intimacy has waned and sexual activity has become ritualistic, some people may try too hard to be "successful" in bed. Paradoxically, the results are frequently disappointing, aggravating an already troubled relationship (Weg, 1985, 1987b).

Another source of stress in sexual behavior at any age, particularly among singles, is the fear of AIDS. This new societal crisis may result in longer-term monogamous relationships—same sex or other sex.

Drugs

Polypharmacy and other treatments that accompany illness and disease often have serious consequences for libido, erectile capacity, lubrication, and orgasm. Antihypertensives are a major group of drugs that affect physical expression of sexuality. Although not inevitable, the effects can include decreased libido, erectile failure, and ejaculatory retardation. Drugs for coronary disorders (such as beta-adrenergic blockers) may also cause impotence. Any tranquilizing drug can also act as a libido depressant in both men and women. Abuse of tranquilizers, alcohol, and marijuana, which can diminish lubrication in the female and weaken erection and delay ejaculation in the male, may exacerbate responsivity that is already slowed (Butler & Lewis, 1986; Kayne, 1976; Weg, 1978).

Surgeries

Pelvic surgery has frequently been the signal for an end to sexual activity for many middle-aged men and women. Clinical reports have indicated that prostatectomies and hysterectomies depress libido and orgasmic capacity. No definitive data indicate that these are inexorable results (Butler & Lewis, 1986; Weg, 1978, 1985). Surgery for excessive benign hyperplasia of the prostate has improved measurably, and rarely does potency have to be affected. Transurethral resection appears to be the surgery of choice in terms of trauma and safety, and its record for maintaining potency is excellent (Weg, 1985). An experimental laser procedure may avoid surgery altogether.

Hysterectomy and/or oophorectomy represent a loss of "womanhood" and "femininity" for some women. They feel and behave as if they are unworthy of loving, sexual interaction. While there have been studies that suggest decreased sexual activity postmenopause, a retrospective inquiry of women who experienced surgical menopause concluded that the altered behavior of the sexual relationship was a major function of psychological rather than physiological factors (Cosper, Fuller, & Tobinson, 1978).

Mastectomy has been an even more significant symbol for middle-aged women who view this body insult as a threat to self-image and acceptance as a woman. Added to the fear of cancer and death may be the fear of loss of

a loving partner. Unfortunately, some men confirm this fear. These presenting negative attitudes of the cancer patient often trigger equally negative
responses in intimate others and friends. Relaxed, loving encounters can
become fewer, augmenting frustrations and depression for both partners
(Weg. 1985).

Colostomies and ileostomies also delay a return to prior sexual activity.
These (as with the aforementioned surgeries) are assaults on body image and
conjure up images of deformed bodies that do not encourage loving relationships. These losses can lead to embarrassment, shame, and self-hate, which
interfere with feelings and behavior that communicate "sexy" and loving
messages (Butler & Lewis, 1986; Rollin, 1976; Weg, 1985). Helping organizations of similarly affected individuals make up a self-help group of
willing volunteers who provide emotional and informational support.

No Time for Loving

Midlife is a time when men and growing numbers of women are in the
workplace striving for satisfaction, appreciation, and reward; a time when
the lingering, intimate dinner is bypassed for the quick bite; and when the
major ambiance for a "loving" experience is late at night after too many
drinks, and when a weary couple finally bids good night to the last departed
guest. What can be a delightful, warm, sharing of affection and sexual drive
becomes an unfeeling release of sexual tension (Appleton, 1982; Weg,
1983c, 1987b). Simply, many couples do not make enough time for a
meaningful sexual exchange and the nurturing of intimacy. A clinical study
of 30 middle-aged married couples found that a major, common quality
among these couples was the minimal time or energy they gave to their
marital and sexual relationships (McCarthy, 1982). Similarly, other problematic aspects of a marriage can have a "dampening" effect on the sexual
dimension of the relationship.

The recent emphasis on technique and multiorgasm in the lay media has
done a disservice to all ages—as if all of human sensuality/sexuality comes
to rest only on genital pleasures. The majority of articles and books on
sexuality characterize sexual behavior in quantitative values for intercourse,
orgasm, and masturbation. The amazing gap, which is just beginning to be
addressed, includes the quality of relationships, the needs and desires of the
whole person (whether or not in a relationship), the meaning of sexual
expression, and the different kinds of supportive, loving ties with or without
the physical, genital expression (Weg, 1983c, 1987b). Needless to say, this
all takes time.

Coping Strategies and
Helping Professionals

Intimacy/Communication

Clearly, any change in the sexual system perceived as decline is a powerful threat to ego and self-esteem. Much of the literature (lay and professional) and individual concern have focused on physical, genital activity. A more positive coping philosophy to deal with the continuum of change in human sexuality would consider the whole person—the partner relationship or lack of it—rather than genitalia, frequency of orgasm, and techniques. Despite much sexual body closeness and intercourse between two people, partners may be unrelated psychologically and emotionally, not sharing feelings or thoughts (McCary & McCary, 1982; Weg, 1987b).

The development and deepening of intimacy beyond its physical aspect promises solutions to conflicts, fears, and apathy of multifaceted relationships. Intimacy nourishes trust, communication, mutual caring, and the exchange of joys and defeats. A relationship in which true feelings can be expressed is mutually supportive and enabling. Professionals in psychology, medicine, and sociology, as well as poets and philosophers, are in agreement that intimacy is essential for children to grow into adulthood with a sense of physical and mental well-being (Erikson, 1963; Maslow, 1970). This is no less true all through life.

The lack of *intimate* relationships often leads to maladaptation, illness, and possibly suicide (Leviton, 1978). Yet, there are many hurdles to overcome in developing intimacy—a person's mores, cultural history, needs, fears, societal customs, and contexts. Men and women differ in their motivation toward intimacy and in their commitment to a satisfying, trusting relationship (Naifeh & Smith, 1984). Basic to this sex differential is the contrasting socialization for boys and girls. Boys learn emotional distancing while girls are encouraged to be emotionally giving and expressive. Male consciousness-raising and encounter groups focus on men learning to establish easy exchanges with women and each other, but large numbers of men are still immersed in the "traditional manhood" approach (Astrachan, 1986; Weg, 1987b). Relationships suffer the resulting silence, misunderstandings, and anger, while honesty and openness wait to emerge. In a survey of 400 psychiatrists who were asked to respond to the question, "Why do marriages fail?," 45% identified the major factor as the husband's inability to communicate feelings (Naifeh & Smith, 1984). Intimacy is not only a reaffirmation of connection with another at many levels during the early and middle years of life, but also functions as an ongoing buffer against "the traumatic changes and losses in many dimensions of living" in the later years (Weg, 1987b, p. 136).

Role Changes

The stereotypic assignations that relegate all males to being aggressive, unemotional, and easily aroused sexually, and females to being passive, emotional, and unaroused, have had significant consequences for relationships. In a romantic sexual encounter, the traditional female is viewed as not taking an active part. She is inclined to let herself be touched rather than touch. She has learned that she must be pretty, passive, and permissive. She has to control her arousal to maintain the conforming "feminine" profile and leave the prerogative to the man. When she has demonstrated sexual interest, her responsivity may have been interpreted as an indication that she was "easy" or oversexed.

As activity initiators, many young males think that touching a female is a signal or sexual starter. The male has been "educated" to believe that as society's aggressor, he must also be so sexually—strong, rough, controlling, and successful in each encounter. If the female's anticipated sexual responsivity does not materialize, he feels angry, bewildered, or put down because she failed to respond as expected. Even if his interest may be in the development of a nonphysical friendship or exchange, he has failed in the physical dimension, an unacceptable affront to his "manliness." The stifling of emotion and tenderness leads many men to view sexual expression as purely physical, and to believe that tenderness is "feminine." This may account for the ritualistic, mechanical overtones in some lovemaking.

The hope for undoing impersonal, mechanical, and predictable genital activity and maximizing the possibility of total human exchange can be found in the tendency toward androgynous behavior in men and women as they move into middle and later years. Increasingly, it appears that although men and women in young adulthood may travel different emotional and social paths, they become more like the other during the middle and later years (Livson, 1983). Women appear to grow more assertive, more committed to self-development and achievement, and more interested in autonomy within the family and in the work world. Men show more tenderness, passivity, and interest in emotional expression. Instead of a reversal of roles, there is a demonstration in each of qualities and behavior that have traditionally been viewed as appropriate only to the other sex.

Livson (1983) found that successful middle-aged men and women with androgynous personalities demonstrated a more fluid expression of self. "Integrated personalities" were both assertive and passive, emotional and instrumental, autonomous and dependent. Both men and women reached out more readily to others, initiated lovemaking, cried, made decisions, and were tender. These are the prerogatives of men and women in exhibiting flexible behaviors suited to situations and feelings, not gender, without threat to identity.

Hormone Therapy

When libido is depressed, when vaginal lubrication is minimal, and partial erections are troublesome, consideration can be given to hormone replacement for the middle-aged man and woman. Hormonal treatment for moderate symptoms (which may, in part, be sex-steroid-related) has long been used for the middle-aged and older female. Up to recent years, estrogen replacement therapy (ERT) was the choice for the range of "complaints" that were diagnosed as peri- or postmenopausal. Consequent to concerns regarding the potentially carcinogenic nature of estrogens, estrogen/progesterone hormone therapy has been widely recommended as superior because together they avoid any retention of uterine lining tissue growth, which occurs in response to estrogen stimulation. Estrogen/progesterone hormone therapy has largely replaced ERT and is now considered protective against cancer. As an additional safeguard against toxic side effects, the concentrations of both female sex hormones have been successfully lowered and remain effective in the elimination of "hot flashes" and contributive to significant maintenance of salt and water balance, protein synthesis, immune surveillance, vaginal lubrication, and calcium balance (Greenblatt, 1977; Masters, Johnson, & Kolodny, 1986; Nachtigall, 1976; Weg, 1987c).

Although disagreements exist regarding the advisability or value of testosterone therapy for the male, there are studies suggesting that a low testosterone level coupled with libidinal and erectile difficulties can be treated with fair to excellent results (Witherington, 1974). A careful physical, medical history is essential, because excessive testosterone therapy could conceivably stimulate further enlargement of an already-at-risk prostate gland to greater benign or cancerous growth. Short-term psychotherapy can sometimes overcome a problem that has interactive, physical, and psychological bases (Weg, 1985).

Psychotherapy

A problematic relationship usually has physical and sexual difficulties such as boredom and impotency in men and lack of responsivity in women. Masters, Johnson, and Kolodny (1986) emphasized sex therapy in short-term, sensate-focused treatment. For more wide-ranging concerns in a relationship, psychotherapy and counseling may be necessary to help the partners identify the problems and their origin (Butler & Lewis, 1986; Kaplan, 1974, 1979, 1983). Psychotherapy encourages self-examination in a number of areas—communication, motivation, and history of certain behaviors in earlier and present relationships. Further, the therapeutic encounter can stimulate new learning about intimacy and establish more appropriate values and goals in a continually changing partnership. There can be improved mutual understanding, intimacy, and caring, which can awaken an inactive or otherwise-occupied libido.

Education

"Sex" education has been customarily relegated to children and adolescents. Educational attention to the changing realities of adult sensual/sexual lives has been minimal. Current role transitions and the blurring of so-called "masculine-" and "feminine"-appropriate behavior have highlighted the urgency for the implementation of lifelong sensual/sexual education.

In preparation for the gradual changes in midlife sexuality, information about expected changes and their relatively minimal consequences for enjoyment and competence could help to prevent unnecessary anger, resentment, fears, withdrawal, or blaming the partner. If the anatomical, physiological alterations that suggest longer, tender lovemaking (at times other than the lateness of night) are responded to positively, the pleasure of intimate, sexual joining might even be greater than in earlier years. Knowledge of facts and potentials of midlife sensual/sexual behaviors is not suggested as the sole mode of support and prevention of sexual and relationship difficulties. Rather, it should be seen as a given without which further attempts for help may be in vain if based on ignorance and stereotypes.

Helping Professionals

There are "givens" as well for the helping professional—current knowledge in sensuality/sexuality and comfort with his or her own sexuality. Most of the readers know there is no one prescription for helping. With the complexity of sexual behavior, sexual dissatisfaction or dysfunction calls for attention to the physiological, psychological, and social aspects of the client. This necessitates not only listening empathically, but also organizing mental and physical health information to expose problems other than sexual. The challenge lies in opening up the multiple dimensions of living that affect sensual/sexual attitudes, libido, and behavior.

Presenting complaints of many middle-aged clients appear to have their origins in contemporary changing roles, values, and life-styles. This does not obviate the possibility that in any one instance, the physiological changes—real or imagined, normative or pathological—may be primary. Although affect and psyche are also involved, it is essential to seek medical allies to diagnose, treat, and eliminate any physical bases.

Conclusion

Victorian myths and stereotypes of adult sensuality/sexuality are slowly succumbing to the impact of new knowledge and behavior. Midlife is a time of psychological, social, and physiological vulnerability. It is a time when self-confidence, self-image, and competence are at risk in a culture that remains, in significant measure, youth-adoring.

There is reason to be optimistic in the present climate, when both men and women increasingly seek authenticity and intimacy rather than power over one another—wholeness of person and relationship. Sexual behavior is learned and is susceptible to relearning with new information in new situations. When women are finally perceived as more than decorative incubator and helpmate, and men become more than the calculating, aggressive, cool providers, relationships will more easily become voluntary, satisfying, affectional connections. The potential for lifelong sensuality/sexuality lies in interdependence, shared caring, and love between people.

References

Adams. C. A., & Turner, B. F. (1985). Reported change in sexuality from young adulthood to old age. *Journal of Sex Research, 21*(2), 126-141.

Albeaux-Fernet, M., Bohler, C. S. S., & Karpas, A. E. (1978). Testicular function in aging male. In R. B. Greenblatt (Ed.), *Geriatric endocrinology: Vol. 5. Aging* (pp. 201-215). New York: Raven.

Appleton. W. S. (1982). Making time for sex. *Medical Aspects of Human Sexuality, 16*(9), 32-39.

Astrachan. A. (1986). *How men feel.* Garden City, NY: Doubleday.

Bart, P. B., & Grossman, M. (1978). Menopause. In M. T. Notman & C. C. Nadelson (Eds.), *The woman patient* (pp. 337-354). New York: Plenum.

Bates, G. (1981). On the nature of the hot flash. *Clinical Obstetrics and Gynecology, 24*, 231-241.

Bell, A. P., & Weinberg, M. S. (1978). *Homosexualities: A study of diversity among men and women.* New York: Simon & Schuster.

Biggs, M., & Spitz, R. (1975). Treating sexual dysfunction: The dual sex therapy team. In R. Green (Ed.), *Human sexuality: A health practitioner's text* (pp. 223-232). Baltimore: Williams and Wilkins.

Brecher, E. (1984). *Love, sex and aging.* Boston: Little, Brown.

British Medical Journal. (1976). 2 (6029), 199-200.

Bullough, V. L. (1976). *Sexual variance in society and history.* New York: John Wiley.

Butler, R. N., & Lewis, M. I. (1976). *Sex after 60.* New York: Harper & Row.

Butler, R. N., & Lewis, M. L. (1986). *Love and sex after 40.* New York: Harper & Row.

Cosper, B., Fuller, S., & Tobinson, G. (1978). Characteristics of post hospitalization recovery following hysterectomy. *Journal of Obstetrics, Gynecology and Neonatal Nursing, 7*, 7-11.

Dilman, V. M. (1971). Age associated elevation of hypothalamic threshold to feedback control and its role in development, aging and disease. *Lancet, 1*, 1211.

Ellenberg, M. (1977). Sexual aspect of female diabetic. *Mount Sinai Journal of New York, 44*, 495-500.

Erikson, E. (1963). *Childhood and society.* New York: Norton.

Featherstone, M., & Hepworth, M. (1983). The midlife style of "George and Lynne": Notes on a popular strip. *Theory, Culture and Society, 1*(3), 85-92.

Featherstone, M., & Hepworth, M. (1985). The male menopause: Lifestyle and sexuality. *Maturitas, 7*(3), 235-246.

Gould, R. E. (1980). Sexual problems: Changes and choices in mid-life: Developmental and clinical issues. In W. H. Norman & T. J. Scaranella (Eds.), *Mid-life crisis: Developmental and clinical issues* (pp. 110-127). New York: Brunner/Mazel.

Greenblatt, R. B. (1977). Estrogens in cancer change the way you treat post-menopausal patients. *Modern Medicine, 45*, 47-48.

Greenblatt, R. B., Nezhat, C., Roesel, R. A., & Natrajan, P. K. (1979). Update on the male and female climacteric. *Journal of American Geriatrics Society, 27*(11), 481-490.

Henker, F. L. (1977). A male climacteric syndrome: Sexual, psychic, and physical complaints in 50 middle-aged men. *Psychosomatics, 18*(5), 23-27.

Hite, S. (1987). *Women and love: A cultural revolution in progress.* New York: Knopf.

Kaplan, H. S. (1974). *The new sex therapy.* New York: Brunner/Mazel.

Kaplan, H. S. (1979). *Disorders of sexual disease.* New York: Brunner/Mazel.

Kaplan, H. S. (1983). *The evaluation of sexual disorders.* New York: Brunner/Mazel.

Kayne, R. C. (1976). Drugs and the aged. In I. M. Burnside (Ed.), *Nursing and the aged* (pp. 436-451). New York: McGraw-Hill.

Kinsey, A., Pomeroy, W. B., & Martin, C. J. (1948). *Sexual behavior in the human male.* Philadelphia: W. B. Saunders.

Kinsey, A., Pomeroy, W. B., Martin, C. J., & Gebhard, P. H. (1953). *Sexual behavior in the human female.* Philadelphia: W. B. Saunders.

Kolodny, R. C., Kahn, C., Goldstein, H., & Barnett, D. (1974). Sexual dysfunction in diabetic men. *Diabetes, 23*, 306.

Levinson, D. J., Darrow, C. N., Klein, E. B., Levinson, M. H., & McKee, B. (1978). *Seasons of a man's life.* New York: Knopf.

Leviton. D. (1978). The significance of sexuality as a deterrent to suicide among the aged. *Death Education*, 2(3), 261-280.

Livson. F. B. (1983). Gender identity. In R. B. Weg (Ed.), *Sexuality in the later years: Roles and behavior* (pp. 105-127). New York: Academic Press.

Maslow. A. H. (1970). *Motivation and personality* (2nd ed.). New York: Harper.

Masters, W. H., & Johnson, V. E. (1970). *Human sexual inadequacy*. Boston: Little, Brown.

Masters. W. H., Johnson, V. E., & Kolodny, R. C. (1982). *Human sexuality*. Boston: Little, Brown.

Masters, W. H., Johnson, V. E., & Kolodny, R. C. (1985). *Human sexuality* (2nd ed.). Boston: Little, Brown.

Masters, W. H., Johnson, V. E., & Kolodny, R. C. (1986). *Sex and human loving*. Boston: Little, Brown.

McArthur. J. W. (1981). The contemporary menopause. *Primary Care, 8*, 141-164.

McCarthy. B. W. (1982). Sexual dysfunctions and dissatisfactions among middle-years couples. *Journal of Sex Education and Therapy, 8*(2), 9-12.

McCary, J. L., & McCary, S. P. (1982). *McCary's human sexuality* (4th ed.). Belmont, CA: Wadsworth.

Melman. A., & Henry, D. (1979). The possible role of the catecholamines of the corpora in penile erection. *Journal of Urology, 121*, 419-421.

Nachtigall. L. (1976). Behind the estrogen-cancer headline. *Medical World News, 17*, 39.

Naifeh. S.. & Smith, G. W. (1984). *Why can't men open up? Overcoming men's fear of intimacy*. New York: Clarkson M. Potter.

Neugarten. B. L., & Datan, N. (1976). The middle years. *Journal of Geriatric Psychiatry*, 9(1), 45-49.

Parker. G. (1985). The search for intimacy in mid-life: An exploration of several myths. *Australian and New Zealand Journal of Psychiatry, 19*(4), 362-371.

Peplau. L. A. (1981). What homosexuals want. *Psychology Today, 15*(3), 28-38.

Pfeiffer. E., & Davis, G. C. (1972). Determinants of sexual behavior in middle and old age. *Journal of American Geriatrics Society, 20*, 151-158.

Porcino. J. (1983). *Growing older, getting better: A handbook for women in the second half of life*. Reading, MA: Addison-Wesley.

Reitz. R. (1977). *Menopause: A positive approach*. Radnor, PA: Chilton.

Renshaw. D. C. (1985). Sex, age, and values. *Journal of American Geriatrics Society, 33*(9), 635-643.

Rollin. B. (1976). *First, you cry*. Philadelphia: J. B. Lippincott.

Rosenberg. S. D., Farrell, M., & Por, D. (1976). Identity and crisis in middle aged men. *International Journal of Aging and Human Development, 7*, 153-170.

Rubin. L. (1982). Sex and sexuality: Women at midlife. In M. Kirkpatricks (Ed.), *Women's sexual experiences—Exploration of the dark continent* (pp. 61-82). New York: Plenum.

Rutherford. R. N. (1956). The male and female climacteric. *Postgraduate Medicine, 50*, 125-128.

Scully. D., & Bart, P. (1973). A funny thing happened on the way to the orifice: Women in gynecological textbooks. *American Journal of Sociology, 78*, 1045-1050.

Sheehy. G. (1976). *Passages: Predictable crises of adult life*. New York: E. P. Hutton.

Sherman. B. M., & Korenman, S. G. (1975). Hormonal characteristics of the human menstrual cycle throughout reproductive life. *Journal of Clinical Investigation, 55*, 699.

Steitz. J. A. (1981-1982). The female life course: Life situations and perception of control. *International Journal of Aging and Human Development, 14*(3), 195-204.

Stoppard, M. (1983). *50-plus lifeguide*. London: Darling Kindersky.

Tannahill, R. (1980). *Sex in history*. New York: Stein and Day.

Trimmer, E. G. (1970). *Rejuvenation*. Cranbury, NJ: A. S. Barnes.

Van Dusen, R. A., & Sheldon, E. B. (1976). The changing status of American women: A life cycle perspective. *American Psychologist, 31*, 106-116.

Verbrugge, L. M. (1983). Multiple roles and physical health of women and men. *Journal of Health and Social Behavior, 24*, 16-30.

Verbrugge, L. M. (1986). Role burdens and physical health of women and men. *Women and Health, 11*(1), 47-77.

Weg, R. B. (1978). Drug interaction with changing physiology of the aged: Practice and potential. In R. C. Kayne (Ed.), *Drugs and the elderly* (pp. 103-142). Los Angeles: University of Southern California Press.

Weg, R. B. (1981). Normal aging changes in the reproductive system. In I. M. Burnside (Ed.), *Nursing and the aged* (2nd ed., pp. 362-373). New York: McGraw-Hill.

Weg, R. B. (1982). Beyond babies and orgasm. *Educational Horizons, 60*(1), 161-170, 196-197.

Weg, R. B. (1983a). Changing physiology of aging: Normal and pathological. In D. Woodruff & J. E. Birren (Eds.), *Aging: Scientific perspectives and social issues* (2nd ed., rev., pp. 242-277). Monterey, CA: Brooks/Cole.

Weg, R. B. (1983b). Introduction: Beyond intercourse and orgasm. In R. B. Weg (Ed.), *Sexuality in the later years: Roles and behavior* (pp. 1-10). New York: Academic Press.

Weg, R. B. (1983c). The physiological perspective. In R. B. Weg (Ed.), *Sexuality in the later years: Roles and behavior* (pp. 39-80). New York: Academic Press.

Weg, R. B. (1985). Sexuality in old age. In M. S. J. Pathy (Ed.), *Textbook of geriatric medicine* (pp. 131-147). New York: John Wiley.

Weg, R. B. (1987a). Biomedical aspects of menopause. In *Encyclopedia of aging* (pp. 433-437). New York: Springer.

Weg, R. B. (1987b). Intimacy and the later years. In G. Lesnoff-Caravaglia (Ed.), *Handbook of applied gerontology* (pp. 127-142). New York: Human Sciences Press.

Weg, R. B. (1987c). Sexuality in the menopause. In D. R. Mishell (Ed.), *Menopause: Physiology and pharmacology* (pp. 127-138). Chicago: Year Book Medical Publishers.

Witherington, R. (1974). The controversial male climacteric. In L. Mastroiani (Ed.), *Clinician: Male and female: An endocrine update* (pp. 51-55). New York: Medcom Press.

2

Menopause and Other Health Issues for Midlife Women

Alice J. Dan
Linda A. Bernhard

Like other menstrual cycle phenomena, menopause has been so mythologized that it is difficult to untangle its reality in women's lives. Different groups view menopause in dissimilar ways: Women who have been through the experience see it mostly in positive or neutral terms, whereas younger women and men report more negative attitudes. The medical community has conceptualized menopause as a sign of decay, as a neurosis, and as an estrogen deficiency disease (Posner, 1979). Despite the recent emergence of more positive views of menopause as a natural life process presenting few problems for healthy women, women still encounter negative stereotypes of menopause in health care situations (DeLorey & Rosenkrantz, in press; McElmurry & Huddleston, 1987).

Cultural meanings of menopause depend on the social value of women in the culture. Where women are largely defined by their reproductive role, menopause is seen as a serious loss of status. In this context, women's functions are viewed as biologically determined, their worth is based on femininity and attractiveness, and aging women are seen as useless and repulsive. In contrast, where age and experience are valued qualities in women, menopause is more positively viewed as one visible sign of ongoing life change. Few writers note that menopause is biologically unique to humans. It has been suggested that there is an evolutionary advantage to the cessation of reproductive function at an age when a woman is still vigorous and able to carry out the arduous responsibilities of parenting for the long period of human immaturity (Alington-MacKinnon & Troll, 1981; Donaldson, 1983).

In this chapter, we present definitions of menopause, perspectives on health care for midlife women, symptom incidence and management approaches for menopausal problems, sociocultural aspects of the menopause experience, and related health issues for midlife women.

Definition of Menopause

Although nearly every midlife woman will experience menopause, it is one of the most misunderstood and little studied aspects of women's health. Terminology relating to menopause is confusing. Strictly speaking, menopause refers to the cessation of menstruation. When women refer to menopause, however, they usually are referring to a time in their lives during which their menstrual cycles change and, ultimately, cease. These changes result from a progressive decrease in the production of hormones by the ovaries, and the period of time is technically known as the climacteric (Utian & Serr, 1976). Women, and men as well, refer to this period of time as the "change of life." The male climacteric is less noticeable, involving a more gradual reduction in fertility, occurring five to ten years later than menopause (Webb, 1985; Weg, 1977).

There are numerous operational definitions for menopause (e.g., Green, 1977; Holzman, 1983; McKinlay & Jefferys, 1974). These often include such terms as premenopause, perimenopause, and postmenopause for which there are no standard definitions. Menopause itself is generally considered to have occurred when a woman has not menstruated for one year. A distinction is also made between "natural" menopause and "artificial" menopause. Artificial menopause results from surgical removal of the ovaries (i.e., surgical menopause) or from destruction of the ovaries by radiation or chemotherapy.

The major differences between natural and surgical menopause are the gradual versus sudden onset and the severity of symptoms. The severity of symptoms experienced during menopause depends on the woman's age and weight, as well as whether she receives estrogen replacement (Kase, 1986).

It is clear that menopause is a socially constructed concept (MacPherson, 1981, 1985), and that how it is used depends on the purposes of the person using the term. Menopause is not synonymous with aging; it appears to be a biologically timed change, rather than a result of atrophy or a breakdown in functioning. Yet the age when it occurs (51 is the current modal age) (Holzman, 1983) is an age when men and women alike believe that they are "getting old." Thus menopause is concurrent with aging and has frequently been "blamed" for many of the problems related to aging. It is difficult to separate the unique effects of menopause from the general effects of aging.

Approaches to
Midlife Women's Health

Until recently biomedical perspectives have dominated the literature on menopause and other health issues for midlife women. Both physiological and psychological symptoms were seen as a result of declining hormone levels, particularly estrogen (Gannon, 1985). Studies of hormonal and tissue changes (e.g., Blum & Eliam, 1979; Studd, Chakravarti, & Collins, 1978) have been used as evidence for the view of menopause as a disease entity, so that the focus for research has been on etiology, diagnosis, symptoms, and treatment of menopause. Based primarily on clinical observation and case studies, this medical literature reflects different sources of information than does the experience of the majority of midlife women (DeLorey & Rosenkrantz, in press). In particular, it reflects problematic rather than normal menopause experiences, and it does not differentiate well between the effects of artificial menopause and natural menopause. Nevertheless, this view is perpetuated by health care providers. A recent study (McElmurry & Huddleston, 1987) found that nurses viewed menopause more negatively than did their menopausal clients. The nurses perceived menopausal women as moody, disinterested in sex, and the victims of "hot flashes." In contrast, the menopausal women reported that they felt freer, more in control of their lives, and enjoyed better communication (including sexual) than they had prior to menopause.

From the mid-nineteenth century on, a wide variety of symptoms and diseases were associated with menopause in the medical literature (Nolan, 1984). With the rise of psychoanalysis, menopause took on the added risk of "involutional melancholia," a diagnosis that appeared in the official *Diagnostic and Statistical Manual of Mental Disorder* until 1979. This diagnosis characterized menopausal depression as endogenously caused, that is, not related to life events, but rather due to the physiological changes of aging and especially the decline in reproductive hormones. Lack of evidence for such hormonally related psychological symptoms led to the deletion of this diagnosis from the psychiatric nomenclature.

More recently, menopause has been characterized as an "estrogen deficiency disease" (Wilson & Wilson, 1963). The identified risks of estrogen "replacement" therapy have resulted in more caution in prescribing estrogen in recent years (Grossman & Bart, 1980). Because estrogen plays a role in moderating the bone loss that leads to osteoporosis, however, it is again being touted as "the single most effective preventive measure" for midlife women (Riis, Thomsen, & Christiansen, 1987).

Psychosocial models for midlife women's health have focused on premorbid personality, stressful life events, and the cultural meanings of menopause. There is evidence that women's previous experiences and adjustment; life events occurring coincident with menopause, such as children leaving home or loss of parents; and the social context for menopause can affect how a woman experiences this process (Gannon, 1985). Recognizing these effects does not mean that a woman's personality or attitudes can be "blamed" for her symptoms, or that her complaints are "all in her head." Rather, these areas offer potential for understanding a particular woman's experience, and for providing support and validation to her.

In promoting the most effective health care for midlife women, it is clearly desirable to integrate aspects of both the biomedical and the psychosocial models of menopause (Koeske, 1982; Nolan, 1984). This integrated model has been called "biosocial," "holistic," or "women's health" (Boston Women's Health Book Collective, 1984). A recent concept paper on nursing practice in women's health (Webster et al., 1986) emphasized illness prevention and health promotion throughout the life span, rather than focusing on reproductive health only. Health care relationships are viewed as egalitarian and collaborative, with a focus on each woman's lived experience, "to enable women to make choices that expand their ability to care for their health and effectively use sources of illness care when necessary" (Webster et al., 1986, p. 143). These concepts seem especially appropriate ways of viewing health in the menopause process.

The Changes of Menopause:
Symptoms and Management

Symptoms. Systematic studies of representative samples of midlife women have generally found few specific symptoms associated with menopause. The only universally identified menopausal symptom is the hot flash (also called hot flush). A hot flash is described as "a sudden, brief wave of heat sometimes accompanied by sweating and chills" (Israel, Poland, Reame, & Warner, 1980, p. 18). Waves usually spread from the chest upward to neck, face, and arms and may last from a few seconds to a minute or more. Hot flashes often occur at night, thus the term *night sweats* (Fogel & Woods, 1981).

There is clear evidence that hot flashes are associated with lower levels of estrogen and higher levels of luteinizing hormone (LH). Atrophic vaginal changes—thinning and dryness of vaginal membranes—are also associated directly with lower estrogen levels. These vaginal changes are less severe in women who are sexually active, however, so they are not universally associated with menopause.

In natural menopause, gradual changes occur in menstrual functioning, with increasingly irregular occurrence of menstruation, increased incidence of anovulatory cycles, and sometimes increased or decreased bleeding during menstruation. Cycle length may be longer or shorter than it was previously, but if the intervals from onset of one bleeding to onset of the next become shorter than 20 days, a woman should check with her health care provider to make sure that she is experiencing a normal variation. Extremely heavy bleeding, interfering with work, for example, should always be investigated, although often no problem is found.

The cessation of menstruation typically occurs between ages 45 and 55. A myth that the age of menopause can be predicted from the age of menarche ("the earlier you begin to menstruate, the later you experience menopause") has recently been disproven (Treloar, 1982). Most frequently, women experience their last period about age 50, so that 51 is commonly listed as the modal age for menopause. Some women begin to experience menstrual changes in their thirties, however, and others not until near 60 years (Graham, 1986).

Estrogen production does not entirely cease with menopause. It is possible that the ovaries and the adrenal gland secrete some estrogen after menopause, but the primary source is fat tissue, which converts androgens to estrogens. For this reason, thin women are at higher risk for experiencing the menopausal symptoms related to estrogen decline (hot flashes and atrophic vaginal changes).

Recent literature has described this period of menstrual cycle changes culminating in cessation of menstruation as the menopause "trajectory" (Voda, 1982). It is problematic for some women because there are so few marking points along this trajectory. If a woman is sexually active and her menstrual periods become irregular, she will be concerned about becoming pregnant. Distinguishing pregnancy or pathology from normal menopausal changes is a salient need for midlife women, requiring further research (McElmurry & Huddleston, 1987).

Hot flashes and night sweats, sometimes called vasomotor symptoms, are the classic signs of menopause. They are experienced in every group studied, except those taking estrogen replacement (Goodman, Stewart, & Gilbert, 1977; Jackson, 1985, in press; Kearns & Christoferson, in press). Jackson (in press) reported that in a sample of 120 Black climacteric women without hysterectomies, 13% experienced considerable difficulty with vasomotor symptoms, 28% experienced no difficulty, and the majority (59%) had some difficulty. These severity rates are similar to those reported for other groups.

Recent studies document that heat and stress can precipitate hot flashes (Freedman, Germaine, & Swartzman, 1987; Guice, 1987). Guice (1987) proposed that the hot flash is a normal temperature-regulating response by the hypothalamus, intended to bring about thermal equilibrium through emergency heat loss. She found that core body temperature, as assessed by digital blood flow, was lower in menopausal subjects, except at the time of the hot flash. It is possible that some as-yet-unidentified metabolic changes are involved in this lowering of finger temperature.

Some group differences in vasomotor symptoms have been found. Nolan (1984) reported that menopausal women with unstable or interrupted careers had greater severity of vasomotor symptoms than those with stable career patterns among a group of 48 midlife nurses. Women with artificial menopause have reported considerably more problems than women with natural menopause (McKinlay & McKinlay, 1986).

Other frequently reported symptoms in midlife women include fatigue, headache, backache and other aches and pains, insomnia, and depression (McKinlay & Jefferys, 1974; Nolan, 1984; Thompson, Hart, & Durno, 1973). Direct relationships to the normal physiological changes of menopause have not been found for these symptoms, but many women do associate these symptoms with menopause.

Bart (1971) found that women who were seriously depressed at menopause were more likely to have been heavily invested in traditional roles of wife and mother. Empty nests are not necessarily associated with menopause, especially now that many women are becoming pregnant in their thirties and forties rather than earlier.

In a study of normal women, Nolan (1984) reported that depression was not significantly related to menopause, but a lowering of life satisfaction was found in women at menopause. This lessening of positive affect was more severe in women with unstable careers. Severne (1982) suggested that there is a period of stress associated with menopause; she found it more severe for working-class employed women than for upper-class women probably not employed outside the home.

Management. The most popular medical approach for addressing menopausal symptoms is hormone replacement therapy (HRT). Controversies about HRT concern purpose of therapy, dosage, length of time used, and drug(s) used.

A woman may be given hormone therapy for several purposes. If the purpose of therapy is to prevent osteoporosis, the approach may be different than if the purpose is to treat climacteric symptoms. Whether or not estrogen is effective in helping women with emotional symptoms is a matter of some dispute, as is the use of estrogen for treating "estrogen deficiency" in the absence of symptoms.

Dosage is problematic because estrogen preparations are available in only a few dosages. Because each woman is different, the dosage optimal for her may not be available. The dosage also varies with purpose of therapy (Gambrell, 1987). Dosage is related to route of therapy—of which there are several, including oral, intravaginal, transdermal, and subdermal. Some studies have been conducted to determine how much estrogen is actually absorbed into the blood stream and how rapidly via the different routes, but much more information is needed (Hammond & Maxson, 1986).

When a woman begins hormone replacement therapy, she may think that it is just to treat the symptoms that she is experiencing, but perhaps her physician assumes that she will continue taking it for the rest of her life. A recently published nursing protocol suggested that estrogen replacement for treatment of menopausal symptoms be used for six months to a year, and then gradually tapered and stopped (Ladewig, 1985).

The length of time estrogen is used should depend partly on whether or not the woman has previously taken exogenous estrogen in other forms— usually oral contraceptives, but possibly diethylstilbestrol (DES) during pregnancy or after a rape; as well as whether or not she was exposed to DES during fetal life. These previous exposures may increase risks; however, the cumulative effects and risks of exogenous estrogen are not well studied.

Some physicians will initiate estrogen "replacement" before a woman has ceased menstruating, whether or not she experiences any menopausal symptoms. Other physicians believe that "treatment" should not begin until after menstrual periods have stopped. Some physicians prescribe estrogen only for symptoms; others believe they should give the drug to prevent osteoporosis.

The specific drug used is another area of controversy. Women can take estrogen, progesterone, or a combination of the two—in natural or synthetic forms. Several drug companies manufacture these drugs, and women's tolerance for the different products can vary. Some women may also be given testosterone to treat menopausal symptoms.

Other controversies about the use of hormone replacement therapy concern the risks of the drugs. The use of exogenous estrogen is well documented as being related to the development of endometrial hyperplasia and carcinoma (Lee, Wingo, Peterson, Rubin, & Sattin, 1986). Its relationship to breast cancer is less clear, but there may be a risk (Lee et al., 1986). The use of progesterone concurrently with estrogen has been shown to be effective in minimizing these side effects and is now believed also to enhance the positive effect of estrogen on prevention of osteoporosis (Gambrell, 1987).

Other potential side effects of estrogen are an increased risk of gall bladder disease including gallstones, and a possible increase in the incidence of hypertension (Hammond & Maxson, 1986). On the positive side, however, studies presently being conducted suggest that taking estrogen may decrease blood cholesterol, and thus have a positive effect in reducing the risk of coronary heart disease with myocardial infarction.

Self-care may well be the best approach for most women to manage menopause. In order for women to know what is happening to their menstrual cycles and their bodies, it is useful for midlife women to keep a journal or calendar record of their menstruation (Voda, 1982). Dates of each period and type of flow should be recorded. It must be emphasized that every woman is different, and individual variation is to be expected. With accurate recordings, a woman will know exactly when she has become menopausal. She will also be better prepared to consult with health care professionals about her cycles. She can also initiate or continue breast self-examination at a regular time each month.

To manage hot flashes, many women find that wearing layers of clothing helps, so that when a hot flash occurs, one or more layers can be removed. Women also find clothing made of natural fiber (e.g., cotton) more comfortable than synthetics. Most women simply do nothing or "wait out" their hot flashes, but other things that help some women include sitting in front of a fan or taking a cool shower to treat hot flashes. Some women find it helpful to avoid drinking hot fluids or eating spicy foods. In Voda's (1981) study of hot flashes, women used a variety of "coping mechanisms" to deal with their hot flashes, including having a cold drink, using air conditioning, and taking off clothing. Sometimes women indicated that they did nothing. Of all the coping mechanisms used, however, none was considered by the women as effective as estrogen.

Although a woman may expect to experience menopause similarly to her mother (if she has that information), she may not have the same experience. Women benefit from talking about menopause with older female relatives or friends who have already had the experience. Self-help groups can be informal and short-term or ongoing groups that discuss many aspects of midlife, including menopause (Schmid-Heinisch, 1985). Some women prefer more intimate private conversation than a support group situation. Women who experience depression at the time of menopause may particularly benefit from a support group experience. They can share their feelings and find out that others feel similarly, as well as find ways to cope with the feelings.

A menopausal woman's capacity for sexual desire and sexual expression is not changed simply by virtue of her menopausal status. When vaginal changes occur, however, they may result in dyspareunia (vaginal pain, especially with sexual intercourse). The best management is prevention: consistent sexual activity, whether intercourse or masturbation, has been shown to prevent or delay the onset of vaginal atrophy (Leiblum, Bachmann, Kemmann, Colburn, & Swartzman, 1983).

If vaginal pain occurs, a woman can do several things to make sexual intercourse more comfortable. She can use a water-soluble lubricant, such as K-Y jelly. Both she and her partner should take plenty of time to be sure that she is fully aroused and as naturally lubricated as possible. In addition, she can try alternate positions to determine if she is more comfortable in a position where she has more control over penetration, such as female superior or side-lying.

Sociocultural Aspects of Menopause

Attitudes toward menopause are generally found to be negative. An early study (Neugarten, Wood, Kraines, & Loomis, 1963) reported that younger women rated menopause significantly more negatively than older women. This finding has been replicated in other reports, with the additional finding that men also rate menopause more negatively than women (Kahana, Kiyak, & Liang, 1980; Perlmutter & Bart, 1982). Thus it seems that having the experience of menopause increases one's positive view of the process. Some women who have been through it speak of "postmenopausal zest," PMZ! These differences in social attitudes indicate the power of inaccurate stereotypes to influence beliefs, and perhaps illustrates how the experience of older women is devalued in the United States because their version is not widely known or accepted.

Very few reports of cross-cultural data on menopause are available. Beyene (in press) studied rural Mayan Indians and rural Greek women, noting both similarities and differences in their menopausal experiences. Both groups perceived menopause as a life stage free of the taboos and restrictions of childbearing years. Freedom to participate in more activities and freedom from the risk of pregnancy and the bother of menstruation characterized reports of menopause. Age at menopause among Mayans (mean age 42) was significantly younger than among Greeks (mean age 47).

In addition, menopause was welcomed among Mayans, while among Greeks it was associated with anxiety, getting old, and having problems. Thus Greek attitudes were more similar to those of women in the United States. Other primarily non-Western groups have also been reported to view menopause positively, and to associate it with few or no symptoms (Dowty, Maoz, Antonovsky, & Wijsenbeek, 1970; Flint, 1975; Griffen, 1977, 1982; Maoz, Antonovsky, Apter, Wijsenbeek, & Datan, 1977). Further study of attitudes toward menopause will be facilitated by the recent development of a valid, reliable semantic differential questionnaire for use in measuring these attitudes (Bowles, 1986, in press). The simple format makes it potentially transferable to a variety of cultural contexts.

Other Health Issues for
Midlife Women

Bleeding and hysterectomy. Any vaginal bleeding in a woman who has experienced a natural menopause must be considered seriously. Roughly one-third of postmenopausal bleeding, and also irregular or heavy bleeding perimenopausally, results from hyperplasia, polyps, and either benign or malignant tumors in the uterus (Casey, 1983). Diagnosis usually requires tissue examination by endometrial biopsy or dilatation and curettage (D & C).

One circular myth is that menopausal women need a hysterectomy; and that having a hysterectomy causes a woman to experience menopause. To counter this myth, all menopausal women do not need hysterectomies. Hysterectomy is not necessarily the answer for "curing" symptoms that occur during midlife. Having a hysterectomy results in menopause only if the woman is premenopausal at the time, and if both ovaries are also removed.

The most common reason for having a hysterectomy in midlife is uterine myomas (that is, fibroid tumors). These are benign tumors that are more common in Black than in White women (Silverberg & Wallach, 1984). Most myomas are asymptomatic; the most common symptom is a change in menstrual bleeding—usually either heavier periods or bleeding between periods. There may also be abdominal pain, often described as pelvic pressure or fullness. The growth of myomas may be increased during pregnancy or with the use of exogenous estrogen, and myomas may diminish in size after menopause (Silverberg & Wallach, 1984). Consequently, if a woman can cope with the symptoms until after her periods cease, she may be able to avoid a hysterectomy.

Breast and lung cancer. Breast cancer is the most common cause of cancer in woman; lung cancer is the most common cause of cancer deaths in women (American Cancer Society, 1987). One in eleven women can expect to develop breast cancer. Unfortunately, that rate has not changed for many years. More women than ever are surviving breast cancer, however, because of early diagnosis and better treatment. Women who regularly perform breast self-examination (BSE) can develop a secure feeling about their ability to detect changes in their breasts. Mammography, as well as BSE, is now recommended by the American Cancer Society as a method of diagnosing breast cancers too small to be palpated.

Throughout their reproductive years, women should perform BSE each month, after their menstrual period. As cycles change during menopause, women should continue to perform BSE after their periods; however, if two or three months go by without periods, women should perform BSE at the time they would regularly expect their periods. Because this can become difficult to remember unless one keeps a calendar, some women select one day (like the first of the month) and perform BSE on that day each month, regardless of when their periods occur. That becomes an easy way to remember to perform BSE after periods have stopped. Because the incidence of breast cancer increases with age, it is important for women to continue BSE after menopause.

Lung cancer has now surpassed breast cancer as the leading cancer killer of women. Two reasons account for this finding. First, because lung cancer is difficult to detect at an early stage, treatment is still fairly ineffective. Second, and more important in women, the increased incidence of lung cancer can be directly correlated with increased cigarette smoking by women.

Osteoporosis. National attention has recently focused on the mortality and health costs associated with bone fractures in elderly women (Kelsey & Hoffman, 1987; Ray, Griffen, Schaffner, Baugh, & Melton, 1987). In midlife, women need to be concerned about preventing excessive loss of bone mineral that would later increase their risk of brittle bones. Bone loss begins in the thirties and proceeds at a slow rate of 1% per year in both men and women. Women are at greater risk of fractures largely because their bones are less dense than men's. Around the time of menopause, some studies have reported an increase up to 4%-5% per year of bone loss in some women. Reasons for this increase are not yet completely understood, but estrogen plays a role in preventing excessive bone loss. Dietary calcium and weight-bearing physical activity also contribute to bone maintenance.

Slender women, those with light skin, and those who smoke are at higher risk for greater bone loss. A family history of bone fractures and early removal of ovaries are other factors contributing to a high risk of osteoporosis. Women with these risk factors should consider taking estrogen supplements around the time of menopause. Women who have hysterectomies before menopause need to know if their ovaries are also removed, because that will significantly affect their risk of bone loss. Adequate dietary calcium is important throughout life, but especially after age 40. Regular walking or other weight-bearing exercise is also recommended.

Weight control and fitness. Many midlife women experience difficulty in controlling their weight. Our society encourages a near phobia about obesity or even being slightly overweight and women may become anxious about adding pounds more easily as they age. Mechanisms for explaining the increased tendency to gain weight have not been clearly documented, yet many midlife women have this problem. The health risks associated with weight more than 20% over ideal weight, as given in insurance tables, are high blood pressure, increased risk of uterine cancer, and diabetes (Norsigian, 1986). But recent studies have shown that dieting to lose weight is ineffective and possibly dangerous.

Many of the risks traditionally associated with excess weight may actually be the result of chronic dieting (Kano, 1985). Of those who lose weight dieting, 95% regain more weight than they lost (Norsigian, 1986). The body is stressed by repeatedly going on and off diets. There are also some benefits to "excess weight" of 10%-30% over the ideal weight on the insurance tables (Norsigian, 1986). These include the production of estrogen by fat tissue, which eases the menopausal transition; the extra weight-bearing of a few pounds, which helps to prevent osteoporosis; and the body reserves that help to survive trauma. In the famous Framingham heart study (Wilson, Garrison, & Castelli, 1985), women with the lowest mortality rates were within this weight range. A long-term follow-up of over 34,000 adults showed that thinness and weight loss were associated with higher mortality, particularly for cigarette smokers (Sidney, Friedman, & Siegelaub, 1987). Diet suggestions for minimizing health risks include eating more whole grains and vegetables, more iron and calcium-rich foods, and minimizing intake of sugar, salt, fat, and highly processed foods. Rather than focusing on losing weight, the more effective approach is to improve the nutritional content of one's diet and exercise regularly to keep fit (Kano, 1985; Norsigian, 1986).

Conclusion

Despite considerable medical concern with menopause, we still lack knowledge based on women's experiences of normal menopause. Conceptualizations of menopause as disease, deficiency, or decline are detrimental to healthy midlife women. These myths help maintain a stereotype of the menopausal woman as unattractive, old, no longer sexually active, and crabby. They result in women being anxious about menopause and uncomfortable talking about it.

A major myth of menopause today is what Pauline Bart refers to as the "myth of the myths" (Grossman & Bart, 1980). That is, in the past the myth of menopause was that menopause was a terrible experience. More recently, the myth is that menopause is easy—it just happens, and women will not have any symptoms or problems. The truth for most women is somewhere in between, and it is important in working with midlife women to recognize the full range of possible menopause experiences.

References

Alington-MacKinnon, D., & Troll, L. E. (1981). The adaptive function of the menopause: A devil's advocate position. *Journal of the American Geriatrics Society, 29*(8), 349-353.

American Cancer Society. (1987). *Cancer facts and figures.* New York: Author.

Bart, P. B. (1971). Depression in middle-aged women. In V. Gornick & B. K. Moran (Eds.), *Woman in sexist society* (pp. 99-117). New York: Basic Books.

Beyene, Y. (in press). Menopause: A biocultural event. In A. J. Dan & L. L. Lewis (Eds.), *Menstrual health in women's lives.* New York: Basic Books.

Blum, M., & Eliam, I. (1979). The vaginal flora after natural or surgical menopause. *Journal of the American Geriatrics Society, 27*(9), 395-397.

Boston Women's Health Book Collective. (1984). *The new our bodies ourselves.* New York: Simon & Schuster.

Bowles, C. (1986). Measure of attitude toward menopause using the semantic differential model. *Nursing Research, 35*, 81-85.

Bowles, C. (in press). The development of a measure of attitude toward menopause. In A. J. Dan & L. L. Lewis (Eds.), *Menstrual health in women's lives.* Champaign: University of Illinois Press.

Casey, M. J. (1983). Abnormal genital bleeding. In B. M. Peckham & S. S. Shapiro (Eds.), *Signs and symptoms in gynecology* (pp. 384-418). Philadelphia: Lippincott.

DeLorey, C., & Rosenkrantz, P. S. (in press). Differing perspectives of menopause—an attribution theory approach. In A. J. Dan & L. L. Len (Eds.), *Menstrual health in women's lives.* Champaign: University of Illinois Press.

Donaldson, J. F. (1983). Letter to the editor. *Maturitas, 5*, 47-48.

Dowty, N., Maoz, B., Antonovsky, A., & Wijsenbeek, H. (1970). Climacterium in three cultural contexts. *Tropical and Geographical Medicine, 22*, 77-86.

Flint, M. (1975). The menopause: Reward or punishment? *Psychosomatics, 16*, 161-163.

Fogel, C. I., & Woods, N. F. (1981). *Health care of women: A nursing perspective.* St. Louis: C. V. Mosby.

Freedman, R. R., Germaine, L. M., & Swartzman, L. (1987). *Laboratory and ambulatory monitoring of menopausal hot flashes.* Paper presented at the 7th Conference of the Society for Menstrual Cycle Research, Ann Arbor, MI.

Gambrell, R. D., Jr. (1987). Estrogen replacement therapy: Guidelines for safe use. *Drug Therapy, 17*(1), 68-81.

Gannon, L. R. (1985). *Menstrual disorders and menopause.* New York: Praeger.

Goodman, M. J., Stewart, C. J., & Gilbert, F., Jr. (1977). Patterns of menopause: A study of certain medical and physiological variables among Caucasian and Japanese women living in Hawaii. *Journal of Gerontology, 32*, 291-298.

Graham, E. A. (1986). Menstruation and menopause. In J. Griffith-Kenney (Ed.), *Contemporary women's health* (pp. 434-448). Menlo Park, CA: Addison-Wesley.

Green, T. H., Jr. (1977). *Gynecology.* Boston: Little, Brown.

Griffen, J. (1977). A cross-cultural investigation of behavioral changes at menopause. *Social Science Journal, 14*(2), 49-55.

Griffen, J. (1982). Cultural models for coping with menopause. In A. M. Voda, M. Dinnerstein, & S. R. O'Donnell (Eds.), *Changing perspectives on menopause* (pp. 248-262). Austin: University of Texas Press.

Grossman, M., & Bart, P. B. (1980). The politics of menopause. In A. J. Dan, E. A. Graham, & C. P. Beecher (Eds.), *The menstrual cycle: A synthesis of interdisciplinary research* (pp. 179-185). New York: Springer.

Guice, E. E. (1987). *A parsimonious hypothesis of the mechanism of the menopausal hot flash.* Paper presented at the 7th Conference of the Society for Menstrual Cycle Research, Ann Arbor, MI.

Hammond, C. B., & Maxson, W. S. (1986). Estrogen replacement therapy. *Clinical Obstetrics and Gynecology, 29*, 407-430.

Holzman, G. B. (1983). Menopausal and perimenopausal problems. In R. W. Hale & J. A. Krieger (Eds.), *Gynecology* (pp. 321-332). New Hyde Park, NY: Medical Examination.

Israel, J., Poland, N., Reame, N., & Warner, D. (1980). *Surviving the change: A practical guide to menopause.* Detroit: Cinnabar.

Jackson, B. B. (1985). Role of social resource variables upon the satisfaction in Black climacteric hysterectomized woman. *Nursing Papers, 17*(1), 4-21.

Jackson, B. B. (in press). Black women's responses to menarche and menopause. In A. J. Dan & L. L. Lewis (Eds.), *Menstrual health in women's lives.* Champaign: University of Illinois Press.

Kahana, E., Kiyak, A., & Liang, J. (1980). Menopause in the context of other life events. In A. J. Dan, E. A. Graham, & C. P. Beecher (Eds.), *The menstrual cycle: A synthesis of interdisciplinary research* (pp. 167-178). New York: Springer.

Kano, S. (1985). *Making peace with food.* Allston, MA: Amity.

Kase, N. (1986). Estrogen deprivation: The physiology, pathophysiology, and informed management of female menopause or castration. In L. Mastroiani, Jr., & C. A. Paulsen (Eds.), *Aging, reproduction, and the climacteric* (pp. 263-285). New York: Plenum.

Kearns, J., & Christoferson, V. A. (in press). Mexican-American women's perceptions of menopause. In A. J. Dan & L. L. Lewis (Eds), *Menstrual health in women's lives.* Champaign: University of Illinois Press.

Kelsey. J. L., & Hoffman, S. (1987). Risk factors for hip fracture. *New England Journal of Medicine, 316*(7), 404-406.

Koeske. R. D. (1982). Toward a biosocial paradigm for menopause research: Lessons and contributions from the behavioral sciences. In A. M. Voda, M. Dinnerstein, & S. R. O'Donnell (Eds.), *Changing perspectives on menopause* (pp. 3-23). Austin: University of Texas Press.

Ladewig. P. A. (1985). Protocol for estrogen replacement therapy in menopausal women. *Nurse Practitioner, 10*(10), 44-47.

Lee. N. C., Wingo, P. A., Peterson, H. B., Rubin, G. L., & Sattin, R. W. (1986). Estrogen therapy and the risk of breast, ovarian, and endometrial cancer. In L. Mastroiani, Jr., & C. A. Paulsen (Eds.), *Aging, reproduction, and the climacteric* (pp. 287-303). New York: Plenum.

Leiblum, S.. Bachmann, G., Kemmann, E., Colburn, D., & Swartzman, L. (1983). Vaginal atrophy in the postmenopausal woman. *Journal of the American Medical Association, 249,* 2195-2198.

MacPherson, K. I. (1981). Menopause as disease: The social construction of a metaphor. *Advances in Nursing Science, 3*(2), 95-113.

MacPherson, K. I. (1985). Osteoporosis and menopause: A feminist analysis of the social construction of a syndrome. *Advances in Nursing Science, 7*(4), 11-22.

Maoz. B.. Antonovsky, A., Apter, A., Wijsenbeek, H., & Datan, N. (1977). Perception of menopause in five ethnic groups in Israel. *Acta Obstetrica et Gynecologica Scandinavica, 65,* 35-40.

McElmurry. B. J., & Huddleston, D. (1987). *The perimenopausal woman: Perceived threats to sexuality and self-care responses.* Paper presented at the 7th Conference of the Society for Menstrual Cycle Research, Ann Arbor, MI.

McKinlay, S., & Jefferys, M. (1974). The menopausal syndrome. *British Journal of Preventive and Social Medicine, 28,* 108-115.

McKinlay. S. M., & McKinlay, J. B. (1986). Health status and health care utilization by menopausal women. In L. Mastroiani, Jr., & C. A. Paulsen (Eds.), *Aging, reproduction, and the climacteric* (pp. 243-262). New York: Plenum.

Neugarten. B., Wood, V., Kraines, R., & Loomis, B. (1963). Women's attitudes toward the menopause. *Vita Humana, 6,* 140-151.

Nolan. J. W. (1984). *Midlife female nurse: Work patterns, general health and psychological well-being.* Unpublished doctoral dissertation, University of Illinois at Chicago.

Norsigian, J. (1986). Dieting is dangerous to your health. *The Network News, 10*(6), 4-6.

Perlmutter. E., & Bart, P. B. (1982). "Changing views of the change": A critical review and suggestions for an attributional approach. In A. M. Voda, M. Dinnerstein, & S. R. O'Donnell (Eds.), *Changing perspectives on menopause* (pp. 187-199). Austin: University of Texas Press.

Posner. J. (1979). It's all in your head: Feminist and medical models of menopause (strange bedfellows). *Sex Roles, 5,* 179-190.

Ray, W. A., Griffin, M. R., Schaffner, W., Baugh, D. K., & Melton, L. J. (1987). Psychotropic drug use and the risk of hip fracture. *New England Journal of Medicine, 316,* 363-369.

Riis. B., Thomsen, K., & Christiansen, C. (1987). Does calcium supplementation prevent postmenopausal bone loss? *New England Journal of Medicine, 316*(4), 173-177.

Schmid-Heinisch, R. (1985). Fair to middling. *Nursing Mirror, 161*(17), 29.

Severne. L. (1982). Psychosocial aspects of the menopause. In A. M. Voda, M. Dinnerstein, & S. R. O'Donnell (Eds.), *Changing perspectives on menopause* (pp. 239-247). Austin: University of Texas Press.

Sidney, S., Friedman, G. D., & Siegelaub, A. B. (1987). Thinness and mortality. *American Journal of Public Health, 77*, 317-322.

Silverberg, A., & Wallach, E. E. (1984). Uterine leiomyomas. *Postgraduate Obstetrics and Gynecology, 4*(22), 1-6.

Studd, J. W. W., Chakravarti, S., & Collins, W. P. (1978). Plasma hormone profiles after the menopause and bilateral oophorectomy. *Postgraduate Medical Journal, 54*, 25-30.

Thompson, B., Hart, S. A., & Durno, D. (1973). Menopausal age and symptomatology in a general practice. *Journal of Biosocial Science, 5*, 71-82.

Treloar, A. E. (1982). Predicting the close of menstrual life. In A. M. Voda, M. Dinnerstein, & S. R. O'Donnell (Eds.), *Changing perspectives on the menopause* (pp. 289-304). Austin: University of Texas Press.

Utian, W. H., & Serr, D. (1976). The climacteric syndrome. In P. A. Van Keep, R. B. Greenblatt, & M. Albeaux-Fernet (Eds.), *Consensus on menopause research* (pp. 1-4). Baltimore: University Park Press.

Voda, A. M. (1981). Climacteric hot flash. *Maturitas, 3*, 73-90.

Voda, A. M. (1982). Coping with the menopausal hot flash. *Patient Counselling and Health Education, 4*(2), 80-83.

Webb, C. (1985). *Sexuality, nursing and health.* New York: John Wiley.

Webster, D., Leslie, L., McElmurry, B., Dan, A., Biordi, D., Boyer, D., Swider, S., Lipetz, M., & Newcomb, J. (1986). Nursing practice in women's health—concept paper. *Nursing Research, 35*, 143.

Weg, R. (1977). More than wrinkles. In L. E. Troll, J. Israel, & K. Israel (Eds.), *Looking ahead: A woman's guide to the problems and joys of growing older* (pp. 22-42). Englewood Cliffs, NJ: Prentice-Hall.

Wilson, P. W. F., Garrison, R. J., & Castelli, W. P. (1985). Postmenopausal estrogen use, cigarette smoking, and cardiovascular morbidity in women over 50: The Framingham Study. *New England Journal of Medicine, 313*, 1038-1043.

Wilson, R. A., & Wilson, T. (1963). The fate of non-treated post-menopausal women. *Journal of the American Geriatrics Society, 11*, 347.

Part II
Cognitive Structures

The two chapters in this part are concerned with cognitive structures, including adult thought and adult intelligence. In Chapter 3, Labouvie-Vief and Hakim-Larson observe that changes in thought processes in middle adulthood are often interpreted in terms of decline and deficit, so that such changes are believed to indicate regression. The authors propose, instead, that adults can experience a qualitative restructuring of the cognitive system that is progressive and adaptive, and brings increasing flexibility and openness in both cognitive and emotional functioning.

Labouvie-Vief and Hakim-Larson point out that youth-centered criteria for cognitive maturity are formal, abstract, and objectified. Adults, however, often think in a pragmatic, concrete, and subjective manner. The authors suggest that these two modes of thought are qualitatively different from each other. They propose that in middle adulthood individuals begin to integrate the two modes of thought in their cognitive and emotional functioning and that optimal mature thought is based on this integration. The two modes of thought are interactive and enrich each other.

The authors conclude that acknowledgment of the two modes of thought can stimulate important research on adaptive processes in adulthood. Professional helpers can facilitate understanding of the two modes of thought to help their clients recognize the adaptive uses of integrating them in their cognitive sytem. This can result, for example, in increased acknowledgment of emotions and other private experience. Such inner knowledge can lead to more productive ways of dealing with problems and relating to intimate others. Performance of workers at midlife might also be different from that of younger workers, which implies that both employers and workers could benefit from increased knowledge of adult thought and its relevance for appraising the behavior and job performance of middle-aged adults.

In Chapter 4, Willis examines issues related to adult intelligence in middle age. Research indicates that, contrary to assumptions of general decline in intellectual functioning, middle age is a period of relative stability. In fact, some abilities, such as verbal ability, do not even show a peak level of performance until late middle age.

Willis discusses several variables associated with individual differences in intellectual development and change, including gender, health, occupation, and life-style. For example, cardiovascular disease has been associated with declines in intellectual functioning, although social status indicators may also be involved. Individuals in occupations involving complex decision making and independent judgment seem to maintain their intellectual abilities. Active engagement in life and challenging tasks requiring flexibility are also related to the maintenance of intellectual performance.

Counselors, educators, and others working with clients at midlife can inform them that their intellectual functioning can be maintained and possibly even boosted if they pursue and remain actively involved in challenging intellectual activities. Employers and educational institutions can contribute to the challenges by developing policies and opportunities that would enable middle-aged adults to acquire new information and technologies for keeping up with changes in their occupations. Also, the adverse effects of cardiovascular disease on intellectual functioning such as memory deficits call for a greater emphasis on prevention in health care.

3

Developmental Shifts in Adult Thought

Gisela Labouvie-Vief
Julie Hakim-Larson

Much recent interest has been stimulated by the notion that adulthood brings major positive and adaptive reorganizations or shifts in thought. This interest in growth has confronted us, however, with a paradoxical situation. Historically, changes in adult thought often have been interpreted from the standpoint of decline and deficit (for reviews, see Labouvie-Vief, 1985; Labouvie-Vief & Schell, 1982). Thus many of the changes unique to middle and late adulthood were often said to indicate regression, and this pervasive view of regression as typical of later adulthood has only occasionally been moderated by the notion that, at best, some individuals are able to maintain or stabilize the achievements of their youth.

In this chapter, we propose that the difficulty in thinking about adulthood in terms of growth and progression, rather than decline and regression, is a consequence of the concept of development that underlies our notions of what 'mature' behavior and cognition are. Life-span developmental researchers describing adulthood and aging have often relied on youth-centered criteria in describing maturity. In doing so, however, they focused on only *one* mode of thought. Specifically, the youthful ability to think about reality in an increasingly formalistic, abstract, and objectified manner has been considered the apex of mature adult thought. Yet, it appears that adults often respond in ways that indicate an interest in the pragmatic, concrete, and subjective aspects of reality. Traditionally, such findings were accounted for by means of the concept of regression.

We propose that this interest in the pragmatic and subjective aspects of reality signals the maturity of a second mode of thought. We describe evidence that indicates that this second mode of thought is not necessarily regressive, but is rather qualitatively different from the first one. Like the first mode, it is subject to developmental change; thus, although it may occur in immature forms, mature forms also emerge, and adulthood brings the unique potential to integrate those mature forms with more objective and rational modes of thinking (e.g., Labouvie-Vief, in press).

Indeed, we propose that, ideally, cognition in middle and later adulthood brings such a transformation in which the individual incorporates optimal use of both modes of thought. This integrative aspect of adult cognition is quite in contrast to the primary task of early development, so that early and late adaptation need to be gauged by somewhat different standards. In childhood and youth, there is a push toward the acquisition of cultural symbol systems, and rules and norms of appropriate social behavior. As a consequence, the first mode of thought takes precedence over the second. That is, knowing in youth is oriented to notions of formal correctness, abstract detachment, and objective validation, while more informal, concrete, and subjective ways of knowing are subordinated and repressed. During adulthood, however—once the symbols, rules and norms of the culture are well learned—the individual may begin to attend to previously neglected facets of the self. The potential emerges to integrate the two modes of thought in one's cognitive and emotional functioning. This integration, often captured by the term *wisdom,* has profound implications for research on adaptive processes in mature adulthood.

The review to follow is structured by a developmental perspective, in which we assume that certain progressive movements in understanding reality are part of the transition from early through middle adulthood and possibly into later life. In proposing such a movement, however, we can only suggest approximate ages. This is true for several reasons. First, as argued later, the kinds of developmental movements we propose are profoundly influenced by cultural and historical changes that will significantly influence the specific time at which a certain form of thinking emerges. Second, they are to be understood as an ideal and as functional, rather than a statistical norm—like the notion, for example, of optimal physical health. And just as optimal health is but an ideal for most adults, we would expect many adults to deviate from an idealized time line of the emergence of a particular form of thought. Finally, the research we will focus on is still new; it examines new frontiers but has as yet established few agreed-upon patterns. Thus, although we believe that the type of thought processes we will discuss in this chapter provide a cognitive underpinning for the popular notion of a midlife transformation, we expect that whether or when an adult experiences this transformation will vary widely with his or her unique historical, cultural, and familial background.

In the following sections, we first provide an overview of the two modes of thought and their proposed relationship throughout the first and second halves of the life span. Then we describe this developmental shift, first, as it occurs in domains pertinent to cognitive development, and then, as it applies to the more general adaptive processes pertinent to the study of self and emotion.

Two Modes of Thought

The notion that two modes of thinking underlie the organization and development of cognition is pervasive in theories of development. Piaget's (1951) theory is an example. One of Piaget's main tenets was that development can never be a pure copy or internalization of outer reality. Rather, it must also incorporate an opposing movement in which we externalize inner tendencies.

That duality is reflected in Piaget's distinction between *assimilation* and *accommodation*. Assimilation is best exemplified by play. Here, a playful or ludic attitude prevails in which the individual is not concerned with the demands of outer reality. Rather, those of an inner reality prevail, and the outer reality is adjusted to an inner one of desires and private images. Accommodation, in contrast, occurs when we adjust to the outer constraints of the world of personal and impersonal objects. Piaget believed that imitation is the prototype of accommodation.

The same duality between two modes of thinking is, indeed, a theme pervading many systems of thought—not only psychological theories, but also theories of philosophy and religion. On one hand, we can relate to reality in a mode that is primarily intuitive, subjective, and imaginative. Here, the world seems animated—as it does, for example, in myth—with the forms our inner world has projected onto it. Meaning in this mode is based on the organic, on feeling, on the imagination: What seems 'true' is what impresses itself on us with gripping conviction. On the other hand, we can relate to reality in a mode that is distanced and objective; now the world is measured in terms of sharable frameworks that are stable and repeatable, and in which phenomena are evaluated not in terms of affective criteria, but by rational categories.

There has been much dispute during the course of history whether the two modes should be held in equal regard (Labouvie-Vief, in press). In that debate, classical Greek thought, as exemplified in the writings of Plato, has profoundly shaped contemporary views of the nature of reason and its development. Plato conceptualized reason as one pole of a duality of ways of knowing. On one hand, that duality is defined by forms of knowing that are tied to an intimate interpersonal context. Such interpersonal contexts were the settings for cognitive activities in pre-Platonic times. The prototypical activity was oral transmission, such as in the scene of an orator reciting an epic to an audience. Such settings highlight what we now would term *context-sensitive* forms of knowing. Imitation, intuition, the analogical and the figurative, the organic and the instinctual, change and conflict all define that pole of Plato's theory of knowledge. The second pole, in contrast, is defined by *context-free* forms of knowing: abstract understanding, rational analysis, the intellectual and the analytical, the mental and the voluntary, and stability and harmony all refer to what Plato thought of as the better parts of the human being.

Recently, in similar fashion, Olson (1977) made the distinction between the "oral" and "written" traditions of language in relation to thought. Bruner (1986) labeled subjective, expressive, holistic, or context-sensitive processing as the "narrative" mode, and objective, logical, analytic, or context-free processing as the "paradigmatic" mode. In keeping with its Greet roots, the first author has elsewhere described the two modes as "mythos" and "logos," respectively (Labouvie-Vief, in press).

Plato's theory proposed a definite value differential between the two modes. The nonrational functions, he thought, were a lesser, reduced version of the rational. They made us similar to animals and children and were associated with illusion, darkness, and ignorance. The result is a vertical or hierarchical arrangement of the two modes (Labouvie-Vief, in press).

As is true of Plato's conception, many contemporary cognitive developmental theories (e.g., Werner & Kaplan, 1963) adhere to such a vertical model. In doing so, they fall short of adequately specifying mature thought as a balanced state in adulthood. The result is that they deal with "nonrational" modes of adaptive functioning only in pejorative terms. As Langer (1942, pp. 292-293) stated, "everything that falls outside the domain of analytical, propositional, and formal thought is merely classified as emotive, irrational, and animalian. . . . All other things our minds do are dismissed as irrelevant to intellectual progress; they are residues, emotional disturbances, or throwbacks to animal estate" and indicate "regression to a pre-logical state."

Contemporary theories of cognition are based on a devaluation of the inner, subjective, and organic dimension of self-experience. Such models have served to enhance and clarify our understanding of child development; they have not, however, served well as models of adult thought. Child development, as many theorists have noted, requires that more state-dependent, organic, and private modes of experience give way to ones that are more abstract and collective. This adaptation to a collective language occurs as children dissociate inner meanings from impersonal outer ones. Thus meaning systems that originate in the organismic, sensorimotor, figurative, dynamic, and personal facets of the self are gradually displaced by ones that are abstract, conceptual, stable, conventional, and impersonal. The former meaning systems are often characterized as immature, while the latter are viewed as indicative of developmental maturity and appropriate socialization.

The adaptive advantage of this process of dissociation and hierarchic organization in earlier development is the acquisition of culturally relevant symbol systems and language systems. These systems permit the novice adult to categorize experience in a stable and reliable manner. In adulthood, however, this hierarchical structure can become a liability. The devaluation of inner and personal experience, on which the success of childhood development largely depends, can result in structures that are limited, closed, and rigidified in adulthood. More mature cognitive development is aimed at an organization that reacknowledges the importance of more private ways of knowing. The new goal now is to establish a lateral and more balanced relationship between the two modes of knowing. Such a lateral relationship yields a different model of knowing, one in which the two modes participate in an interactive, mutually enriching relationship.

In summary, the vertical model is of particular significance in the acquisition of culturally appropriate or conventionalized systems of self-regulation; it is more relevant to earlier than to later development. Adulthood, however, brings the potential for a different type of organization—one that places a balanced and "lateral" emphasis on the use of the two modes.

Using the modes-of-knowing approach in this chapter, we describe a series of studies that provide support for a developmental shift from the "vertical" to the "lateral" organization of the two modes of knowing in adult thought. Our contention is that an adaptive model of such developmental shifts in adult thought must incorporate multiple research domains; and, therefore, bodies of data pertinent to cognitive, self-, and emotional development are addressed in the following sections.

Intelligence and Problem Solving

A brief history. Early studies of adult cognition were launched near the beginning of this century, when the intellectual climate was one of logical positivism. The belief then was that the mind was to be described in terms of a vertical model in which logos processes were superordinate to those of mythos. Adaptive cognition, hence, was believed to be best indexed by the ability to engage in context-free thinking. With that criterion, we quickly amassed an enormous body of evidence suggesting that such abilities for context-free thinking peaked early in the adult life span, with dramatic declines as early as the late twenties and early thirties (e.g., Jones, 1959; Welford, 1958). In contrast to childhood, adulthood was seen as a period of deficit and regression; indeed, the notion was prevalent that the aging of cognitive functioning reflected a reverse mirror image of the process of development. Ribot's (Rubenstein, 1968, p. 409) law of the aging of cognitive functioning stated this principle of regression as follows:

> Regression first affects more complex organizations. In mnemonic organization, the "new" dies prior to the "old," the complex before the simple. . . . Volitional control is lost first, the control of automatic action later. In this way cognitive organization follows the reverse order of its development through sequential stages.

This *simple regression* view of cognitive aging offered a conceptual umbrella for most of the then-available evidence. For example, psychometric tests of intellectual functioning consistently reported that deficits were most pronounced on tests of abstract thinking and problem solving, figural-spatial thought, and the performance scale of the WAIS—those functions termed "fluid" by Cattell (1963) and Horn (1970). Similarly, extensions of Piagetian methodology into adulthood (see Reese & Rodeheaver, 1985, for a review) suggested that many elderly functioned at concrete levels. Hence, the assumption was that aging brought a loss of abstract, formal-operational thought. These "regressive" changes were thought to be manifestations of inner biological changes resulting from a universal and irreversible biological aging program.

It was evident, however, that on many measures middle and elderly adults did not show decrements but actually continued to improve. In particular, tests related to cultural knowledge, such as vocabulary, general information, and arithmetical operations, often favored middle and sometimes even quite old adults. How could this fact be accommodated within a vertical model? By positing that the observed changes were merely of the "concrete" variety—thus the gains of adulthood were looked at as a mere accumulation of facts and information. This interpretation, then, led to a *modified regression model.* That model maintained that even though abstract, context-free abilities declined under the relentless influence of biological deterioration, concrete, context-sensitive abilities continued to accumulate or, at least, remain stable throughout most of adulthood.

The theory of fluid and crystallized intelligence originally proposed by Cattell (1963) and extended by Horn (Horn, 1970; Horn & Donaldson, 1980) illustrates how specific age-related changes in intellectual functioning are thought to mirror regressive changes in the central nervous system (see Labouvie-Vief, 1985, for a more extensive discussion). In this model, fluid intelligence, in particular, is dependent on the proper functioning of the nervous system and is measured by tasks that show age-related declines (e.g., speeded tasks, tests of reaction time). Crystallized intelligence, in contrast, demonstrates the cumulative effect of culture and learning of task performance (for example, tests of verbal ability, general cultural knowledge). Because regressive change in the nervous system occurs gradually, these crystallized abilities are thought to continue to compensate for the early declines in fluid ability and, eventually, to be superseded by the accumulation of losses and regressive changes in the nervous system.

A new way of thinking about these issues gradually emerged in the 1970s when it became apparent that the differentiation between context-free fluid abilities and context-sensitive crystallized ones was not always so clear. Especially under the influence of Schaie's efforts (e.g., Schaie, 1980; Schaie & Labouvie-Vief, 1974; Schaie & Parham, 1977), it became obvious that much of the variance in adult intellectual functioning was not so much a matter of individual decremental change. Instead, age group differences in intellectual functioning often reflected the fact that different age groups in cross-sectional research represent quite different backgrounds in terms of educational and cultural experience. This century has witnessed a profound educational revolution, which made education accessible to more and more younger age groups or cohorts. The result of this revolution was to create a marked differential between younger and older cohorts. Rather than indicating individual age-related decline, that differential is a result of historical changes. As Schaie and Labouvie-Vief (1974, p. 15) noted:

> Most of the adult life span is characterized by an absence of decisive intellectual decrements. In times of rapid cultural and technological change it is primarily in relation to younger populations that the aged can be described as deficient, and it is erroneous to interpret such cross-sectional age differences as indicating ontogenetic change patterns.

Schaie's demonstration of cohort differences stimulated a host of studies predicated on a more *contextual view* of adulthood and aging. These studies suggest that age differences in intellectual performance are not primarily tied to age, but are affected by education, training, life-style, and health variables (for a review, see Labouvie-Vief, 1977). In contrast to the predictions of the regression model, such context effects cannot be readily aligned along a simple fluid/biology versus crystallized/culture duality, but hold for the total of the cognitive system. Thus some biological deficits affect primarily context-sensitive processes, while others may have more impact on fluid, context-insensitive ones. In turn, many "fluid" abilities represent skills that are specifically fostered by culture.

Contextualism, then, rejects the biology-culture dualism. Instead, it argues that all adaptation is biocultural (see Baltes, Dittmann-Kohli, & Dixon, 1984; Baltes & Kliegl, 1986; Labouvie-Vief & Chandler, 1978; Lerner, 1976, 1984). Further, it rejects the notion of major universal patterns of change that transcend context and proposes instead that age-related changes can simply be reduced to variations in context. This view provides a wholesome corrective to the biases of a logos-oriented regression model. It shows us that, in many arenas of cognition, performance is due to variations in context rather than a presumed failure of some generalized adaptive capacity. Nevertheless, in proposing that adult age differences can be explained purely in terms of differences in context and familiarity, it implicitly adheres to the standard of excellence set by those models. Thus, at best, researchers can demonstrate that intelligence remains stable; there is no room, however, for genuine qualitative changes.

In contrast, an emerging view is to propose that adulthood may actually bring qualitative changes of a *progressive* nature. Because the standard by which adaptive intelligence has been gauged was developed for the purpose of predicting the intellectual accomplishments of youth, it is possible that many mature adult accomplishments are misclassified. Youth often require a rule-based orientation in which they disregard the more concrete, intuitive, and subjective facets of their own experience. Rather, they view problems in terms of the abstract, "objective" structure and reference this structure by specifying rules and culturally appropriate classification systems. Although this represents an advance in thought over childhood abilities, it may only be a transition to a more integrated approach in which this dualism is no longer operative.

As an example of this transition, consider a study by Benner (1984) in which novice nurses inappropriately overgeneralized the rules they had learned concerning the caretaking of infants. Novices took a narrow and literal interpretation of their newly acquired system of operation. In the absence of rich experience, they stuck to clearly defined, deductive rules. Experienced nurses, however, were unabashedly intuitive in their approach and not as rule-bound as the novices. More is involved in this shift than mere quantitative variation in experience. Rather, as individuals acquire expertise, their knowledge becomes too complex and richly organized to conform to a simple rule-oriented system, and flexible functioning is enhanced by a less explicit and more intuitive approach (see also Dreyfus & Dreyfus, 1986; Rybash, Hoyer, & Roodin, 1986).

Postformal cognition. An argument similar to the novice-to-expert shift has emerged in current attempts to extend Piaget's theory of formal thought and mature cognition to the adult years. Piaget's emphasis on formal, abstract thinking was motivated by the belief that, in order to relate to collective knowledge systems, children must be able to dissociate from their personal, concrete experience. Further, in order to function effectively in society, they must be able to integrate concrete aspects into a coherent system. When this is accomplished they are capable of a degree of autonomous and objective functioning in which behavior is no longer dictated by immediate concrete fluctuations. Much recent work in the field, however, suggests that such autonomy is not yet achieved with the advent of formal thinking.

Many of these studies took their impetus from Perry's (1968) study on intellectual development in the college years. Perry found that formal, abstract thinking, with its absolutism and dualism of right and wrong, created a number of cognitive distortions in the thought of youth. For example, young college students were found to believe that only one "right" perspective exists on such abstract notions as "truth" or "reality." In their concern with this absolute view, they were not able to define autonomous criteria or procedures for how to arrive at such judgments, but were instead extremely vulnerable to the external sources that defined those concepts for them. Hence, a high degree of conceptual dependence remains an important feature of youthful thought. Consistent with the pluralism of college life, some students were found to progress to a more relativistic mode of thought in which context played a greater role in decision making. Finally, some students reached a point where they were able to take a committed stance within such a relativistic framework.

Similarly, Kitchener and King (1981) found an age-related progression in how youths and adults construed reality according to its "subjective" and "objective" elements. Participants in their study were given tasks that assessed their reasoning on competing interpretations of the same phenomenon (e.g., evolution versus creationism). Younger participants merely sided with their own belief system and construed the competing one as wrong on this basis. Thus less mature individuals polarized the two elements and afforded greater weight to the presumed "correct" and "objective" viewpoint. Mature subjects, on the other hand, were able to see that one's belief system is influenced by characteristics of the self. As a result of incorporating an awareness of these subjective elements into their thinking, they were less likely to distort and to be dogmatic about a particular belief. Further, they were better able to specify the procedures by which their beliefs could be subjected to objective verification.

The tendency of younger subjects to distort information was also examined in a recent study conducted by Blanchard-Fields (1986) on the social-cognitive reasoning of adolescents and adults. The tasks, which varied in their emotional saliency as rated by the subjects themselves, involved the presentation of two disparate accounts of the same event or situation. One task, for example, presented the accounts of a fictional war as given by two historians of each of the two warring countries; each account construed its victories as indisputable and its losses as minor. The other tasks involved more emotionally laden real-life arguments between two opposing parties. After the presentation of each task, participants were asked to describe the actual event and were probed for their understanding. A six-level postformal coding scheme was used to score the responses. At the two lower levels, the individual polarizes the discrepant accounts and chooses one as right and the other as wrong. At the middle two levels, multiple outcomes are acknowledged but an insistence on an objective orientation to what factually happened is retained. Finally, at the last two levels, the individual makes a clear differentiation between an event and how it is to be interpreted. Now, judging what is true or what has "really" happened is no longer a matter of "objective" facts; rather it involves taking into account how individuals interpret events. Objectivity can no longer be ascertained by appeal to facts, but rather by discussing the process of interpretation and how that process is intercoordinated among thinkers (e.g., Belenky, Clinchy, Goldberger, & Tarule, 1986; Kuhn, Pennington, & Leadbeater, 1982).

Using a similar postformal developmental framework in a study on logical inferencing and text interpretation, we have examined age-related differences in processing the narrative and paradigmatic features of problem solving (Labouvie-Vief, Adams, Hakim-Larson, Hayden, & DeVoe, 1987). Preadolescents, adolescents, and adults up through their forties were given a series of problems in which a simple logical sequence was embedded in a brief narrative text. The problems were such that individuals could respond literally to the story structure and affirm the logical influence implied, or respond in a variety of other ways based on their own psychological interpretation of the story characters. Consider the following problem:

John is known to be a heavy drinker, especially when he goes to parties. Mary, John's wife, warns him that if he gets drunk one more time, she will leave him and take the children. Tonight, John is out late at an office party. John comes home drunk.

Does Mary leave John?

How certain are you of your answer?

Our preadolescents and most adolescents adopted a logical approach. At the least differentiated level, they were not aware that different conclusions follow under different interpretations. Instead, they simply affirmed the truth value of the premises as stated—thus, in the example, Mary was said to leave "because it says so." Their style was highly literal and text-dependent, and conclusions seemed to spring from the text rather than the reader. When requested to provide a rationale for their answers, young adolescents were perplexed at being asked to justify the obvious. They pointed to the text, stating "it says so right here!"

Somewhat older adolescents, in contrast, had a beginning awareness that conclusions are related to some activity located within the self. These individuals had also become aware that the problem had a degree of ambiguity. Their reactions to that realization, however, was that they would then seek to eliminate it. Increased self-monitoring resulted in the apparent hope that the logical dimensions of the problem could be preserved.

More mature adolescents and young adults, in contrast, became more sensitive to issues of interpretation. They realized that variability in interpretation is not just due to the problem's ambiguity, but is a matter of principle. A strong conceptual dualism emerged at the level of reflective language, and individuals talked about two strategies that were, in essence, different. One strategy was based on an approach called "logical," "objective," "mathematical," or "rational," while the second was called a matter of "opinion," "subjective," or "emotional." These strategies are seen as antagonistic, often suggesting a struggle between two inner voices. Consider this answer of a man in his thirties:

> The key is "one more time." Mary's simple statement—if she meant it—is weighted off of John's drunkenness. The logic is clear, clean—if you choose to ignore human dimensions. If A happens, then B will result—a gross simplification of cause and effect, or event and result—again, when my creative urge is not suppressed, I can misfire, hear what I want, distort the story and place a wrong answer, firmly convinced that it is correct.

Notice that this individual had a metalanguage available in which the duality of the problem could be described. The structure of that metalanguage was one of conflict, however, as in the example above. The two strategies were pitted against each other in an either-or, antagonistic fashion. Some adults did, however, proceed to a final level in which this dualism was transcended. These individuals recognized that the "logical" and the interpretive are intricately interwoven. Hence, ambiguity is no longer a result of the problem's ambiguity, or of the self's tendency to "misfire;" rather it is a necessity and arises from the fact that equally competent individuals nevertheless can bring different perspectives to the same problem.

It is interesting that, while these results were significantly associated with age, the lower levels were almost exclusively occupied by the preadolescents and adolescents. Among the adults, however, age was not the primary predictor. Rather, what differentiated the adult groups was not age, but another indicator of cognitive complexity—namely, their understanding of issues of certainty and logical conclusions. As discussed later, this finding emerges as a frequent one in the new field of adult developmental processes.

In sum, the major limiting feature of adolescent thought in postformal models is the dualism that pervades the youth's understanding of both physical and social reality. Because youth can operate only within a single abstract system, a choice must often be made between seemingly opposing conceptualization. Thus youths have been found to polarize absolute right and wrong (e.g., Colby, Kohlberg, Gibbs & Lieberman, 1983; Perry, 1968), subjective and objective reality (Kitchener & King, 1981), mind and body (Broughton, 1980), the inner and outer self (e.g., Broughton, 1981), and logic and emotion (e.g., Labouvie-Vief, 1982). Although the evidence suggests that these dualisms become better integrated with maturity, during youth they oftentimes result in a one-sided orientation to reality.

Memory. Research on aging changes in the memory system also originated from a logos-oriented view of the mnemonic system. That view was first stated by Ebbinghaus (1913). Ebbinghaus was well aware of the methodological problems posed by the fact that individuals' memories come in so many idiosyncratic versions related to differences in context. He felt that these complexities could be circumvented by bracketing contextual factors and by offering "a possibility of indirectly approaching the problem . . . in a small and definitely limited sphere and, by means of keeping aloof for a while from any theory, perhaps of constructing one" (Ebbinghaus, 1913, p. 65).

It is not surprising that the elderly were found to do particularly poorly on memory tasks fashioned after this view, such as word lists of low semantic structure (see Labouvie-Vief & Schell, 1982, for review). Thus that aging changes in the memory system were interpreted within a *regression model.* Several versions of that model still are influential. According to one, the elderly adult is less likely to process information "deeply," because she or he often fails to relate it to the lexical and categorical systems of culture. Thus aging is said to bring a loss of deep, and a prevalence of more "shallow," ways of processing (Craik, 1977). According to a second—and more general, though complementary—interpretation, aging is accompanied by a general restriction of processing capacity: thus older individuals are less able to manipulate information in their memories and a variety of regressive phenomena is the consequence (see Hultsch & Dixon, 1084; Labouvie-Vief & Schell, 1982).

That simple regression view soon was reformulated under the weight of evidence showing that it was not possible to separate the study of memory from the context in which it occurred. Bartlett (1932) already demonstrated that what we remember is profoundly influenced by the schemata we bring to a memory task. Moreover, the effect of those schemata is not necessarily better recall. Often schemata distort recall so as to make it fit better with already available knowledge. Thus many authors now subscribe to a view of the aging of memory that is *contextual.* Accordingly, aging does not necessarily bring a loss of processing capacity, but often reflects differences between the young and the old in terms of familiarity, expertise, motivation, life-style, and health variables.

Although the contextual interpretation delineates alternatives to a simple regression view of aging and memory, it does not delineate options for positive and progressive forms of memory development in later life. This problem was addressed in a research project by the first author (Adams, Labouvie-Vief, Hobart, & Dorosz, 1987; Labouvie-Vief, Schell, & Weaver-dyck, 1982). The proposal stated that new adaptive forms of memory development may well emerge if we enlarge our criteria for successful memory performance.

In most research, "successful" memory performance is assessed by just one of two possible modes of relating to text. Olson (1977) described these modes by referring to written and oral traditions, arguing that the introduction of literacy and writing introduced a new style of thinking. Eventually, these styles were no longer exclusively related to the type of setting in which a message was transmitted, but came to constitute more general modes by which the meaning of a message can be defined.

According to Olson (1977), meaning in "oral" settings is interpersonal and defined by the shared experience of speaker and listener. In such a setting, meaning is highly context-sensitive. Psychological and social considerations, rather than purely logical ones, structure discourse: Does a message have subjective, intuitive appeal? Does the listener understand it? If the answer to these questions is yes, the message is successful; if no, it fails. Thus the meaning of a message resides not only "objectively" in a statement or text, but also in the interpersonal bond between participants. They co-construct meanings, relying on interpretation, filling in gaps in messages, and so forth.

Written language, in contrast, disembeds the construction of meaning from the interpersonal dyadic bond. The process of interpretation is no longer open to the whims of one's subjectivity, but rather is highly constrained and standardized. Explicit premises, rules of logic, lexical knowledge, and precise rules all characterize the allocation of meaning.

The two languages employ different criteria of truth and validity. Oral language appeals to the intuitions and feelings. A good message is one that is plausible, that makes common sense, that grips us, that has the appeal of beauty, authority, faith. In contrast to these mythos criteria are the logos criteria of the validity of a written message: formal consistency, logical precision, and explicit propositions all enhance its truth value. And, finally, these different truth functions are best maximized with different language forms. Oral language is poeticized and particularized. It freely employs rhythm, illustrations, figures of speech, and proverbs—in contrast to the propositional, universalizing, analytical, and definitional approach of written messages.

Olson (1977) maintained that in both cultural and individual development, primary emphasis has been on the optimization of the logos mode. The adolescent or young adult is specialized at dealing with conventionalized, propositional knowledge in which reality is represented in terms of outer, "objective," and collective symbols. There is a bias, therefore, in which the meaning of texts is construed as objective rather than subjective, as literal rather than interpreted, as logical rather than psychological. Yet, this cognitive orientation brings with it a suppression of other forms of knowing: those embodied by figurative, narrative, and psychological ways of knowing.

In our research we found evidence that middle and older adults relate to text in a more interpretative and psychological mode. We reasoned that if these adults became experts at the processing of information relating to subjective processes and inner dynamics, this processing style would result in deficits in tasks that require more objective and formal ways of processing. These deficits should be particularly pronounced in tasks of relatively formal structure, but less so in material that can be approached more informally. We, therefore, turned to narrative material. For example, in one study we gave a fable to elders, averaging 74 years in age, and college students (Labouvie-Vief, Schell, & Weaverdyck, 1982). The fable concerned a wolf who had promised a reward to a crane for removing a bone stuck in his throat. When, after sticking his neck down the wolf's throat and dislodging the bone, the crane asked for the reward, the wolf told him that his reward was to get away alive!

Subjects read the fable and then were told either to recall as much of it as they possibly could, or to provide a summary. For college students, there was no significant difference between these two conditions: they always gave highly detailed recall protocols. But for the older adults, the difference was marked. In the summary condition, they gave terse though structurally complete summaries. In the recall condition, however, their recall was just as detailed as that of the young.

One interesting feature was that many of the summaries of the older adults showed an approach qualitatively different from that of the college students. They did not deal with inferences that were explicitly called for by the text, but rather with the text's metaphorical, moral, or social-normative meaning, as in this example:

> The moral of the story, as I understand it, was that people should not seek a reward for their well-doing, but to be content with having done a good deed. It also depicts a certain shrewdness, as noted by the wolf who sought help in time of need, but was unwilling to give of himself, even in a small way, to show any appreciation of the help he had received from the crane. Many times, people who do good deeds receive only a spiritual reward for their well doing.

Older adults were found to represent the meaning of the fable in such a way as to highlight its moral tone. Yet, in doing so, their responses were also coherently tied to features of the text (Adams & Labouvie-Vief, 1986).

In a recent replication of this study with narrative texts, a similar age-related pattern was found (Adams, Labouvie-Vief, Hobart, & Dorosz, 1987). The results again indicated that young adults focus on literal, text-based features, whereas older adults summarize the gist of the text along with its psychological and metaphoric meaning. One important issue that arises in this work is whether such changes in processing among older adults reflect a compensation for the inability to recall literal, detailed information, or whether such changes reflect a mature capacity to integrate the complexities of the underlying meaning structures (Adams & Labouvie-Vief, 1986).

Within a decrement model, the finding that older adults concentrate on more integrative and interpretative features could be interpreted as a shift toward a more global response style that compensates for a decline in processing skill. Our analyses indicate, however, that the shift we have discussed is not necessarily accompanied by a deficit in the processing of the more objective base.

This conclusion is further corroborated in a study by Adams (1986). As part of that study, participants were asked to read, recall, and summarize a Sufi teaching tale. While most research on memory processes in later adulthood has focused on just two age groups—college students in their twenties and elders about 60 or older—Adams included a middle-aged group as well. Analyses indicated no age differences between adolescents and the middle-aged in the ability to retell and summarize the text-based information. Age differences were found, however, with respect to the tendency to interpret the text and go beyond its explicit meaning. The middle-aged adults tended to integrate the text-based actions and events with the implicit psychological and metaphorical meanings of the text. They did not "lose" their ability to attend to the text base, but rather they were able to function at two levels simultaneously: the mature adult thus developed a kind of two-layered language in which both the text's objective structure (the structure of its actual events) and its more subjective and psychological meanings (the structure of its psychological significance) were represented.

In the Adams (1986) study, the older adults did, indeed, show a tendency to focus more exclusively on the integrative mode. To the extent that they mastered the text-based structure with less facility than the young, their response style could be said to compensate for a loss of detailed memory. Because the tendency toward an integrative response style appeared to emerge in middle adulthood—when there was no loss whatever of the objective text base—rather than later in old age, however, a simple compensation interpretation does not seem to be entirely appropriate. Rather, it is possible that the older adult who experiences some difficulty in effortful processing falls back on a processing style already well mastered—that is, to concentrate on less effortful interpretive processing.

The skill of the middle-aged adults who were able to coordinate logical and psychological dimensions of information can have profound adaptive significance for the individual and society. Gutmann (1977) argued, for example, that in many societies it is the elders who can encode important truths about the human condition in a highly symbolic form, thereby providing guidelines for the behavior and experiences of younger generations. It is possible, then, that a change to a more symbolic and integrative response style prepares the elder in many cultures to take a unique role as a moral and spiritual leader.

In another vein, the mature adult is likely to become aware that it is often not the event, but our interpretation of it, that decides its impact upon our lives. To induce this distinction between an event and its interpretation is, for example, at the heart of psychoanalytic and other therapeutic efforts that take as their assumption that many psychological disturbances involve an overly narrow interpretation of early autobiographical events. In turn, healing is often accompanied by the individual's recognition that more healthful interpretations of the event are possible than the one that has formed the basis for his or her suffering (Schafer, 1980). This effect was well demonstrated, for example, in Main's (1987) research in which adult adjustment was not related to the actual objective attachment history between mothers and their adult daughters, but rather by the daughters' flexible perspectives in constructing their narratives of their mothers.

Some evidence indicates that similar changes in autobiographical reconstruction are not just a matter of pathological adaptation, but are a normal part of the transition from early to middle and late adulthood. Young adults with their literal bias tend to take their interpretations of events (for example, their life histories) as objective. In that perspective, events take on singular, determined meanings. Middle-aged adults, in turn, are aware that we view events through our interpretive lenses: this ability can confer on the adult a more flexible perspective in which interpretation is related to a degree of choice (McAdams, 1985).

Self and Emotion

Our perspective on cognitive self-regulation—as evidenced in the domains of intelligence, problem solving, memory, and language processing—carries important implications for how the individual construes the social world. Similar to theories of cognition, many theories of social and emotional adaptation point out that adaptation results from an interplay of two modes of organizing and understanding experience. In Freud's theory, for example, rational thought is governed by the "secondary process" of the ego, whereas more primitive impulses stemming from the id are linked with "primary process" thinking (e.g., Giovacchini, 1977). As with cognitive development, secondary process thought comes to superordinate primary process thought in a vertically arranged hierarchy.

More cognitively oriented views also adopt this two-mode structure. George Herbert Mead (1934), for example, differentiated between the "I" and the "me." Strauss (1977, p. 286) described Mead's (1934) notion of the self as follows:

> The "I" represents the impulsive side of behavior—what the individual is just as likely to surprise himself as anyone else with. In contrast, "the me" refers to the community internalized in the person; it represents the community's social control of the individual's behavior.

We have suggested that the primary task of early development is to produce a vertical arrangement between these two sides of the self. The growing child learns conventional modes of regulation according to the culture's dictates of rationality. In childhood and youth the self is objectified and it is primarily the "me" that is emphasized in the self-concept. The "me" comprises a self that is increasingly rational as defined by the culture.

The notion that early development is aimed at conventionalization is also expressed in several other theories. Kohlberg's "conventional" level of moral reasoning (e.g., Colby, Kohlberg, Gibbs, & Lieberman, 1983), in particular, involves thought whereby the rules and norms of the culture are adopted and followed. Similarly, Loevinger's "conformist" level of ego development (e.g., Loevinger & Wessler, 1978) and Kegan's "interpersonal" level (e.g., Kegan, 1982) are defined as thought that indicates an embeddedness in group belonging and interpersonal relationships.

Although such a conventional and conformist understanding of the "me" is an important developmental achievement during childhood, it also has drawbacks. Commenting on early life, Stern (1985) noted that our increased ability to communicate in terms of the concepts of our culture is usually acquired at the expense of a sense of relatedness with the self's own personal and interpersonal experiences:

> Infants' initial interpersonal knowledge is mainly unsharable, amodal, instance-specific, and attuned to nonverbal behaviors in which no one channel of communication has privileged status with regard to accountability or ownership. Language changes all of that. With its emergence, infants become estranged from direct contact with their own personal experience. Language forces a space between interpersonal experience as lived and as represented. And it is exactly across this space that the connections and associations that constitute neurotic behavior may form . . . with the advent of language and symbolic thinking, children now have the tools to distort *and* transcend reality. (Stern, 1985, p. 182, emphasis added)

Hence, early development often results in the loss of spontaneity and the disconnection of private and public modes of knowing. In contrast, later development may bring a more adaptive reconnection of the two modes. Once the individual is able to constrain his or her impulses according to the culture's symbol system, it then becomes possible for the "self" to loosen the constraints and restore the lost sense of intimacy and immediacy.

This notion of the potential for reconnection of the two modes is illustrated in several contemporary views of adult thought. In Kohlberg's theory (Colby, et al., 1983), the "postconventional" movement beyond conventional thought involves the use of self-chosen principles in making moral judgments concerning the self, others, and the broader community. Such reconnection is also evidenced in Jung's (e.g., Campbell, 1971) analytic view of the second half of life, in which previously suppressed, basic psychological functions become integrated with those functions that were enhanced in the first half of life. Consistent with Jung's analysis of such integrated personality processes in midlife and beyond is the growing body of research on sex roles and coping and defense processes in adulthood. Mature adults, in contrast to youth and less highly developed adults, are more likely to adopt a flexible stance with respect to sex roles and to use less distorting defense mechanisms and means of coping with stress (e.g., Haan, 1977; Kegan, 1982; Loevinger & Wessler, 1978; Vaillant, 1977).

In our research on emotional self-regulation, we found support for this adaptive reconnection in some adults. A broadly based foundation of theory and supportive research on emotional regulations from childhood through adulthood provided the backdrop for our studies.

Similar to the two modes of knowing described previously in relation to cognitive development, theorists on emotion also emphasize that human behavior is regulated by two modes. Buck (1984), for example, described a dual control system for emotional communication. At first, built-in programs of emotional expression regulate the infant. Gradually, these built-in programs become modified under the effect of cultural symbol systems.

With development, the child often needs to suppress spontaneously felt emotion and comes to express emotion symbolically according to the culture's rules and roles of appropriate convention within certain contexts (e.g., Lewis & Saarni, 1985). Children learn to control their feelings in accordance with "feeling rules" (e.g., Hochschild, 1979), and to control the expressions on their faces according to "display rules" (e.g., Ekman & Oster, 1979; Malatesta & Haviland, 1985; Saarni, 1979). As a consequence, the child's inner life comes to be defined along the lines of what is considered culturally appropriate; more spontaneous and private aspects of inner life and experience become disconnected.

With development in adolescence and beyond into the adult years, more complex relationships occur between the outer social controls placed on emotional expression and the experience and conceptualization of inner feeling states. Adults have acquired the ability to conceal their inner feelings through the use of masks, to convey ambivalent or subtle nuances through affect blending, and to miniaturize their expressions (compress or fragment the components) to avoid affect contagion in social situations (e.g., Malatesta & Izard, 1984).

The private, spontaneous expression of emotion comes to be vertically and hierarchically subordinated to cultural symbols of emotion expression. Such disconnection appears to be a normal and adaptive feature of emotional self-regulation in early development. In order for younger individuals to acquire the cultural rules of feeling and display, it is necessary that they control or modify their inner feelings or natural tendencies to express the emotion. The use of mental control often comes to take precedence over bodily feedback in regulating one's emotional states (e.g., Lowen, 1972). Suppressed or "backed-up" affect is the end result (e.g., Tomkins, 1980).

Such efficiency of control is not always adaptive. If it leads to a continuous and prolonged lack of conscious attention to inner feedback, it may have serious repercussions for both mental and physical health as the person ages (e.g., Schwartz, 1982). Indeed, we propose that the adaptively functioning adult is able to validate inner biological states, coordinate inner experience with cultural conventions, and effectively act upon both in ways that reflect a complex and more lateral understanding of self, others, and society.

We investigated this process of reconnection in a large-scale research project on the development of self-regulation in adulthood. As part of this project, we compared how individuals from preadolescence through older adulthood experienced the emotions of anger, sadness, fear, and happiness (Labouvie-Vief, Hakim-Larson, & DeVoe, Schoeberlein, in press).

During a taped interview, 100 male and female participants (10 to 77 years) first described a recent incident relevant to each emotion. They were then asked questions about the description and control of their internal states for each emotion. A four-level coding scheme was constructed from the interview responses of a subsample of participants using the postformal theory of the first author (Labouvie-Vief, 1982). Before describing the results as they relate to age, it will be useful to outline that theoretical structure.

This theory broadly encompasses the domains of cognitive, affective, ego, and interpersonal development. The levels are named *presystemic*, *intrasystemic*, *intersystemic* and *autonomous*. The presystemic self is unable to coordinate the elements that constitute a single abstract system; therefore, the individual demonstrates only a partial understanding and adoption of cultural rules, roles, and conventions. Children at this level are concrete in their thinking and tied to relatively direct dyadic supervision by a significant other. At the intrasystemic level, the self is able to coordinate the elements that constitute a single abstract system. The individual is limited, however, to the use of only one such abstract system at a time. Within that system, absolute and certain truths are upheld. The self does not regulate behavior in a mature manner, but rather behaviors are oriented toward the given truths provided by authority and social rules. The concept of the "other" is thereby generalized and more abstract. The intersystemic thinker, in contrast, is able to move away from logical absolutes and certainty. Multiple perspectives are acknowledged, and logical relativism coupled with uncertainty emerges. The self can see many alternatives, and truth is viewed as being particular to a given context. The self may have to confront many previously ignored issues, however, to make effective choices from among the many available alternatives. Such decisions may create an inner crisis and the individual may need to engage in a major restructuring of his or her inner life. The final, autonomous, level highlights the importance of the "self" as a regulating structure for thoughts, emotions, and actions. Responsibility for one's development is acknowledged and the historical self over time can be reflected upon. Truth is no longer absolute but understood to be created by individuals, and has characteristics that are pragmatic, social, ethical, moral, and personal.

Using this theory, we examined the development of emotion language in participant responses from the project on emotional self-regulation. Responses were coded according to a coding scheme consistent with the four levels described above. Our results (Labouvie-Vief, DeVoe, & Bulka, in press; Labouvie-Vief, Hakim-Larson, DeVoe, & Schoeberlein, in press) showed a developmental progression: older individuals were significantly more likely to use higher levels, whereas younger participants were more likely to use lower levels. Overall, the progression continued at least until midlife, when individuals reached the highest emotional maturity. For the oldest adults (aged 60 and over) scores were somewhat lower than those for the middle-aged adults—a finding that may well reflect the impact of historical changes on the organization of emotion and defense.

In addition to this age-related progression, however, we also found a significant relationship of these four levels with ego development as assessed by Loevinger's sentence-completion test (Loevinger & Wessler, 1978). At each of the adult age levels, a wide range of ego levels is represented, and it is this indicator rather than age per se that predicts level of emotional maturity most strongly.

In general, the progression showed that younger individuals, or adults with less advanced ego development, used a language of emotions that was almost entirely devoid of feeling. Feelings were described not in terms of inner feedback, but in terms of an outer conventional language. Conventionality comprised two dimensions. First, feelings were described in terms of formal and technical processes. For example, when asked to describe the felt experience of anger, the individual said, "my adrenaline was high," or "my heart rate increased." The language was distanced, framed in terms of parameters observable from the outside with the help of technical monitors. Metaphors, if used, were static and conventional, conveying a diffuse and nonspecific sense of inner process. Second, feelings were described in terms of how one should feel: external rules and standards of conduct rather than the felt experience characterized by individuals' expressions of emotions. Thus many individuals described their feelings not in terms of felt quality, but rather their efforts to control them, and their frustrations at how difficult they were to control. Overall, then, there was a concern not with flexible affective expression, but rather with how to control feeling.

As we anticipated, our mature adults—those around middle adulthood—gave evidence of a significantly reorganized emotion language. Feelings were described in terms of a vivid felt process: for example, individuals might say "my heart felt like bursting," or "I felt a rush of energy." Their language was inner and personal rather than outer and technical. Metaphors became dynamic, dealing not with static states, but with process and transformation. At the same time, the individuals began to differentiate an inner realm of emotional experience from an outer realm of convention. The conflict between these realms was acknowledged, and the individual was concerned with accepting impulses and thoughts that previously seemed too overwhelming to accept.

This progression in how individuals describe their emotions was paralleled by the control strategies mentioned. Two broad categories of control emerged in this analysis. One means of control concerned the use of inner mental or reflective strategies (such as thinking about a feeling and/or delaying or inhibiting it through the use of such mental strategies as forgetting, diverting, and so on) and the other concerned interpersonal encounters of self and others (such as recruiting the help or support of others or allocating responsibility in an interpersonal frame). We found that the young person or less mature adult often controlled emotions through active metacognitive strategies such as forgetting, ignoring, and redirecting one's thoughts. The primary end of emotion control appeared to be repression of emotional tension and freedom from emotional conflict. The individual also looked to others to affirm the self's feelings. In conflict situations, others are often blamed for the self's negative emotional states; therefore, others must change for the self's feeling state to change.

These controls contrasted with the language of the mature adult who was open to acknowledging periods of intense inner conflict and rumination. Aware that emotions have a lawful regularity of their own, which may oppose our concepts about them, these individuals evolved means of control that allowed more full acknowledgment of their emotional experience. For example, realizing that "you can't paper your emotions over," individuals often made an effort to examine their felt experience rather than inhibiting it under a layer of "shoulds" and "oughts." Emotions were accepted as motivating energy to assist the self in either acting upon or accepting the prevailing situation. Others were no longer blamed for the self's emotional state, but were viewed as part of a more complex system of interaction and communication. Again, the adults here traversed the two modes. In becoming more flexible and spontaneous, they did not "lose" the ability to regulate emotional experience. Rather, they united knowledge relating to the presentation of the emotional self with the need for personal expressivity.

As part of the same project and with the same research participants, we have examined how such developmental variations influenced coping, stress, and defense processes (Labouvie-Vief, Hakim-Larson, & Hobart, 1987). In this study, the 100 male and female participants (10 to 77 years) were administered a number of well-known measures of coping, defense, and ego development. In addition, we assessed a brief narrative of stressful experience for the quality of its content and for the developmental level of the source of stress.

Our results provided evidence for a developmental progression in processes of coping and defense. Individuals who were younger or less mature were more likely to use the defenses of turning against others and projection, and the coping strategies of escape/avoidance and distancing. Older and more developmentally mature individuals used these strategies to a lesser degree. Instead, they used inner-focused control strategies whereby they accommodated negative events and reassessed them in a more positive light. Relative to less mature individuals, more mature adults demonstrated an inward turn and a flexible reassessment of negative conditions.

These results suggest, then, that there are significant progressive changes from early to middle adulthood in individuals' ability to cope with simple emotional situations. These results join an increasing body of evidence that has reported similar early-to-middle-adult changes in the flexibility of coping and defense. At the same time, our findings link such adaptive gains to the more general area of changes in cognitive organization—the integration of mythos and logos processes—which we believe underlie and give direction to changes in coping and self. There is a growing body of data suggesting that changes related to self and emotion have important adaptive implications for middle and later adulthood.

Conclusion

There is increasing evidence for developmental shifts in adult thought that are progressive and adaptive, and that bring increasing flexibility and openness. In both cognitive and emotional functioning, this progression moves from a vertical organization of the two modes in childhood and youth to one that is more lateral and balanced in mature adulthood. In this chapter, we have summarized evidence indicating that this reorganization occurs in many domains of adult development—intelligence, language and problem solving, memory, emotion, stress, coping, and defense.

The proposal that adulthood brings a broad restructuring of the cognitive system immediately raises questions about the universality of such a developmental trend. At this juncture, this remains an open question. There is now increasing evidence, however, that these two modes of experience—and their disconnection or integration—have a biological basis seated within the functioning of the central nervous system (e.g., Tucker & Williamson, 1984). Many cultures throughout history appear to have acknowledged a link between self-regulation and biology. The importance of the movement toward the integration of opposing tendencies has long been recognized by Eastern philosophers and scientists (e.g., Logan, 1986; Paranjbe, 1987). More recently, the field of transpersonal psychology has attempted to apply this same issue to concepts of individual development in the West (e.g., Wilber, 1983).

There is evidence that the progression beyond cultural conventionality discussed here captures a phenomenon that may apply to many highly civilized, literate cultures. This progression, however, is an ideal trajectory—ideal in the sense that it describes a potentiality that is not necessarily realized by every adult. Rather, whether or not the individual realizes this potential will depend on a number of conditions, including historical and cultural processes and individual life history. In allowing such contextual flexibility, however, specifying such "ideal" pathways also calls for an analysis of the conditions that detour individuals into less optimal trajectories, indicative of less-well-integrated functioning. For example, Tucker and Williamson (1984) summarized evidence that indicates that failures of integration are the result of specific physical and mental health dysfunction. Thus failures of some or even most adults to live up to a standard of optimal development does not necessarily invalidate the usefulness of such an ideal concept. Rather, it points to the need for investigating the conditions that may foster optimal development throughout mature adulthood and later life.

References

Adams, C. (1986). *Qualitative changes in text memory from adolescence to mature adulthood.* Unpublished doctoral dissertation, Wayne State University, Detroit, MI.

Adams, C., & Labouvie-Vief, G. (1986, November). *Modes of knowing and language processing.* Paper presented at Developmental Dimensions of Adult Adaptation: Perspectives on Mind, Self, and Emotion Symposium, conducted at meeting of the Gerontological Society of America, Chicago, G. Labouvie-Vief (Chair).

Adams, C., Labouvie-Vief, G., Hobart, C., & Dorosz, M. (1987). *Adult age group differences in story recall style.* Unpublished manuscript, Wayne State University, Detroit, MI.

Baltes, P. B., Dittmann-Kohli, F., & Dixon, R. A. (1984). New perspectives on the development of intelligence in adulthood: Toward a dual-process conception and a model of selective optimization with compensation. In P. B. Baltes & O. G. Brim, Jr. (Eds.), *Life-span development and behavior* (Vol. 6, pp. 33-76). New York: Academic Press.

Baltes, P. B., & Kliegl, R. (1986). On the dynamics between growth and decline in the aging of intelligence and memory. In K. Poeck, H. J. Freund, & H. Gansshirt (Eds.), *Neurology* (pp. 1-33). Heidelberg: Springer.

Bartlett, F. C. (1932). *Remembering.* Cambridge: Cambridge University Press.

Belenky, M. F., Clinchy, B. M., Goldberger, N. R., & Tarule, J. M. (1986). *Women's ways of knowing.* New York: Basic Books.

Benner, P. (1984). *From novice to expert: Excellence and practice in clinical nursing practice.* Reading, MA: Addison-Wesley.

Blanchard-Fields, F. (1986). Reasoning on social dilemmas varying in emotional saliency: An adult developmental perspective. *Psychology and Aging, 1,* 325-333.

Broughton, J. (1980). Genetic metaphysics: The developmental psychology of mind-body concepts. In R. Rieber (Ed.), *Body and mind* (pp. 177-221). New York: Academic Press.

Broughton, J. (1981). The divided self in adolescence. *Human Development, 24,* 13-32.

Bruner, J. (1986). *Actual minds, possible worlds.* Cambridge, MA: Harvard University Press.

Buck, R. (1984). *The communication of emotion.* New York: Guilford.

Campbell, J. (Ed.). (1971). *The portable Jung.* New York: Viking.

Cattell, R. B. (Ed.). (1963). Theory of fluid and crystallized intelligence: A critical experiment. *Journal of Educational Psychology, 54,* 1-22.

Colby, A., Kohlberg, L., Gibbs, J., & Lieberman, M. (1983). A longitudinal study of moral judgment. *Monographs of the Society for Research in Child Development, 48* (1, Serial No. 200).

Craik, F. I. M. (1977). Age differences in human memory. In J. E. Birren & K. W. Schaie (Eds.), *Handbook of the psychology of aging* (pp. 384-420). New York: Van Nostrand Reinhold.

Dreyfus, H. L., & Dreyfus, S. E. (1986). *Mind over machine: The power of human intuition and expertise in the era of the computer.* New York: Free Press.

Ebbinghaus, H. (1913). *Memory.* New York: Teacher's College Press.

Ekman, P., & Oster, H. (1979). Facial expressions of emotion. *Annual Review of Psychology, 30,* 527-554.

Giovacchini, P. L. (1977). Psychoanalysis. In R. J. Corsini (Ed.), *Current personality theories* (pp. 15-43). Itasca, IL: F. E. Peacock.

Gutmann, D. (1977). The cross-cultural perspective: Notes toward a comparative psychology of aging. In J. E. Birren & K. W. Schaie (Eds.), *Handbook of the psychology of aging* (pp. 302-326). New York: Van Nostrand Reinhold.

Haan, N. (1977). *Coping and defending: Processes of self-environment organization.* New York: Academic Press.

Hochschild, A. R. (1979). Emotion work, feeling rules, and social structure. *American Journal of Sociology, 85,* 551-575.

Horn, J. L. (1970). Organization of data on life span development of human abilities. In L. R. Goulet & P. B. Baltes (Eds.), *Life-span developmental psychology: Research and theory* (pp. 424-466). New York: Academic Press.

Horn, J. L., & Donaldson, G. (1980). Cognitive development in adulthood. In O. G. Brim & J. Kagan (Eds.), *Constancy and change in human development* (pp. 445-529). Cambridge, MA: Harvard University Press.

Hultsch, D. S., & Dixon, R. A. (1984). Memory for test materials in adulthood. In P. B. Baltes & O. J. Brim, Jr. (Eds.), *Life-span development and behavior* (Vol. 6). New York: Academic Press.

Jones, H. E. (1959). Intelligence and problem solving. In J. E. Birren (Ed.), *Handbook of aging and the individual* (pp. 700-738). Chicago: University of Chicago Press.

Kegan, R. (1982). *The evolving self.* Cambridge, MA: Harvard University Press.

Kitchener, K. S., & King, P. M. (1981). Reflective judgment: Concepts of justification and their relationship to age and education. *Journal of Applied Developmental Psychology, 2,* 89-116.

Kuhn, D., Pennington, N., & Leadbeater, B. (1982). Adult thinking in developmental perspective. In P. B. Baltes & O. J. Brim, Jr. (Eds.), *Life-span development and behavior* (pp. 157-195). New York: Academic Press.

Labouvie-Vief, G. (1977). Adult cognitive development: In search of alternative interpretations. *Merrill-Palmer Quarterly, 23,* 227-263.

Labouvie-Vief, G. (1982). Dynamic development and mature autonomy: A theoretical prologue. *Human Development, 25,* 161-191.

Labouvie-Vief, G. (1985). Intelligence and cognition. In J. E. Birren & K. W. Schaie (Eds.), *Handbook of the psychology of aging* (pp. 500-530). New York: Van Nostrand Reinhold.

Labouvie-Vief, G. (in press). Modes of knowledge and the organization of development. In M. L. Commons, C. Armon, F. A. Richards, & J. Sinnott (Eds.), *Beyond formal operations: The development of adolescent and adult thinking and perception.* New York: Praeger.

Labouvie-Vief, G., Adams, C., Hakim-Larson, J., Hayden, M., & DeVoe, M. (1987). *Modes of text processing from preadolescence to mature adulthood.* Unpublished manuscript, Wayne State University, Detroit, MI.

Labouvie-Vief, G., & Chandler, M. (1978). Cognitive development and life-span developmental theory: Idealistic versus contextual perspectives. In P. B. Baltes (Ed.), *Life-span development and behavior* (pp. 181-210). New York: Academic Press.

Labouvie-Vief, G., DeVoe, M., & Bulka, D. (in press). Speaking about feelings: Conceptions of emotion across the life span. *Psychology and Aging.*

Labouvie-Vief, G., Hakim-Larson, J., DeVoe, M., & Schoeberlein, S. (in press). Emotion and self-regulation: A life-span model. *Human Development.*

Labouvie-Vief, G., Hakim-Larson, J., & Hobart, C. J. (1987). Age, ego level, and the life-span development of coping and defense processes. *Psychology and Aging, 2,* 286-293.

Labouvie-Vief, G., & Schell, D. (1982). Learning and memory in later life. In B. Wolman & G. Stricker (Eds.), *Handbook of developmental psychology* (pp. 826-846). Englewood Cliffs, NJ: Prentice-Hall.

Labouvie-Vief, G., Schell, D. A., & Weaverdyck, S. E. (1982). *Recall deficit in the aged: A fable recalled.* Unpublished manuscript, Wayne State University, Detroit, MI.

Langer, S. (1942). *Philosophy in a new key: A study in the symbolism of reason, rite, and art.* Cambridge, MA: Harvard University Press.

Lerner, R. M. (1976). *Concepts and theories of human development.* Reading, MA: Addison-Wesley.

Lerner, R. M. (1984). *On the nature of human plasticity: Implications for intervention with children and adolescents.* New York: Cambridge University Press.

Lewis, M., & Saarni, C. (1985). *The socialization of emotions.* New York: Plenum.

Loevinger, J., & Wessler, R. (1978). *Measuring ego development.* San Francisco: Jossey-Bass.

Logan, R. K. (1986). *The alphabet effect.* New York: William Morrow.

Lowen, A. (1972). *Depression and the body.* New York: Penguin.

Main, M. (1987, April). *Working models of attachment in adolescence and adulthood.* Symposium presented at the Society for Research in Child Development, Baltimore, MD.

Malatesta, C. Z., & Haviland, J. M. (1985). Signals, symbols, and socialization: The modification of emotional expression in human development. In M. Lewis & C. Saarni (Eds.), *The socialization of emotion* (pp. 89-116). New York: Plenum.

Malatesta, C. Z., & Izard, C. E. (1984). The facial expression of emotion: Young, middle-aged, and older adult expressions. In C. Z. Malatesta & C. E. Izard (Eds.), *Emotion in adult development* (pp. 253-273). Beverly Hills, CA: Sage.

McAdams, D. P. (1985). The "Imago": A key narrative component of identity. In P. Shaver (Ed.), *Self, situations, and social behavior: Review of personality and social psychology* (Vol. 6, pp. 115-141). Beverly Hills, CA: Sage.

Mead, G. H. (1934). *Mind, self and society.* Chicago: University of Chicago Press.

Olson, D. R. (1977). From utterance to text: The bias of language in speech and writing. *Harvard Educational Review, 47,* 257-281.

Paranjbe, A. C. (1987). The self beyond cognition, action, pain, and pleasure: An Eastern perspective. In K. Yardley & T. Honess (Eds.), *Self and identity: Psychosocial perspectives* (pp. 27-40). New York: John Wiley.

Perry, W. G. (1968). *Forms of intellectual and ethical development in the college years.* New York: Holt, Rinehart & Winston.

Piaget, J. (1951). *Play, dreams, and imitation in childhood.* New York: Norton.

Reese, H. W., & Rodeheaver, D. (1985). Problem solving and complex decision making. In J. E. Birren & K. W. Schaie (Eds.), *Handbook of the psychology of aging* (pp. 474-499). New York: Van Nostrand Reinhold.

Rubenstein, S. L. (1968). *Grundlagen der allgemeinen Psychologie.* Berlin: Volkseigener Verlag.

Rybash, J. M., Hoyer, W. J., & Roodin, P. A. (1986). *Adult cognition and aging: Developmental changes in processing, knowing, and thinking.* New York: Pergamon.

Saarni, C. (1979). Children's understanding of display rules for expressive behavior. *Developmental Psychology, 15,* 424-429.

Schafer, R. (1980). *Narrative action in psychoanalysis.* Worcester, MA: Clark University Press.

Schaie, K. W. (1980). Intelligence and problem solving. In J. E. Birren & R. B. Sloane (Eds.), *Handbook of mental health and aging* (pp. 262-284). Englewood Cliffs, NJ: Prentice-Hall.

Schaie, K. W., & Labouvie-Vief, G. (1974). Generational versus ontogenetic components of change in adult cognitive behavior: A fourteen year cross-sequential study. *Developmental Psychology, 10,* 305-320.

Schaie, K. W., & Parham, I. A. (1977). Cohort-sequential analysis of adult intellectual development. *Developmental Psychology, 13,* 649-653.

Schwartz, G. E. (1982). Physiological patterning and emotion. In K. R. Blankstein & J. Polivy (Eds.), *Self-control and self-modification of emotional behavior* (pp. 13-27). New York: Plenum.

Stern, D. (1985). *The interpersonal world of the infant.* New York: Basic Books.

Strauss, A. (1977). Sociological theories of personality. In R. J. Corsini (Ed.), *Current personality theories* (pp. 277-302). Itasca, IL: F. E. Peacock.

Tomkins, S. (1980). Affect as amplification: Some modifications in theory. In R. Plutchik & H. Kellerman (Eds.), *Emotion: Theory, research, and experience: Vol. 1. Theories of emotion* (pp. 141-163). New York: Academic Press.

Tucker, D. M., & Williamson, P. A. (1984). Asymmetric neural control systems in human self-regulation. *Psychological Review, 91,* 185-215.

Vaillant, G. (1977). *Adaptation of life.* Boston: Little, Brown.

Welford, A. T. (1958). *Aging and human skill.* London: Oxford University Press.

Werner, H., & Kaplan, B. (1963). *Symbol formation.* New York: John Wiley.

Wilber, K. (1983). *Up from Eden: A transpersonal view of human evolution.* Boulder, CO: Shambhala.

4

Adult Intelligence

Sherry L. Willis

This chapter discusses issues related to adult intelligence in middle age. Two middle-aged adults facing intellectual challenges are briefly described. In 1964 Wayne Hazelwood joined IBM as a typewriter assembler (*New York Times*, May 17, 1985, p. 15). He was good at his job, but IBM made changes in the way they manufactured typewriters. Wayne's job was no longer necessary. So, in 1975 Wayne began an intensive training program and became a Selectric typewriter quality inspector. He did well, but new developments in typewriter technology again required the learning of new skills. In 1980 Wayne took a training course in manufacturing instruction. Most recently, in 1985 Wayne began his fourth career at IBM as a member of the electronic card assembly technical staff. Over his 21-year work life, Wayne has repeatedly applied his intellectual abilities to learn new information and technical skills.

Susan graduated from college, married, and is now the mother of two preadolescent children. She and her husband are concerned about the financial strain of having two children in college in a few years. In addition, Susan is eager to continue her own professional development. She is applying for graduate studies in library science. Part of her graduate program will focus on computer technology involved in information management and retrieval. Susan, at age 40, will be acquiring a number of complex, new analytical skills.

Societal stereotypes have suggested that childhood and adolescence are the primary periods for intellectual development (Willis, 1985). Our society has concentrated virtually all of formal schooling within the early part of the life span. It was assumed that the individual could acquire during the early years the knowledge and intellectual abilities required to carry out the responsibilities of adulthood. Just as the individual reached biological maturity in adolescence or early adulthood, there was the assumption that intellectual development also "peaked" early in the life span. As early signs of biological aging began to become evident in middle age (e.g., gray hair, changes in body composition), it was assumed that the individual's level of intellectual functioning was beginning to diminish.

In our rapidly technologically advancing society, however, it becomes increasingly important for middle-aged adults to perform at a high level of intellectual competence (Cross, 1981). It is in middle age that many adults assume major familial, professional, and societal responsibilities (Havighurst, 1972). These require not only the application of previously developed knowledge and abilities but also the acquisition of new information and skills. Can adults in middle age be expected to meet these intellectual demands?

In this chapter, the literature on developmental changes in intellectual functioning across adulthood will be reviewed, with particular focus on middle age. We will begin by considering the construct of intelligence and how it has been measured. Second, we will discuss age-related changes in intellectual performance. Third, we will examine several variables that contribute to individual differences in the level of intellectual functioning in adulthood.

Measurement of Intelligence

When asked to nominate individuals considered to be extremely intelligent, one often begins by identifying certain behaviors "characteristic" of intelligent people, and then chooses individuals who exhibit these behaviors. Such behaviors may include solving problems efficiently or learning new tasks quickly. It is important to note that intelligence is a theoretical construct and is not directly observable. It must be inferred from observing an individual's behavior. The more situations in which we observe intelligent behavior, the more confident we become in our estimate of a person's intelligence. Assessment of intelligence via IQ tests works according to the same principle: the individual is presented with a series of tasks, and his or her responses are judged in terms of level of competence.

Intelligence is not identical with competent behavior. Many factors can affect competent behavior in addition to intelligence. Consider, for example, an individual's performance on a math test. Certainly, the individual's intelligence is an important factor in performance on a math test. The individual's prior educational training in mathematics, the motivation to do well on the test, and the individual's anxiety in test-taking situations, however, are additional factors that will affect performance.

Of particular concern in this chapter are factors other than intelligence that might differentially affect the performance of adults of different ages. For example, many young adults, still in school, will have had more recent experience in taking tests, thereby being more "test-wise" and suffering less test anxiety than many middle-aged and older adults, who have had little recent experience with test taking. Likewise, when IQ tests are administered under speeded conditions, many older adults suffering sensory or behavioral (e.g., arthritis) handicaps may be disadvantaged in their ability to respond quickly. The role of factors other than intelligence needs to be taken into consideration in interpreting test performance, particularly when performance of adults of different ages is to be compared.

Multidimensionality of Intelligence

A perennial question in the study of intelligence is whether intelligence is a single, general ability, or several different abilities. Binet, one of the early investigators of intelligence, favored the idea of general ability, known as the "g" factor (Anastasi, 1976). In the study of adult intelligence, however, the importance of studying several distinct abilities has been increasingly recognized (Willis & Baltes, 1980). The importance of studying different abilities will become evident later in the chapter, as we examine changes in level of performance across the life span. Longitudinal research indicates that there are different patterns of developmental change for different abilities.

How many abilities are involved in adult intelligence? Different models of adult intelligence have focused on different numbers and types of abilities. Some models focus on only a few salient abilities (Thurstone & Thurstone, 1941); other models have suggested as many as 120 distinct factors of intelligence (Guilford, 1967). Many of these ability factors have been identified using the statistical procedure of factor analysis. Some of the more commonly recognized ability factors are verbal, number, space, memory, perceptual speed, and reasoning. Verbal ability has been assessed by tests of reading comprehension, verbal analogies, and vocabulary. Number ability involves competence in basic mathematical computations (addition, subtraction, multiplication, division). Space ability involves competence in visualization, and mental rotation of figures in two- and three-dimensional space. Memory has been examined in terms of memory span (e.g., recall of a list of words), and associative memory (e.g., recall of pairs of words). Perceptual speed involves the ability to make simple visual discriminations quickly and accurately. General reasoning, or induction, involves the ability to identify a rule or pattern in a problem and to utilize that rule in solving subsequent problems.

Abilities and Activities in Adulthood

The abilities described above were initially studied in research with children. Early investigators, such as Binet, identified these abilities as being important predictors of children's ability to achieve in academic settings (Anastasi, 1976). While schooling is an important developmental task of childhood, adults frequently apply their intellectual abilities in other pursuits. Are these same abilities useful in studying adult intelligence? Findings from recent research indicate a qualified "yes" to the above question. For example, performance on traditional intelligence tests has been shown to be a useful predictor of entry-level competence in a number of professions (e.g., engineering, piloting, computer programming; Hills, 1957; Smith, 1964). Moreover, recent research indicates that these abilities are significant predictors of middle-aged and older adults' performance on a number of tasks of daily living (e.g., reading a medicine bottle label, comprehending a newspaper editorial, interpreting a bus schedule; Willis & Schaie, 1986, 1987).

Many activities of daily living are complex tasks that involve multiple abilities. For example, reading and interpreting a medicine bottle label certainly involves verbal ability, but the competence to determine the size of dosage required for a given individual also requires reasoning ability (Willis & Schaie, 1986). Likewise, reading a road map involves spatial ability and verbal ability. Thus it is useful to think of abilities as basic "building blocks" of competent behavior. Several "blocks" (i.e., abilities) are involved in order to perform a given complex task, such as reading a road map.

Developmental Changes in
Intellectual Ability

A primary question of developmental psychologists focuses on how intellectual functioning changes as the individual progresses from young adulthood to middle age to old age (Willis & Baltes, 1980). Does the individual's performance on all abilities go "downhill" after young adulthood, as some societal stereotypes suggest? In order to examine this question, one needs some understanding of the two major research designs used in developmental research on adult intelligence.

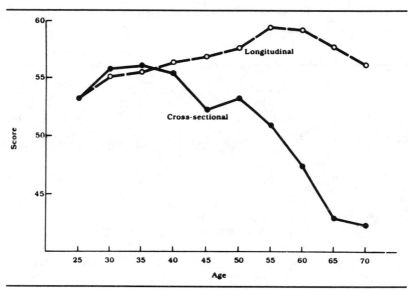

Figure 4.1.   Comparable Cross-Sectional and Longitudinal Age Gradients for the Verbal Meaning Test

SOURCE: K. W. Schaie and C. R. Strother (1968). A cross-sequential study of age changes in cognitive behavior. *Psychological Bulletin, 70,* 671-680. Copyright 1968 by the American Psychological Association. Reprinted by permission.

Cross-Sectional Studies

The most widely used design in studying intellectual functioning has been the cross-sectional method (Botwinick, 1977). Using this method, the researcher compares the intellectual performance of adults of different ages at one point in time. For example, in 1960, the researcher might have compared the verbal ability performance of adults aged 20, 30, 40, 50, 60, 70, 80, and 90 years. The common finding across a number of cross-sectional studies was that young adults perform at a somewhat higher level than middle-aged adults, and that middle-aged adults perform at a somewhat higher level than older adults. This pattern of age differences is shown in Figure 4.1 (Schaie & Strother, 1968).

The interpretation of early cross-sectional studies was that these age differences in performance between young, middle-aged, and older adults reflected age-related decline. It was assumed that the middle-aged and older adults had performed at the same level as the younger adults when they were in their twenties and thirties. Their performance was assumed to have declined with increasing age.

Longitudinal Studies

Findings from longitudinal studies of intellectual functioning presented quite a different picture than those from cross-sectional studies (Schaie, 1983a). In longitudinal studies, the same individuals are studied across time. Longitudinal findings indicate that verbal ability, for example, continues to develop throughout middle age (Schaie & Strother, 1968). In contrast to cross-sectional findings, verbal ability peaks in late middle age, rather than in young adulthood. Reliable age-related decline in verbal ability does not occur until the late sixties.

Figure 4.2 presents longitudinal data from Schaie's longitudinal study (Schaie, 1983a) across the age range from young adulthood to old age for men and women for five different abilities. Note that, for all of the abilities studied, intellectual functioning in middle age is stable. There is no reliable decline until the early sixties. Note also that there are different patterns of age-related change for different abilities. Reliable age-related decline occurs somewhat earlier for some abilities than for others. Abilities such as numerical computations and spatial reasoning that involve speeded performance, and abstract reasoning, show earlier patterns of decline than abilities such as verbal ability. In addition, there are gender differences in intellectual performance. On average, men perform at a somewhat higher level than women on spatial ability, whereas women perform at a higher level than men on reasoning ability. There are also gender differences in patterns of age-related change. Men and women exhibit onset of age-related decline at somewhat different ages for certain abilities.

The findings from longitudinal studies, then, indicate that middle age is a period of relative stability in intellectual functioning. There is no reliable decline in intellectual performance in the middle years. Indeed, for some abilities, such as verbal ability, peak level of performance occurs in late middle age rather than in young adulthood. Thus findings from longitudinal studies indicate that intellectual ability continues to develop throughout the middle years.

Cohort Differences

What accounts for the difference between findings of cross-sectional and longitudinal studies? Cohort or generational differences are at issue (Schaie, 1983a). Cross-sectional studies compare individuals of different ages *and*

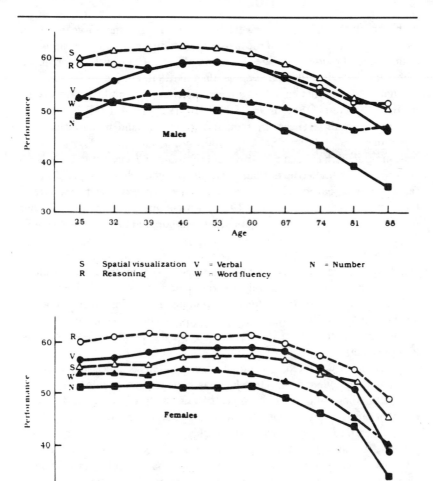

Figure 4.2. Longitudinal Changes for Five Thurstone Primary Mental Abilities

SOURCE: K. W. Schaie (1983). The Seattle Longitudinal Study: A twenty-one year exploration of psychometric intelligence in adulthood. In K. W. Schaie (Ed.), *Longitudinal studies of adult psychological development*. New York: Guilford Press. Used by permission.

different cohorts. That is, age and cohort are confounded in cross-sectional studies. For example, if 40- and 75-year-olds are compared in 1985 in a cross-sectional study, these individuals differ not only in age, but also in birth cohort; the 75-year-olds were born in 1910 and the 40-year-olds in 1945. The life experiences of these two cohorts differ, even when examined at the same chronological age. For example, the 1945 birth cohort has a higher level of education, on average, than the 1910 cohort.

Figure 4.3 presents cumulative mean differences in ability performance for 10 birth cohorts (1889, 1896, 1903, 1910, 1917, 1924, 1931, 1938, 1945, 1952). Cohort differences for inductive reasoning and numerical ability performance are shown (Schaie, 1986; Willis, in press). For inductive reasoning, there has been a positive cohort trend. Successive cohorts have performed at a higher level than previous cohorts, when compared at the same chronological age. On the other hand, there is a curvilinear cohort trend for numerical ability. The 1910-1924 birth cohorts performed at a higher level than did earlier or later cohorts, when compared at the same chronological age.

These data indicate that there are cohort differences in performance level, and that the pattern of these cohort differences vary by the ability studied. The distinct life experiences of the various cohorts contribute to these cohort differences in level of intellectual functioning. The experiences of cohorts are known to differ on important variables, such as educational level, medical care, nutritional resources, and historical events (e.g., war, economic depression).

Interpretations of cross-sectional studies often assume that older individuals functioned at the same level as younger individuals when at the same chronological age. Cohort comparisons, as shown in Figure 4.3, indicate that this is rarely the case. There are distinct cohort differences in level of intellectual functioning across the adult years. It is only when successive cohorts are studied longitudinally across the same age range that these cohort differences are identified. Thus cohort longitudinal studies contribute valuable information on how individuals change in intellectual functioning across the adult years and on cohort differences in level of intellectual performance.

It should be noted, however, that there are some limitations to longitudinal studies (Schaie, Labouvie, & Barret, 1973). As individuals are studied over time, less advantaged individuals (e.g., in education, health, occupation) are more likely to drop out of the study, such that the remaining subjects are more advantaged than the original sample. Thus the findings of longitudinal studies are somewhat positively biased. The significance of these limitations, however, can often be assessed and controlled for via independent sampling and statistical procedures (Schaie, 1983a; Siegler, McCarthy, & Logue, 1982).

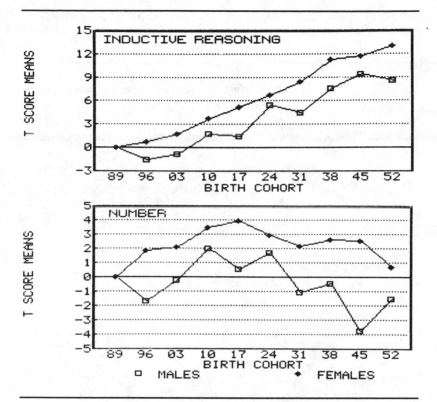

Figure 4.3. Cumulative Cohort Differences for Two of the Three Thurstone Primary Mental Abilities (inductive reasoning, number)

SOURCE: K. W. Schaie (1986, September). *Social context and cognitive performance in old age.* Paper presented at the meeting of the American Sociological Association, New York.

Health, Life-Style, and Intellectual Functioning

The findings presented thus far on intellectual functioning have focused on normative, or average, patterns of age-related change. While normative patterns of age-related change in intellectual functioning do not occur until the early sixties, there are wide individual differences in performance. Some individuals show significant changes in intellectual performance in midlife, while a few remarkable individuals show little decline even into the eighties. In this section, some of the variables associated with these individual differences are considered. The focus is on variables of particular relevance in midlife.

Health

In middle age, individuals begin to experience some early signs of normative aging, such as graying of hair, change in body composition, and menopause. These types of biological changes occur in most, if not all, individuals; however, there are wide individual differences in the timing of these changes. In addition to these normative changes, some individuals in midlife begin to experience signs of pathological aging as manifested by the presence of chronic diseases. Although chronic disease is not necessarily a part of normative aging, the likelihood of developing at least one chronic disease increases with increasing age (Shock, 1985; Siegler & Costa, 1985). It is important, then, to study intellectual development in the absence of chronic disease, as well as to examine how specific diseases affect cognitive functioning throughout adulthood.

Some diseases affect intellectual behavior directly, by damaging the brain. An example is Alzheimer's disease, which was originally identified in middle-aged adults (Butler & Lewis, 1982). Currently, more attention is given to diseases of the Alzheimer's type found in older populations, because the prevalence of this disease increases in advanced old age. Other chronic diseases (for example, arthritis, diabetes) affect intellectual functioning indirectly by making it more difficult for adults to perform in a competent manner. The distraction of pain and financial concerns that accompany illness may also affect the quality of intellectual performance.

Cardiovascular disease is one of the most important diseases affecting intellectual functioning (Siegler & Costa, 1985). Its increasing importance in midlife is evidenced by the fact that heart disease is one of the two most prominent causes of death in middle age (Levy & Moskowitz, 1982).

Cerebrovascular diseases that affect the blood flow to the brain might have a direct effect on mental functioning. The reduced blood flow decreases the oxygen supply to brain cells, resulting in temporary "malnutrition" or permanent "starvation" and death of affected tissue. Even mild cardiovascular disease has been shown to be related to deficits in memory (Klonoff & Kennedy, 1966), and lower scores on the Wechsler Adult Intelligence Scale (Wang, Obrist, & Busse, 1970). Intellectual decline has been associated with blood pressure that was pathologically high (Eisdorfer & Wilkie, 1973).

Cardiovascular disease was also found to be related to generally lowered mental functioning in Schaie's longitudinal study (Hertzog, Schaie, & Gribbin, 1978). It was also noted, however, that cardiovascular disease was more common among people who were older and in the lower social class. When people of the same age and social class were compared, cardiovascular disease was related to significantly lower functioning on only two measures: number and a composite measure of intellectual ability. These findings indicate that one must be cautious in interpreting studies that compare individuals with and without a disease. Factors (for example, age, social class) correlated with the disease may be more important predictors of intellectual functioning than the disease per se.

Work

Does the type of work one engages in affect intellectual functioning in middle adulthood? A 10-year longitudinal study of the relationship between work complexity and intellectual flexibility showed that the two factors were reciprocally related (Kohn & Schooler, 1983). The complexity of the work environment was studied along three dimensions: routinization, closeness of supervision, and substantive complexity of work. Substantively complex work requires the worker to deal with ideas and people, and involves the use of initiative, thought, and independent judgment. Men who had jobs that required independent decision making and that involved working with a complex set of environmental circumstances tended to become more intellectually flexible through adulthood. These findings were maintained when prior levels of intellectual flexibility were controlled for. Thus the work one does affects how one thinks. Research indicates that the reciprocal relation between work and intellectual flexibility is evident for both men and women (Miller, Schooler, Kohn, & Miller, 1979).

Life-Style

There is also evidence that one's life-style can affect intellectual functioning. The relationship between changes in intellectual functioning over the prior 14-year period and the individual's life-style were examined within Schaie's longitudinal study of intellectual development (Gribbin, Schaie, & Parham, 1980). Four types of participants were identified. First, there were the "average" adults, average in social status, family continuity, and involvement in their environment. These individuals maintained their level of intellectual functioning over the 14-year period studied. Second, there were the "advantaged" adults, who were of high social status and who lived lives that required them to engage in new activities and learn new things. These advantaged individuals often showed improved intellectual performance over the 14-year period.

The third and fourth groups, in contrast, showed some decline in level of intellectual functioning. One group was labeled the "spectators," given that they tended to live a rather passive, static life-style and rarely were actively involved in challenging, new endeavors. The most unfortunate group in terms of intellectual decline were the "isolated older women," who had experienced some form of family dissolution (for example, divorce, widowhood) and had become isolated or disengaged. Thus these findings suggest that active engagement in life and successful involvement in tasks that require flexibility and new challenges are related to maintenance of intellectual functioning in the adult years.

Threat of Professional Obsolescence

One type of intellectual challenge that is particularly salient in midlife deals with professional obsolescence. Professional obsolescence has been defined as the use of information, concepts, or techniques that are less effective in solving problems than others currently available in one's field of specialization (Dubin, 1972). Obsolescence does not reflect an age-related loss of ability, rather it reflects individuals not continuing to learn and update themselves as new knowledge and techniques become available.

Obsolescence is particularly relevant in midlife because most middle-aged individuals have terminated formal schooling years earlier. The length of the work life has been increasing since the turn of the century. In 1900, the average worker spent only 21 years in the labor force, often in the same job. In 1980, the average working life had grown to 37 years and many individuals were experiencing multiple job changes over the work life. In addition, our society is experiencing a knowledge explosion, such that the relevant knowledge one needs in one's career cannot be fully obtained in the years of formal schooling. The individual must continue to update throughout the adult years.

It is now estimated that 75% of all occupations involve some knowledge of computers (Naisbitt, 1984). Few middle-aged adults today, however, had experience with computers in their formal schooling. With the knowledge explosion and technological advances, the knowledge and skills one uses in one's occupation can change rapidly. The term *professional half-life* has been coined to describe the time it takes for 50% of one's professional knowledge to become invalid or obsolete (Dubin, 1972). For computer scientists, the half-life is only two or three years; among engineers, it is five or six years (Cross, 1981).

Thus middle-aged individuals must continually seek mechanisms for updating their professional knowledge and skills. Given rapid technological change, occupations also become obsolete and individuals may be required to learn several new jobs within their work lives. Learning is, indeed, becoming a lifelong process (Willis, 1985). Individuals who are flexible, are willing to accept new assignments, and possess the basic cognitive abilities and skills needed to engage in learning new tasks are better prepared to deal with the challenges of professional updating.

Summary

Findings from longitudinal research present a picture of intellectual functioning in middle age that is somewhat different from that suggested by our stereotypical views. For a number of mental abilities, middle age is a period of stability in intellectual functioning. Indeed, some abilities, such as verbal ability, actually "peak" in middle age. Continued development in midlife is most evident for abilities that are extensively employed in tasks and responsibilities of daily living.

While there is a normative pattern of stability in intellectual functioning in middle age, there are wide individual differences in developmental patterns of change. Some adults exhibit decline in intellectual functioning in midlife, while others demonstrate growth patterns in many abilities. A number of variables have been found to be associated with individual differences in intellectual development and change. These variables include health, occupation, and life-style. Cardiovascular disease has been associated with earlier declines in intellectual functioning; however, social-status indicators may be more important predictors of intellectual change than cardiovascular disease per se. On the positive side, individuals who are actively engaged in life, seeking and experiencing new learning challenges, are particularly advantaged in maintaining intellectual functioning. Likewise, occupations that involve complex decision making and independent judgment appear to foster intellectual development.

Longitudinal studies that have examined the intellectual functioning of several generations at the same chronological ages have shown significant cohort differences in level of intellectual performance. For some abilities, such as inductive reasoning, a positive cohort trend has been found. For other abilities, however, negative or curvilinear cohort trends have been identified. Thus the influence of sociocultural change on intellectual performance appears to be differential for various abilities. Given rapid sociocultural change in some sectors of our society, it becomes important to consider both age and cohort, when comparing the performances of middle-aged and older adults with that of younger adults.

Although there is little evidence for significant normative decline in intellectual functioning in middle age, the adult in midlife is increasingly faced with the threat of technical or professional obsolescence. Obsolescence does not reflect age-related cognitive loss, but ineffective efforts to keep up to date with rapid informational and technological changes. Obsolescence is most evident in certain professions directly affected by technological advances. Virtually all adults, however, are vulnerable to becoming obsolete, unless updating occurs, as certain technologies (for example, computer-driven devices) are becoming more widespread in our society. Longitudinal research findings indicate that the mental abilities needed to acquire new information and technologies are intact and available to individuals in middle age. Individuals in midlife, however, must continue to develop and apply their intellectual abilities to meet the challenges of our technological society.

References

Anastasi, A. (1976). *Psychological testing* (4th ed.). New York: Macmillan.

Botwinick, J. (1977). Intellectual abilities. In J. E. Birren & K. W. Schaie (Eds.), *Handbook of the psychology of aging* (pp. 580-605). New York: Van Nostrand Reinhold.

Butler, R. N., & Lewis, M. I. (1982). *Aging and mental health* (3rd ed.). St. Louis: C. V. Mosby.

Cross, K. P. (1981). *Adults as learners* . San Francisco: Jossey-Bass.

Dubin, S. (1972). Obsolescence or lifelong education: A choice for the professional. *American Psychologist, 17* , 486-498.

Eisdorfer, C., & Wilkie, F. (1973). Intellectual changes with advancing age. In L. F. Jarvik, C. Eisdorfer, & J. E. Blum (Eds.), *Intellectual functioning in adults* (pp. 21-29). New York: Springer.

Gribbin, K., Schaie, K. W., & Parham, I. (1980). Complexities of life style and maintenance of intellectual abilities. *Journal of Social Issues, 36* , 47-61.

Guilford, J. P. (1967). *The nature of human intelligence*. New York: McGraw-Hill.

Havighurst, R. J. (1972). *Developmental tasks and education* (3rd ed.). New York: McKay.

Hertzog, C., Schaie, K. W., & Gribbin, K. (1978). Cardiovascular disease and changes in intellectual functioning from middle to old age. *Journal of Gerontology, 33*, 872-883.

Hills, J. R. (1957). Factor analyzed abilities and success in college mathematics. *Educational Psychological Measurement, 17* , 615-622.

Klonoff, H., & Kennedy, M. (1966). A comparative study of cognitive functioning in old age. *Journal of Gerontology, 21* , 239-243.

Kohn, M. L., & Schooler, C. (1983). *Work and personality: An inquiry into the impact of social stratification* . Norwood, NJ: Ablex.

Levy, S. M., & Moskowitz, J. (1982). Cardiovascular research: Decades of progress, a decade of promise. *Science, 217*, 121-129.

Miller, K., Schooler, C., Kohn, M. L., & Miller, K. (1979). Women and work: The psychological effects of occupational conditions. *American Journal of Sociology, 85*, 66-94.

Naisbitt, J. (1984). *Megatrends*. New York: Warner.

Schaie, K. W. (Ed.). (1983a). *Longitudinal studies of adult psychological development*. New York: Guilford.

Schaie, K. W. (1983b). The Seattle longitudinal study: A 21-year exploration of psychometric intelligence in adulthood. In K. W. Schaie (Ed.), *Longitudinal studies of adult psychological development* (pp. 64-135). New York: Guilford.

Schaie, K. W. (1986, September). *Social context and cognitive performance in old age*. Paper presented at the meeting of the American Sociological Association, New York.

Schaie, K. W., Labouvie, G. V., & Barret, T. J. (1973). Selective attrition effects in a fourteen-year study of adult intelligence. *Journal of Gerontology, 28* , 328-334.

Schaie, K. W., & Strother, C. R. (1968). A cross-sequential study of age changes in cognitive behavior. *Psychological Bulletin, 70* , 671-680.

Shock, N. (1985). Longitudinal studies of aging in humans. In C. E. Finch & E. L. Schneider (Eds.), *Handbook of the biology of aging* (pp. 721-743). New York: Van Nostrand Reinhold.

Siegler, I. C., & Costa, P. T., Jr. (1985). Health behavior relationships. In J. E. Birren & K. W. Schaie (Eds.), *Handbook of the psychology of aging* (2nd ed., pp. 141-166). New York: Van Nostrand Reinhold.

Siegler, I. C., McCarthy, S. J., & Logue, P. E. (1982). Wechsler memory scale scores, selective attrition, and distance from death. *Journal of Gerontology, 37* , 176-181.

Smith, I. M. (1964). *Spatial ability: Its educational and social significance*. London: University of London.

Thurstone, L. L., & Thurstone, T. G. (1941). Factorial studies of intelligence. *Psychometric Monographs* , no. 2.

Wang, H. S., Obrist, W. D., & Busse, E. W. (1970). Neurophysiological correlates of the intellectual function of elderly persons living in the community. *American Journal of Psychiatry, 126* , 1205-1212.

Willis, S. L. (1985). Towards an educational psychology of the older adult learner: Intellectual and cognitive bases. In J. E. Birren & K. W. Schaie (Eds.), *Handbook of the psychology of aging* (2nd ed., pp. 818-847). New York: Van Nostrand Reinhold.

Willis, S. L. (in press). Cohort differences in cognitive aging: A sample case. In K. W. Schaie & C. Schooler (Eds.), *Social structure and the psychological aging processes*. Norwood, NJ: Ablex.

Willis, S. L., & Baltes, P. B. (1980). Intelligence in adulthood and aging: Contemporary issues. In L. Poon (Ed.), *Aging in the 1980's: Psychological issues* (pp. 260-272). Washington, DC: American Psychological Association.

Willis, S. L., & Schaie, K. W. (1986). Practical intelligence in later adulthood. In R. Sternberg & R. Wagner (Eds.), *Practical intelligence: Origins of competence in the everyday world* (pp. 236-270). New York: Cambridge University Press.

Willis, S. L., & Schaie, K. W. (1987, July). *Mental abilities and real life tasks*. Paper presented at the International Society for the Study of Behavioral Development, 10th Biennial Meeting, Tokyo, Japan.

Part III
Mental Health and
Personality Development

The three chapters in Part III focus on mental health, personality development, and work, family, and social relationships of men. In Chapter 5, Chiriboga points out that men and women at midlife face a number of challenges and potential stressors. The author shows, however, that there is scant research support for the popularly described phenomena of "midlife crisis" and "empty-nest syndrome." Instead, adults at midlife are generally more efficient and productive than ever before. And, through anticipatory socialization, midlife and its tasks do not come as a shock.

Chiriboga acknowledges that there are role losses and burdens related to this time in life; however, adults are more capable of dealing with stress and problems than ever before. Social workers, psychologists, and other professional helpers can encourage and support their clients' use of personal and social resources to cope with their circumstances. They can also provide information on the empirical findings about midlife crisis and the empty-nest syndrome, so that clients can more accurately assess their situations.

In Chapter 6, Haan presents research findings from the Berkeley Institute of Human Development's longitudinal study of approximately 100 persons in two samples over a 50-year span. The researchers found that the transition between late adolescence and early adulthood showed marked personality shifts and was the time of least stability. The findings revealed that personality, along some dimensions more than others, is not set in childhood and adults can change at middle age. The research findings countered two prevalent myths: the midlife crisis and middle-aged immutability and stodginess. Both men and women were found to be more assertive and cognitively committed, and the women were more outgoing than ever.

According to Haan, the results indicate that adults may change most markedly when life conditions change—men changing from early to middle adulthood as they become more comfortable in their careers, and women from middle to later adulthood as they return to the workplace. The studies also showed that the women changed more frequently than the men as a group. Haan suggests that women's multiple and conflicting role commitments are conducive to more frequent change. Counselors, therapists, and educators can help women assess the trade-offs between their various role commitments and personality emphases, and learn ways to prevent or cope with stressful conditions.

Professional helpers may do middle-aged clients a disservice by expecting them to be either crisis-ridden or unable to adopt new ways of living. Haan implies that personality is more fluid, adaptive, and innovative than is usually thought; however, environmental change can have more immediate and clearer effects on personality change than counseling or psychotherapy with clients.

The author cautions that the participants in the studies were mostly White, middle-class Northern Californians, so that the results might not be generalizable to other groups. Similar studies need to be conducted with people in other social classes, ethnic groups, and at various historical periods.

In Chapter 7, Tamir examines myths related to the work, family, and social relationships of men at midlife. She reviews research studies that show social-class differences between the lower and working classes and the upper-middle classes for age at perceived onset of midlife, life patterns, societal integration, and coping strategies. For example, the blue-collar worker often considers himself to be middle-aged by 40, whereas the upper-class man often does not consider himself entering middle age until his early fifties. Research has also shown that men from the lowest socioeconomic classes are the most alienated from society, work, self, and others.

Tamir cites studies showing that although most men in their forties do not directly indicate that they are in crisis, they are confronted by transitional issues. Tamir examines major issues for men at midlife, including mortality, reaching one's peak, and consideration of leaving a legacy. Each of these issues requires a certain degree of self-analysis and decision making in order to move on to a fulfilling second half of life.

Tamir examines myths related to men at work, and concludes that men at middle age are the most highly satisfied with their jobs and often achieve their highest incomes and level of prestige at this period of life. She reviews literature that refutes the myth that men at middle age are obsolete at work. Research has also shown that middle-aged men begin to rely more on interpersonal relations than on the workplace for emotional fulfillment.

The myth that middle-aged men are contemplating leaving their wives is also countered by research findings, according to Tamir. Most marriages continue through middle age even if the partners are dissatisfied with their relationship. Studies show that a man's self-perceived happiness in his forties is highly related to his marital happiness. Major points of conflict in midlife marriages, however, include the stress of parenting adolescent children, or the woman's increasing assertiveness or unwillingness to meet her husband's desires for dependency and nurturance. Tamir's review of research data shows the diversity in coping patterns for men in their forties that correlate with social class, societal integration, and educational background. She cautions, however, that the literature reported might involve a cohort factor that would be different from the forthcoming middle-aged baby boom cohort. There may be an even greater diversity of midlife patterns among this group.

Helping professionals working with middle-aged men should be informed regarding the positive aspects of middle age for men and become familiar with the mythology that could be detrimental to these clients. Tamir points out various issues regarding therapy approaches. For example, the middle-aged male, Tamir suggests, is likely to benefit more from relating to the therapist as an equal rather than from a dependent position.

5

Mental Health at the Midpoint:
Crisis, Challenge, or Relief?

David A. Chiriboga

The premise underlying this chapter is a simple one: that during the middle years, a heightened awareness of personal abilities and a solid grounding of self in society will tend to overcome a host of midlife problems resulting from physical and social stressors. In providing evidence in support of this premise, some of the myths and stereotypes of middle age will be discussed, as well as the realities.

The Midlife Crisis:
Fact or Fantasy?

The myths surrounding the mental health of middle-agers generally focus on what has come to be known as "the midlife crisis." Deriving from clinical impressions of persons who seek help in dealing with the issues and challenges of their stage of life, this crisis is usually attributed to the male or female menopause, and to the other health problems described by Dan and Bernhard (Chapter 2 in this volume). The so-called empty-nest syndrome, a hypothesized midlife pathology triggered by the departure of children, has also been suggested as commonplace among middle-agers. Central to both variants of midlife problems is the sense of loss, both of physical health and social opportunities, and a sense of closing options in many areas of life (Lifton, 1979).

Although the midlife crisis and empty-nest syndrome remain popular topics in books and articles written for lay audiences, the research support for these problems is surprisingly slight. What support there is tends to be based either on clinical populations or on other nonrandomly selected samples. In one of the most comprehensive clinically oriented studies conducted, approximately 500 middle-aged men completed questionnaires and another 200 were interviewed (McGill, 1980). One conclusion reached was that up to one-third of middle-aged American men go through a midlife crisis. The evidence backing this conclusion, however, consisted basically of evidence for change per se:

> Many men in mid-life, ages forty to sixty, experience events which cause them to dramatically and significantly change their personality and behavior. This change in personality and behavior may be appropriately called a "crisis." (McGill, 1980, p. 267)

To equate "change" with "crisis" seems to either inflate the importance of the former concept or weaken the latter.

On the other hand, there is mounting evidence from research studies that serious midlife problems are actually experienced by only 2% to 5% of middle-agers (Cooper & Gutmann, 1987; Farrell & Rosenberg, 1981; Krystal & Chiriboga, 1979; Schlossberg, 1987). In one study, for example, a Midlife Crisis Scale was completed by over 300 men between the ages of 30 and 60. Of these, only about 2% reported feelings that in any way suggested crisis conditions (Cooper, 1977). These findings were subsequently replicated in a second study, where once again a group of approximately 300 middle-aged men completed the Midlife Crisis Scale and no evidence was found for a crisis (Costa & McCrae, 1978).

In another study, Lowenthal and Chiriboga (1972) found that most of a randomly selected group of middle-aged parents were looking forward to the empty-nest stage of life with great anticipation. On one hand, this extremely positive attitude was based on the expectation of greater personal freedom and more quality time to spend with their husbands or wives. On the other hand, many of the respondents commented that the chief source of marital disputes was the children, and they looked forward to the departure of this source of problems.

The disparity between the estimates for midlife problems made by helping professionals and by researchers is rather mystifying. Its origins may derive from the fact that most empirical research has drawn respondents from the community while helping professionals generally focus on clinical populations. It may well be that the prevalence of midlife crises tends to be overestimated by members of the helping professions, whose practice would by definition include a disproportionate number of persons who are suffering from emotional problems.

Helping professionals, in fact, may be falling victim to the same "guilt by association" thinking that can lead law enforcement officers to view all citizens as potential criminals simply because so many of their clients are criminals. In other words, counselors and therapists should bear in mind that those who seek their help represent only a small fraction of middle-agers, and that the crises these people bring with them are more likely to stem from long-standing problems than from their current stage of life (McCrae & Costa, 1984).

Overreadiness to view midlife as a time of crisis can lead to an automatic acceptance of this as the basic issue, coupled with an overreadiness to treat the surface problem instead of seeking to identify its roots. Such a predisposition to treat on the basis of life stage rather than specific etiology is not uncommon even in the medical profession. For example, depressed women in midlife who seek help from the medical establishment often encounter a "medicalization" of their problems because the practitioner views these as the result of physiologic disturbance (McKinney, 1987). The result may be a prescribed course of estrogen replenishment or psychotropic drugs as opposed to a potentially more appropriate scrutiny of the personal and social conditions faced by the client.

Mental health and the midlife crisis. If the middle years were associated with the turmoil and distress depicted in the more pessimistic accounts of this life stage, one would assume that the incidence of mental illness in all its various guises would rise dramatically. In fact, such is not the case. Suicide peaks at young adulthood and late life for White males, peaks and then declines during the middle years among White females, and also declines among middle-aged Black men and women. In fact, suicide rates for persons over the age of 44 have actually declined during the past 35 years, while rates for young adults are more than twice what they were in 1950 (U.S. Bureau of the Census, 1986; U.S. Department of Health and Human Services [DHHS], 1985).

Depression and other signs and symptoms of stress and crisis demonstrate no major shift during this stage. For example, mental health admissions to state and county mental institutions, private psychiatric hospitals, and non-federal hospitals decline for the 45-64 age group (U.S. DHHS, 1986). Alcoholism, however, reaches a peak during middle age, and alcohol-related deaths are the fifth-ranked cause of death for this age group in the United States (Pan American Health Organization, 1986; U.S. DHHS, 1986).

Midlife as a Boring Plateau

The midlife crisis is, at the very least, an interesting myth, although there is no disputing the fact that some individuals do indeed experience such a crisis (Lifton, 1979). Ironically, another prevailing stereotype of middle age concerns anything but a crisis. Many researchers seem to hold to a stereotypic image of middle age as a time of comparative equilibrium and uneventfulness, during which the individual plays out the roles in life he or she established and developed during young adulthood. In consequence, relatively little attention has been paid to the middle years, with many researchers appearing to prefer study of the presumably more tumultuous younger or later years (Michels, 1984).

Both the myths and the stereotypes of middle age depart considerably from the realities. For some individuals it is a time of beginning decline, for others a time of peak ability, a time of challenge, or a time of relief. As Dickens wrote of another age, "It was the best of times, it was the worst of times."

To understand better the diversity of experiences, and especially the challenges of mental health faced by persons at midlife, this chapter will present several theories concerning mental health during this period, then conclude with a discussion and examples of stress experiences and how they may affect mental health.

Mental Health and the
Tasks of Living

One of the more accepted ways of studying issues in adult development is to consider how the demands of a particular stage of life interact with personal characteristics to help shape the structure and functioning of the self. Such an approach is particularly appropriate to the study of mental health at midlife because most definitions of mental health suggest that it generally is problematic only to the extent that the individual fails to live up to the demands and obligations imposed by society and social relations (Albee, 1986; Offer & Sabshin, 1984).

From the perspective of the helping professional, it is also relevant to note that developmental theory generally treats the mental health of middle-aged persons as something that evolves not only from their current situation but from their past experiences and characteristics. Mental health is also considered to be strongly influenced by whether individuals recognize that they have entered a new stage of life: a stage in which the demands and expectations are beginning to change from those that existed during young adulthood.

The remainder of this section will review the works of five stage theorists whose ideas have been especially influential in the study of mental health during the middle years: Carl G. Jung, Robert J. Havighurst, Erik H. Erikson, David L. Gutmann, and Daniel Levinson. In each case, the theorist has sought to explain why people during this life stage either grow, remain the same, or deteriorate in well-being. In his own way, each of these theorists has emphasized the growth and challenges associated with the stage, and sees the crises as evolving only in those instances where the individual fails to meet these challenges.

The Developmental Theory of
Carl Jung

One of the more influential writers on the psychology of middle age, Carl Jung described this stage of life as one with potential for both growth and stagnation. Departing from his preceptor, Sigmund Freud, on the issue of when the primary thrust of development ended, Jung divided psychological development into two phases, with the break between the two occurring at about age 40.

Up until the forties, according to Jung, men and women are often principally concerned with meeting obligations that revolve around the dual responsibilities of raising a family and establishing one's place in society. The expectations and demands created in the push to meet these obligations shape the directions in which personality develops. A gender difference emerges. Men, for example, often focus on the instrumental and achievement-oriented side of their personalities because of their need for outward success in the employment arena. Women, in contrast, were seen to focus on the more expressive and nurturant dimensions of personality as a result of the greater salience of their parenting role.

The cost of this one-sided development may not be immediately obvious to the individual, but the need to recognize its existence intensifies with age:

> The nearer we approach to the middle of life, and the better we have succeeded in entrenching ourselves in our personal attitudes and social positions, the more it appears as if we had discovered the right course. . . . We overlook the essential fact that the social goal is attained only at the cost of a diminution of personality. (Jung, 1960, p. 772)

In other words, Jung felt that people who appear to have successfully come to terms with life may in fact have established a blind and narrow accommodation. They have ignored the fact that middle age is not simply a continuation of young adulthood. Change is in the wind and must be heeded.

As the demands of the family lessen, at about the age of 40, Jung suggested that many individuals get a chance to balance their hitherto uneven development. The initial stages of this balancing-out are often preceded by what Butler (1974) labeled the "life review," which Jung, however, described simply as a period of stock-taking:

> Instead of looking forward one looks backward, most of the time involuntarily, and one begins to take stock, to see how one's life has developed up to this point. The real motivations are sought and real discoveries are made. The critical survey of himself and his fate enables a man to recognize his peculiarities. (Jung, 1954, p. 331)

With these words Jung also suggested that a growing concern with one's inner self is a normal part of middle age. In this he anticipated Neugarten's (1964) concept of "interiority," a concept she developed on the basis of empirical studies of middle-aged men and women, which she cast as a precursor of psychological aging. Jung made the interesting point that self-concern, if prominent at an earlier life stage, might well be viewed as unhealthy: "For a young person it is almost a sin, or at least a danger, to be too preoccupied with himself; but for the ageing person it is a duty and a necessity to devote serious attention to himself" (Jung, 1960, p. 785).

The balancing of personality characteristics can be attained by giving expression to suppressed qualities. Individuals can achieve this "union of opposites" by paying greater heed to the inner world, and bringing parts of this world to consciousness. This confrontation with the inner world may be a threatening experience because it involves giving up the image of youth and recognizing the finitude of life. The transition to an inner orientation is, therefore, often associated with a period of "storm and stress" and is a transition people may seek to avoid, preferring instead to continue with a way of living more appropriate to earlier stages of life. Whether welcomed or avoided, this balancing-out is not only a possibility afforded by the growing freedom from obligations and social demands, but something Jung saw as a requirement for successful adjustment during the middle and later years.

Reinforcing this need to reorient one's life, Jung proposed that one of the major causes of neurosis at midlife is the perseveration of a life-style that is no longer appropriate:

> They cling to the illusion of youth or to their children, hoping to salvage in this way a last little scrap of youth. One sees it especially in mothers, who find their

sole meaning in their children and imagine they will sink into a bottomless void
when they have to give them up. (Jung, 1953, p. 114)

In describing the need to withdraw from old involvements with the world,
Jung foreshadowed the theory of disengagement expressed so eloquently by
Cumming and Henry (1961). He was also addressing some of the conditions
that lead to the often-cited empty-nest syndrome and midlife crisis: holding
on to the parent role or denying the aging process.

To the extent that the individual successfully completes the transition to
an inner orientation, Jung suggested that she or he can continue to grow and
thrive. Acquiring a mature sense of responsibility for oneself also involved
developing a feeling of responsibility to the community, and the balanced
person in later life often becomes a spiritual or social leader. While an
increased awareness of the inner world can sensitize the individual to early
signs of the aging process, Jung (1953) portrayed acceptance of diminishing
capacity and increasing losses as a first step toward coping with the
problems, as well as the potentials, of later life.

Havighurst and Developmental Tasks

Unlike Jung and many other theorists of personality in adult life, Robert
J. Havighurst is neither a clinician nor oriented to psychoanalysis. His initial
training was in engineering, although he subsequently pursued careers first
in education and later in gerontology. But as was the case with Jung, his
distinguished Viennese counterpart, Havighurst proposed a model of personal development suggesting that successful resolution of past challenges
can help future adjustment.

For Havighurst (1952), each period of life is associated with a set of
"developmental tasks" that confront the individual. While recognizing that
the actual tasks arise from more or less unique combinations of biological,
psychological, and social forces, Havighurst provided lists of developmental
tasks that generally must be addressed at different stages of life. Failure to
deal with these tasks, or an inadequate resolution of the tasks, can set the
stage for maladjustment.

Of particular relevance to this chapter are those tasks that pertain to the
middle years. During these years, which for Havighurst (1952) encompassed
roughly the period from age 30 to 60, the tasks are to

(1) achieve adult civic and social responsibility;
(2) establish and maintain an economic standard of living;

(3) assist teenage children to become responsible and happy adults;
(4) develop adult leisure-time activities;
(5) relate to one's spouse as a person;
(6) accept and adjust to the physiological changes of middle age; and
(7) adjust to aging parents.

The first three of these "tasks" seem to reflect the kinds of social obligations considered by Jung as exerting more dominance in the first half of life. The remainder come close to what Jung (if asked) might have referred to as the tasks of the second half of life.

A perusal of the literature on later life produced during the almost four decades since Havighurst first published his model demonstrates its continuing vitality. Some tasks, such as providing care to aging parents, have only recently begun to receive attention from researchers. Others, such as the use of leisure, still await the attention they deserve.

From the perspective of the counselor and therapist, one of Havighurst's central contributions is the notion that in the lives of each and every one of us there are certain tasks that confront us. How we identify and manage these confrontations, or even how we ignore them, can help in the understanding of the client at midlife. Havighurst's work, in fact, suggests the strategy of asking clients to list those major demands or tasks they are currently dealing with, and identifying those in which they feel problems remain. Overall, he presents an optimistic viewpoint on the so-called crises of midlife. Rather than crises, the individual confronts basically clear-cut and expectable tasks everyone must face in the same way they have faced developmental tasks at earlier stages.

Erikson's Life Cycle
Theory of Personality

Trained as a child analyst and steeped in the psychoanalytic tradition of Freud, Erik Homberger Erikson's theoretical formulations were strongly influenced by his years as a clinician and by his involvement in the studies of child development conducted at the Institute of Human Development, University of California, Berkeley. A pervasive theme in Erikson's writings is the close relationship of the individual's personal life evolution to the historical period and to the society in which one lives. Like many contemporary theorists, Erikson sees adaptation over the life course as evolving through a series of transactions between the developing organism and the social order:

Personality can be said to develop according to steps predetermined in the human organism's readiness to be driven toward, to be aware of, and to interact with, a widening social radius, beginning with the dim image of a mother and ending with mankind. (Erikson, 1980, p. 54)

The interactive "steps" or crises take the form of a series of eight developmental stages, during each of which the individual is confronted by opposing tendencies either to grow or to decline. These stages occur in a predetermined and sequential ordering that draws on biological and psychosocial maturation, as well as interactions with society. At the end of each stage, the individual will have developed a psychosocial feature that will continue to characterize that person during the rest of his or her life, and that might be considered a building block in the construction of mental health or illness. For example, at the conclusion of the first stage an individual will have developed a sense either of trust or of mistrust in other people.

How the individual adjusts to the crises posed by each stage depends in part on what Erikson refers to as an "epigenetic" principle. As presented by Erikson (1980), the concept of epigenesis has its intellectual roots in the biological principle that development of an embryo proceeds according to an overall ground plan. Within this plan each distinct organ has its own time of maximum growth and differentiation, and development continues until all parts have developed sufficiently to form an integrated, functional whole.

Translating this biological principle into psychosocial terms, Erikson hypothesized that the success with which the demands of any stage are resolved lays the groundwork, good or bad, for resolution of any further crisis. This would be comparable to a poorly developed vascular system creating strains leading to an enlarged heart. In the realm of adjustment, how well the individual copes with the problems of midlife depends at least in part on how well the crises of youth and young adulthood have been faced. A person with a poorly developed sense of self, for example, could be expected to have difficulties in developing a sense of sharing and oneness with others.

Other assumptions by Erikson include (a) that each of the eight psychosocial characteristics exists in interrelation to the rest; (b) the viability of each characteristic rests upon its emergence at the appropriate time in development; (c) each characteristic exists in some precursor form prior to the time of special ascendance, and continues in yet another form after that time; and (d) achieving growth as the outcome of any stage is not possible without experiencing some elements of the less successful side.

Regarding this last point, the idea is that without conflict and challenge, there can be no growth. As an example, an individual must experience distrust to establish trust fully, and have some uncertainties about personal identity in order fully to achieve an integrated self. Moreover, once trust or any other quality is established, it continues to operate in relationship to other qualities. From the perspective of the health professional concerned with middle age, one implication of this theoretical perspective is that in order to resolve present dilemmas, the whole historical development of the individual must be treated—an awesome task!

All in all, Erikson posed eight stages in personality development over the life course. He based these stages on the classic psychosexual stages of development outlined by Freud, but incorporated additional psychosocial stages. The stages are described in many standard texts and will not be repeated here, but a few additional words are in order concerning the two stages that occur in middle and later life: generativity versus ego stagnation, and ego integrity versus despair and disgust.

Not too long ago, Erikson (1982) reconsidered the significance of these two stages from the perspective of both a changing society and his own advanced age (in 1982 he was 80). For example, he extended the notion of sexuality past Freud's genital stage to include procreativity in adulthood and "generalized sensuality" in later life. He also began to speak of the last stage of life in terms of a quest for coherence and wholeness, a sense of kinship not just with one's family but with the past and future world. This amounts to an extended sense of the generativity that plays an important role at an earlier stage.

Before leaving Erikson's theoretical perspectives, it may be worthwhile to mention that there is little empirical evidence that the stages unfold in a true epigenetic sequence. At the same time, the psychosocial characteristics associated with each stage have been demonstrated to have major importance for adult mental health. For example, in her research on middle age, Neugarten (1968) reported that the development of a sense of immortality, through nurturing of children, mentoring, or other attempts to influence the younger generations, was associated with well-being in her sample of highly successful middle-aged professional men and women. Similarly, individuals in the throes of marital separation and divorce may be reconfronted with issues pertaining to the establishment of trust, industry, and identity (Chiriboga, 1982). Divorce may also reawaken in the noncustodial parent those issues pertaining to generativity, because his or her accustomed means of expressing generativity may no longer be appropriate (also see Weick, Chapter 11, this volume).

Gutmann and Ego Mastery Styles

A clinical psychologist with training in anthropological techniques, David L. Gutmann has devoted over two decades to the examination of systematic changes in personality across middle and later life that have implications for how individuals cope with life. In order to evaluate the generalizability of his initial findings, Gutmann studied middle-aged and elderly residents of Kansas City, the Navajo of Arizona, the Highland and the Yucatan Mayas of Mexico, and the nomadic Druze living in Giliean and Syrian territories of the Middle East. For each group, Gutmann used a combination of projective tests, in-depth interviews, and dream analysis to record and assess common themes of middle-aged and older men and women.

One of Gutmann's (1964) earliest findings was the existence of three apparently universal styles with which individuals of different ages relate to demands placed upon them. He referred to these styles as ego mastery styles, because the overt or covert behaviors he assessed seemed rooted in the ego processes. The three mastery styles are as follows:

(1) *Active mastery.* Persons with this ego mastery style tend to take an active and assertive stance toward their environment. They try to change conditions in the outer world rather than change themselves, and they pursue their goals aggressively.

(2) *Passive mastery.* Persons with this ego mastery style are characteristically accommodative. They give in to the situation. Typically they do not see themselves as being in positions of power, and hence try to change themselves rather than the situation.

(3) *Magical mastery.* Use of this ego mastery style is indicated by a distortion of reality. Individuals attempt to cope with situations by means of denial or redefining the situation, rather than by taking action to actually change it. This style is considerably less common than the other two, and clearly less adaptive.

Across all the cultures he studied, Gutmann (1977) saw evidence for a developmental progression from one style to another. Men in the middle years, for example, typically displayed characteristics associated with active mastery, but passive mastery became more common among older subjects. In contrast, women in early middle age were characterized by passive mastery styles but active mastery became more common in later middle age and in old age. Few men and women acted in ways associated with magical mastery, but when they did, it typically was in extreme old age.

The shifts in mastery styles clearly overlap with Jung's postulated "balancing-out" of personality characteristics, and Gutmann (1975, 1985) also postulated social obligations as playing a pivotal role in determining both the sex differences and the developmental trajectory. For Gutmann these social obligations have traditionally centered on parental responsibilities. Men sacrifice their needs for comfort and emotional expression in the interests of enhancing aggressive and competitive characteristics needed to fulfill their role as breadwinners; women sacrifice the more aggressive characteristics in order not to alienate the breadwinner or psychologically damage the vulnerable child. But as parental responsibilities lessen in midlife, a change takes place:

> Particularly for women aging paradoxically brings new beginnings. As parents enter middle age, and as children take over the responsibility for their own security . . . the sex-role reversals that shape our transcultural data occur . . . both sexes can afford the luxury of living out the potentials and pleasures that they had to relinquish early on, in the service of their particular parental task. (Gutmann, 1975, p. 181)

Gutmann's point is that behavior usually identified as either "masculine" or "feminine" is often associated not only with gender but with stage of life. His latest research, based on interviews and testing of women in the pre- and post-empty-nest stage, provided empirical evidence that post-empty-nest women are more likely to demonstrate assertive, aggressive, and "executive" traits usually associated with men (Cooper & Gutmann, 1987). At the same time, he recognized that in today's society, with its new life-styles and parenting styles, what we traditionally view as male or female personality styles and behavior may be changing.

Hence, for the helping professional, one contribution of Gutmann's research is support for the "balancing" notion of Jung. In fact, his clinical findings suggest that those who fail to achieve balance may be more susceptible to emotional problems during the middle years. Adding to the notion that middle age is not a time of crisis and struggle, Gutmann also found that the middle years tend to be characterized by an active mastery style among both men and women. This perspective has been substantiated in other research as well. For example, in the previously cited study of Neugarten (1968), one finding was that a synonym for *middle age* could well be "the executive years." The reason, according to Neugarten, was that during middle age individuals have had sufficient experience with themselves as well as whatever career they chose (including that of homemaker) to develop a heightened awareness of how to solve problems and perform at a peak.

Similarly, Lowenthal, Thurnher, and Chiriboga (1975) found, on the basis of adjective rating list material, that the self-concepts of women in the younger and older stages of middle age show signs of becoming more dominant and assertive, whereas the self-concepts of males show an increasing acceptance of intimacy and sociability. All together, research and theory based on the mastery style approach has clearly defined the middle years as a time of peak performance and influence.

Levinson and the
Seasons of a Man's Life

Basing his work on a study of 40 men aged 35 to 45 who were originally interviewed in 1969 and then reinterviewed approximately two years later, Daniel J. Levinson and his colleagues developed a theory of personal development that blends ingredients of Jung's developmental perspectives, Havighurst's notions of developmental tasks, and more recent work on critical life transitions. A central thrust of Levinson's research is that at each stage of life an individual will be confronted with challenges to his or her established life-style and ways of thinking. Like the other theorists reviewed here, Levinson does not see these challenges as insurmountable. Rather, they simply represent a fact of life that most individuals deal with at the proper time.

Levinson's perspective is that as each individual progresses along the life course he or she will encounter challenges and potential crises. To expand on this point a little further, Levinson postulated the existence of five eras within the course of a human life, each of which represents a relatively stable time with its own distinctive characteristics. Each era is also said to occur within a relatively restricted age range, although proof of this age-linked progression was not furnished and Levinson (1986) himself has questioned this progression. The eras are as follows:

(1)   Childhood and adolescence era (birth to age 22)
(2)   Early adulthood era (age 17 to 45)
(3)   Middle adulthood era (age 40 to 65)
(4)   Late adulthood era (age 60 to 85)
(5)   Late late adulthood era (age 80 and over)

Of particular relevance to this chapter are Levinson's speculations concerning how individuals move from one era to the next. At the beginning of each era is a time of change and transition, what Levinson called "cross-era transitional periods." The midlife transition, for example, extends approximately from age 40 to 45 and, like the transitions that precede it, it represents a time when the individual must attempt to match his or her personal identity with a new stage of life. The kind of self-examination that Levinson sees as becoming central during the midlife transition is reflected in questions such as "What have I done with my life? What do I really get from and give to my wife, children, friends, work, community—and self?" (Levinson et al., 1978, p. 60). These questions can also be seen to typify the life review process Jung portrayed as important to mental health during the middle years.

Levinson also pointed out that as the individual draws near to the close of middle age other issues must be addressed if he or she is to maintain a healthy adaptation to life. In the following comments, he described men approaching age 60 as facing certain critical issues reminiscent not only of Jung, but of Erikson and Havighurst as well:

> The developmental task is to overcome the splitting of youth and age, and find in each season an appropriate balance of the two. . . . During the Late Adult Transition, a man fears that the youth within him is dying and that only the old man—an empty dry structure void of energy, interests or inner resources—will survive for a brief and foolish old age. His task is to sustain his youthfulness in a new form appropriate to late adulthood. (Levinson et al., 1978, p. 35)

In reviewing and evaluating Levinson's theoretical contribution, it becomes clear that he differs from the other theorists presented thus far in not presenting any specific mental health qualities as being linked to a successful middle age. He nevertheless views the individual's life and mental health as being affected by certain regularities associated with each successive stage of life.

Stress and Mental Health

During the past 10 to 15 years, a number of studies have concluded that personality characteristics, including neuroticism, the self-concept, and other dimensions related to mental health, are surprisingly stable over time. Among the most prolific supporters of this position, Costa, McCrae, Zonderman, Barbano, Lebowitz, and Larson (1986; McCrae & Costa, 1984) concluded, for example, that flexibility, introversion/extroversion, and neuroticism are traits that, once established, are borne by the individual during the entire course of life. This is encouraging news to those who reject the concept of the midlife crisis as a universal phenomenon of that stage of life; it suggests that we cannot assume or expect major changes in mental health to occur simply on the basis of entering a new stage of life.

On the other hand, even Costa and McCrae would agree that the situational context, especially social stressors, can affect an individual's mental health. The relationship of stress exposure to mental health at any age is strong, and one that has been replicated in study after study. One of the more common findings is that any kind of significant loss, but especially that of a loved one, is likely to lead to depression (Brown & Harris, 1978; Horowitz & Wilner, 1980). For example, Brown and Harris (1978) and Brown, Bifulco, Harris, and Bridge (1986) found that widows are much more likely to experience depressive episodes in the weeks and months following bereavement.

What then are social stressors? Basically they represent those conditions occurring in our lives that impose demands. According to Lazarus (Lazarus & Folkman, 1984, p. 19), perhaps the most well-recognized stress researcher today, "Psychological stress is a particular relationship between the person and the environment that is appraised by the person as taxing or exceeding his or her resources and endangering his or her well-being."

Historically, most stress researchers have studied only the short-term implications of exposure to stressors. More recently, however, students of adult development and aging have begun to recognize the long-term impact of stress (Chiriboga & Cutler, 1980; Eisdorfer & Wilkie, 1977; Neugarten, 1977). For example, Wallerstein (1986) reported that many of her adult respondents were still suffering from the aftermath of divorce well into the tenth year of her longitudinal study. In another study of divorce, family stressors during early childhood were found to bear a significant relationship to mental health of adults of all ages (Chiriboga, Catron, & Weiler, 1987). In a study of more normative transitions, such as the empty nest and retirem nt, stress was found to exert a major influence on psychosocial functioning over periods of 11 to 12 years (Chiriboga, 1984; Lowenthal et al., 1975).

A Basic Paradigm of Stress

Most stress theoreticians would agree that the basic stress paradigm includes the following three components: stressor, mediating factors, and stress responses. Each is important in itself: together they help us to understand that the stress experience is an interactive process. Simply knowing that the last child left home, for example, does not really help us to predict whether a person will experience an "empty-nest" crisis or not.

The stressor. Stressors are social and physical forces impinging upon the person that may exert a deleterious effect. The most commonly studied are what have come to be known as "life events" after the seminal research of two psychiatrists, Thomas Holmes and Richard Rahe. Life events are potentially disruptive experiences, such as divorce, bereavement, or even a vacation, that upset the day-to-day routine in some way. Using the 42-item Schedule of Recent Events developed by Holmes and Rahe (1967), or any of dozens or more variations, countless researchers have examined the incidence of discrete, more or less nonnormative events that occur in the lives of individuals at any age.

As far as knowledge about middle and later life is concerned, this massive research effort has done little beyond establishing that persons in middle and later life may experience fewer events, whether conceived as positive or negative in nature (Chiriboga & Cutler, 1980). Sex differences have also been reported. In one study incorporating data derived from the 1980 NORC General Social Survey, it was found that men and women aged 40-60 showed no differences in either the incidence or the perceived impact of several middle-age "life events," but that these events showed a greater relationship to life satisfaction among men (Sherman, 1982).

Schulz and Rau (1985) defined life events in terms of their statistical and temporal probabilities of occurrence. Some events, for example, marriage and retirement, are both statistically and temporally "normative" in that they are highly likely to occur, and highly likely to occur within restricted time periods. Other events, such as winning a major state lottery prize, or experiencing some natural disaster or war, are statistically infrequent and may occur at any point in life.

For Schulz and Rau (1985), as well as earlier researchers (Lowenthal et al., 1975), normative and nonnormative events constitute major markers of the adult life course. For example, middle age may be heralded by the expected departure of the first child from home or by the unexpected situation of being passed over for an important work assignment.

The mediators. Mediators are those factors, inside or outside the individual, that act to modify the impact of the stressor. Two of the more commonly studied are coping strategies (Lazarus & Folkman, 1984) and social supports (Thoits, 1982).

Despite voluminous research, extremely little is known about how to define or study coping. The efficacy of social supports is better known but still only partially substantiated. In one major investigation, Berkman and Syme (1979) found that smaller network size was related to an increased risk of mortality over a nine-year period. Other studies have found little evidence that size of social networks, supposedly critical mediators of the relationship between stressors and health, bears a strong relationship to well-being (Lieberman, 1982; Schaefer, Coyne, & Lazarus, 1981).

At least one study from a national probability sample has reported formal and informal agents of social support to have a greater bearing on life satisfaction among middle-aged women than men (Sherman, 1982). Married men, however, seem to have a better life (at least insofar as life satisfaction scores indicate), whereas married women demonstrated lower life satisfaction than did women who were divorced or widowed (Sherman, 1982).

Given that middle-aged men and women today face life situations and challenges that are nontraditional in terms of how previous cohorts of middle-agers lived, one assumption is that social supports may play an increasing role in determining outcome. Today, for example, the markers that shape our lives, such as the birth or departure of children, or one's first full-time job, can vary widely in their timing. One woman may become a grandmother at 35 while another is still waiting at 73. In the research of Hirsch (1980, 1981), there is evidence that the potentially negative impact of experiencing these displaced markers, what Neugarten (1977) called "off-schedule" events, can be mitigated by social supports.

Hirsch (1980) studied young widows and middle-aged women returning to school. These people were experiencing unusual stress loads, but the stress was mediated by the presence of social supports. Interestingly, Hirsch found that more diversified social networks seemed most efficacious, probably because a greater range of skills and experience was represented in such networks. It may also be that in more diverse, heterogeneous networks, there is a greater likelihood of having persons who can empathize and share experiences that are nonnormative.

The responses. Responses to stress exposure can occur on both physical and psychosocial levels, and often involve a developing series of responses that unfold as the person attempts to deal with the stress. Perhaps the best-known description of the evolving stress response can be found in Kubler-Ross's (1969) five stages of responses to one's impending death. These stages occur in the following sequential order: shock and denial, anger, bargaining, depression, and acceptance. Horowitz (1976) developed a more generic portrayal of what he calls the "stress response syndrome," in which the stages consist of initial outcry, denial, intrusive thoughts about the stressor, working through, and completion.

These stages appear to occur in roughly the same order for people at any point in adult life. From a therapeutic perspective, the key to understanding how an individual is dealing with stress lies in determining whether the individual is perseverating at any one stage of the stress response, or is proceeding at a reasonable rate. For example, parents who refuse to accept the fact that they are "empty-nest" parents may experience increasing difficulties with their adult children (Golan, 1986; Krystal & Chiriboga, 1979). The same is true for a worker who ruminates continually about a declining role in company affairs and who subsequently irritates and angers his or her supervisors.

Stress and the Adult
Life Course: One Study

As a means of characterizing the stress experiences of midlife adults, one particular research project will be described in some detail. From 1969 to 1980, a study was conducted of the stress experiences of men and women who were aged 16 to 65 at the initial contact (Fiske & Chiriboga, 1985). The sample consisted of 216 individuals who at their first contact were each facing one of four normative transitions. Subjects included high school seniors facing graduation from high school, newlyweds who were facing decisions about parenthood, middle-aged parents facing the departure of their youngest children from their home, and workers facing retirement.

Although the intent of the study was to examine the impact of transitions on the lives of people at different points along the life course, a life events inventory and other measures of stress were also included. The findings both supported and extended previous reports on the stress exposure of older people. For example, support was found for previous reports that middle-aged adults apparently did report fewer life events than younger adults, but more than those in the retirement stage of life (Lowenthal & Chiriboga, 1973).

At the same time, there was also evidence that middle-aged and older respondents were reporting more life events in certain specific areas of life, especially the areas of health, finances, and family (Chiriboga & Cutler, 1980). The reason for the discrepancy between our findings and those of others rested in part on the fact that we had developed a life event inventory that contained items appropriate to all stages of life (Lowenthal et al., 1975). In contrast, life event inventories generally are designed for younger populations and contain many items that are not appropriate for older and retired populations. For example, events such as "child born" or "child ran away from home" are relatively infrequent for persons aged 40 and over. On inventories that contain mostly events appropriate to younger stages of life, it is impossible for middle-aged or older adults to receive a high score.

As the research continued over an 11-year period, we began to find that social stressors included not only life events but nonevents (for example, not having a grandchild), experiencing life transitions off schedule (for example, getting married for the first time at 40 instead of the early twenties), waiting for some anticipated problems to occur (such as waiting for retirement day), and the minor hassles of everyday life. We also found that for middle-agers some of the most distressing events occurred not to themselves but to their loved ones (Lowenthal et al., 1975). This phenomenon we labeled "altruistic" stress.

Considering the impact of all these stressors on the lives of respondents, we began to identify some important characteristics of stress conditions. For example, life events and other stressors are not necessarily random conditions (Chiriboga, 1984; Fiske & Chiriboga, 1985). For some people, there is continuity over time, in the sense that some people seem continually to have more than their share of stressors while others have much fewer.

In another series of analyses, it was found that components of the personality such as dimensions of the self-concept, life satisfaction, and psychological symptomatology were relatively stable (Chiriboga, 1984) over the entire 11 years during which we followed the subjects. Despite the stability in various aspects of personal functioning, however, life stressors revealed a lot about how people change over the life course. In order to pursue this matter in more detail, the characteristic stress loads of individuals over the 11-year period was contrasted with the degree of change in various dimensions of personality. One finding was that middle-agers who characteristically experienced a relatively low stress load were more stable in symptomatology, self-concept, and morale than were those chronically exposed to higher stress loads (Chiriboga & Fiske, 1987).

Summing Up the Evidence for Social Stressors

The actual degree of exposure by middle-agers to stress is not well established. While a number of early life course studies suggested that older people experience fewer life events presumed to be stressful, other studies have reported that middle-aged and older adults simply experience different kinds of stressors than do younger people. Evaluations of stressors also vary considerably from one individual to another, depending on the adequacy of their mediating resources. For example, two middle-aged people suffering from painful and chronic arthritis may have opposite reactions: one feeling lucky in comparison with others in the same age group, the other feeling depressed and defeated.

Concerning the role of stressors in affecting personal functioning, there is evidence to support the contention that life circumstances play a major role in determining how individuals play out their own personal drama of the life course. These life circumstances include those that arise from the particular fact of being middle-aged: the sense of incompleteness and imbalance associated with devoting the first half of life to meet society's demands (Jung, 1960) and the developmental tasks presented by this stage. At the same time, the helping professional may find that seemingly random and "nonnormative" conditions of life affect personal development in middle age, just as they do at an earlier age.

Stress in the Middle Years

Up to this point in the chapter, general issues were addressed that are relevant to both mental health and stress during the middle years. It was suggested that although mental health tends to be stable, stress factors may intervene. In the remaining sections of this chapter, examples will be provided of midlife stressors, mental health, and their interrelationship. These examples will first be drawn from home and from the workplace, followed by a discussion of additional sources of stress.

Home and work are emphasized because they represent two of the most salient domains in the lives of adults, and perhaps at no time is this more true than during middle age. Both in the home and at the workplace, middle-agers stand in control—or at least they are nominally in charge. For more traditional men and women, there is a clear gender split in terms of which domain is most salient: work for men and home for women. Thirty years ago, Havighurst (1957) investigated the social role performance of middle-aged men and women. His basic finding, and one that still holds true today, was that the lives of women were more likely to be structured around the home and family, whereas the lives of men were structured around both home and work. Subsequent research suggested that more traditional men and women may have difficulties when their central role circumstances change: when work rewards become less frequent or disappear, for example, or when children leave the home (Lowenthal et al., 1975).

Another finding of interest: What Havighurst (1957) called "social competence," or the ability to perform in different roles, was maintained at a peak plateau throughout the middle years, with little or no sign of decline in performance from age 40 to 70. As suggested in several of the chapters contained in this volume, Havighurst's early findings are echoed in more recent research in such diverse areas as intellectual functioning, physical health, and emotional well-being. The importance of this message lies in the fact that, from the standpoint of physical and social psychological functioning, the middle-ager does not experience meaningful levels of decline. Indeed, the middle-ager is often at a peak level of functioning at work and at home.

The World of Work

The world of work exerts a compelling demand on the time of working men and women. For women, the middle years are often enhanced by career entry and reentry, with women reporting gains in both self-esteem and satisfaction (Block, Davidson, & Grambs, 1981). For men, on the other hand, the second half of the midlife period may be fraught with increasing anxiety and frustration as the rewards begin to diminish from what had been a primary source of life satisfaction.

It is clear that work stress can play an important role in the mental health of the middle-aged worker. Most devastating seems to be unemployment. There is substantial evidence that the middle-aged worker, faced with decreased options for reemployment and often labeled as an "older" worker, is hard hit by economic downturns, demotions, and unemployment (Brenner, 1985). On the other hand, middle-aged workers suffer substantially less unemployment than any other age group of workers. In 1985, for example, the unemployment rate for those aged 45-64 was 4.5%, as compared to 11.1% among those aged 20-24 or 6.2% among those 25-44 (U.S. Bureau of the Census, 1986).

A study of successful middle-aged workers. To explore work issues in midlife in more detail, Neugarten (1968) conducted an intensive, in-depth investigation of the issues and coping strategies of successful middle-aged professionals. She found a confluence of factors leading to feelings of dissatisfaction and anxiety. One was the growing recognition that career options were becoming more limited. Many of these professionals were coming to realize that, as a middle-aged worker, their ability to move from one company to another was growing more limited or had already reached the point of no return. In other words, they would have to make the most of where they were.

Another factor was the awareness of reaching a career peak or plateau, both of which can lead to a feeling that one's major accomplishments are now in the past and that one's job will be offering fewer and fewer rewards and challenges (or, perhaps more frustrating, awareness that those higher in the company hierarchy felt that one had reached a career peak or plateau). Still another factor was a growing awareness of the finitude of the time remaining to work, coupled with uncertainties concerning what would come after retirement and an awareness of the finitude of life itself.

The overall tone of the interviews and responses to structured instruments, however, did not reflect a sense of stress and impending decline. Rather, the tone was one of peak performance and challenge. Respondents almost universally spoke of the middle years as a time of challenge, when ability and experience were finally paying off. These middle-aged men acknowledged the downside of middle age, but emphasized, often with wonder and amazement, how well they were managing their lives. Many spontaneously commented on a greater freedom to be truly themselves, both at work and at home. In the following quote, a 55-year-old lawyer in the study commented on this freedom:

> I have discarded a lot of values I was previously stuck with. The values were largely oriented in terms of the conduct of one's life in relation to the community instead of what would be important to myself. So it was a complete flip flop and I decided that if I were to mean anything to society I would first have to mean something to myself. (quoted in Chiriboga, 1966, p. 46)

The lived life. Over and over again, the theme that emerged from these interviews was one of cumulative experience and knowledge, of having lived with oneself and one's profession long enough to know what to expect and what to do. Another man, an executive, gave an example:

> Someone comes in, all wrought up and hot under the collar. You think, this is old stuff, you know, I've been through this fifty times and it really isn't as important as this person is trying to make it. And there are a number of alternatives for a resolution of the problem. I don't mean you are blasé or bored by the situation, but that you have some resources with which to deal. (quoted in Chiriboga, 1966, p. 38)

The World of Home and Family

Work stress and home life. Although work stress during the middle years has received a great deal of attention, surprisingly little research has focused on the consequences of job-related stress for home life. The little information that does exist suggests an interplay of stress across role boundaries. For example, the wives of high-level administrators with Type A personality characteristics were found in one study to report more marital problems and greater social isolation (Burke, Weir, & DuWors, 1979). Similarly, Jackson and Maslach (1982) reported that when police officers were identified as being in the throes of burnout, the wives of these officers were likely to report marital and family problems. Because there is empirical evidence supporting the view that the middle-aged worker is heavily involved and committed to work (Block et al., 1981; Fiske, 1980; Tamir, 1982), it is a reasonable supposition that the impact of work stress may spread to nonwork dimensions. This may be most true in the case of sustained unemployment, where studies have found the middle-aged worker and family to be most affected (Kasl, 1979; Pearlin et al., 1981).

Home life. Research on the subject of marital satisfaction during the middle years has generated contradictory findings. Pineo (1961), for example, found evidence for a decline in marital satisfaction and intimacy, whereas others found evidence for a plateau (Spanier, Lewis, & Cole, 1975) or increase (Lowenthal et al., 1975). One reason may be related to where the couple is in terms of progress toward the "empty nest." In one investigation, for example, Lowenthal and Chiriboga (1972) found that the chief source of arguments for middle-aged parents with children at home were the couples' children. Follow-ups of these parents led to the conclusion that the departure of children, far from being a devastating stressor that precipitated midlife crises, was associated with an improvement in marital satisfaction (Chiriboga & Cutler, 1980; also see Rollins, Chapter 8, this volume). As one 45-year-old housewife in the sample put it: "We're not losing a daughter, we're gaining a den."

Caught in the Middle:
A New Midlife Stressor

At the turn of the century, when 50% of a birth cohort had died by age 47, few middle-agers were facing the death or needs of elderly parents—they were busy facing their own personal demise! In today's world of longer-lived parents, it is expectable that during midlife one's parents will grow increasingly dependent until at some point they die. While their death can provoke anguish and a sense of loss, and may even signal the beginning of the individual's own sense of aging, a parent's need for care prior to death can produce a devastating burden.

There is increasing evidence that the social systems of the elderly have tremendous significance. One major source of support lies in the middle-aged children: not only are they a major provider but they are frequently the preferred care provider (Wan, 1982). Typically, these children are responsive to their parents' needs (Brody, 1985; Cantor, 1983; Neugarten, 1977; Troll, Miller, & Atchley, 1979; see Troll, Chapter 10, this volume). In terms of the physical health needs of older parents, for example, it has been estimated that from 70% to 80% of the help received actually comes from adult children. One recent review concluded that "family members provide an extraordinary amount of assistance to their older family members" (Springer & Brubaker, 1984, p. 16).

The role of middle-aged children as caregivers becomes especially difficult when cognitive deficits appear in the parent (Robinson & Thurnher, 1979). From a health delivery and family intervention perspective, an increased burden is accentuated in the case of Alzheimer's disease. This is a crippling disease whose slow and insidious course imposes a tremendous and continuing strain on loved ones, who typically assume the major responsibilities for care. The economic and emotional cost to families is uncountable, while the cost to society runs into billions of dollars annually. And, to compound the problem facing adult children, it has also been estimated that, of those who live up to the eighties and beyond, approximately one-third will develop the signs and symptoms of Alzheimer's disease before they die (Schneider & Brody, 1983).

Attention to parental need can exert a heavy toll, leading an increasing number of middle-aged and older people, especially women, to become caught in what's called the "generational squeeze." In other words, they are caught between competing obligations to their parents, to their children and spouses, and to their own plans for the remaining years. Responsibilities to the older generation can also keep family members, again primarily women, out of the labor force (Nissel, 1984). These competing and often conflicting demands may become a source of strain, no matter how much care is actually provided to the parents (Cantor, 1983; Neugarten, 1977). At the same time it should be kept in mind that caring for family members more often than not is a fulfilling act, and one that is a source of satisfaction for both parents and their middle-aged children (Brody, 1985; Zarit, Orr, & Zarit, 1985).

Discussion

The focus in this chapter, and throughout the present volume, has been on the fact that men and women at midlife face a number of challenges and potential stressors. Generally at a peak in social responsibility as well as position, the midlifer is also at the threshold of decline and must at some point begin to accept this reality. In this regard it may be useful to divide middle age into two phases, early and late, much as Neugarten (1977) broke old age into the "young-old" and "old-old" phases.

For those in early middle age, the need to deal with role losses and additional burdens such as parental caregiving may still seem remote. Rewards at home and work are still rolling in: children are growing up and becoming independent, achievements at work are satisfying and new responsibilities and challenges are still forthcoming, few if any friends have died, and the probability of spousal bereavement is still relatively remote.

For those in later middle age, from the midfifties on, the probabilities of new challenges and growth may become less and less. Children generally have left the home and are living their own lives as best they can, employers may be thinking twice about offering a new growth position, and heart attacks and cancer are beginning to take their toll. Later middle age, then, becomes a time when the individual must learn to turn loss into challenge, to begin to replace former activities with others that are equally or more satisfying.

After all is said and done, the transition to midlife, and passage through this age period, is probably more often anticlimatic than climatic for most individuals. Regardless of how we view it, we have heard of middle age before we get to that stage and we have some ideas about what to do when we actually reach it. In other words, the relentless process of adult socialization has had its imprint on our lives and on our reactions, and midlife does not come as a surprise and shock.

In sum, there is increasing empirical evidence to suggest that from at least a psychological point of view the middle years are our peak years. For Neugarten (1968) these are the "executive years," and Fiske (1979) speaks of "the prime of life." For most of us, midlife represents a time of life when we have lived with ourselves long enough to know our assets and liabilities, have known our spouses and loved ones long enough to understand them at least a little bit, and have worked in our jobs long enough to feel comfortable and be on top of things.

In essence, midlife represents a time when individuals are more in control of things, at both a personal and an occupational level, than they ever have been before or ever will be again. It is a time when the knowledge they have accrued is most personalized and most usable (see Labouvie-Vief and Hakim-Larson, Chapter 3, this volume). Middle-agers have generally acquired enough knowledge to know what to expect of life. In consequence, they can deal with the world more efficiently and productively than ever before. For most people, middle age is not a crisis but a challenge and a relief.

References

Albee. G. W. (1986). Toward a just society: Lessons from observations on the primary prevention of psychopathology. *American Psychologist, 41,* 891-898.

Berkman, L., & Syme, S. (1979). Social networks, host resistance, and mortality: A nine-year follow-up study of Alameda County residents. *American Journal of Epidemiology, 109,* 186-204.

Block, M. R., Davidson, J. L., & Grambs, J. D. (1981). *Women over forty: Visions and realities.* New York: Springer.

Brenner, M. H. (1985). Economic change and the suicide rate: A population model including loss, separation, illness, and alcohol consumption. In M. R. Zales (Ed.), *Stress in health and disease* (pp. 160-185). New York: Brunner/Mazel.

Brody, E. M. (1985). Parent care as a normative family stress. *Gerontologist, 25*(1), 19-29.

Brown, G. W., Bifulco, A., Harris, T., & Bridge, L. (1986). Life stress, chronic subclinical symptoms and vulnerability to clinical depression. *Journal of Affective Disorders, 11*(1), 1-119.

Brown, G. W., & Harris, T. (1978). *Social origins of depression: A study of psychiatric disorder in women.* London: Tavistock.

Burke, R. J., Weir, T., & DuWors, R. E. (1979). Type A behavior of administrators and wives' reports of marital satisfaction and well-being. *Journal of Applied Psychology, 64,* 57-65.

Butler, R. (1974). Successful aging and the role of the life review. *Journal of the American Geriatric Society, 22,* 529-535.

Cantor, M. J. (1983). Strain among caregivers: A study of experience in the United States. *Gerontologist, 23,* 597-610.

Chiriboga, D. A. (1966). *Self-actualization among successful middle agers.* Unpublished trial research project, University of Chicago.

Chiriboga, D. A. (1982). Adaptation to marital separation in later and earlier life. *Journal of Gerontology, 37,* 109-114.

Chiriboga, D. A. (1984). Social stressors as antecedents of change. *Journal of Gerontology, 39*(4), 468-477.

Chiriboga, D. A., Catron, L. S., & Weiler, P. G. (1987). Precursors of adaptation: A study of marital separation. *Family Relations, 36,* 163-167.

Chiriboga, D. A., & Cutler, L. (1980). Stress and adaptation: Life span perspectives. In L. Poon (Ed.), *Aging in the 1980s: Psychological issues* (pp. 347-362). Washington, DC: American Psychological Association.

Chiriboga, D. A., & Fiske, M. (1987). *Recharting adult life*. Paper presented at the 1st International Conference on the Future of Adult Life, Noordwijkerhout, the Netherlands.

Cooper, M. W. (1977). *An empirical investigation of the male midlife period: A descriptive, cohort study*. Unpublished undergraduate honors thesis, University of Massachusetts at Boston.

Cooper, K. L., & Gutmann, D. L. (1987). Gender identity and ego mastery style in middle aged, pre- and post-empty nest women. *Gerontologist, 27*(3), 347-352.

Costa, P. T., Jr., & McCrae, R. R. (1978). Objective personality assessments. In M. Storandt, I. C. Siegler, & M. F. Elias (Eds.), *The clinical psychology of aging* (pp. 119-143). New York: Plenum.

Costa, P. T., Jr., McCrae, R. R., Zonderman, A. B., Barbano, H. C., Lebowitz B., & Larson, D. M. (1986). Cross-sectional studies of personality in a national sample. Part II: Stability in neuroticism, extroversion and openness. *Psychology and Aging, 1*, 144-149.

Cumming, E., & Henry, W. (1961). *Growing old: The process of disengagement*. New York: Basic Books.

Eisdorfer, C., & Wilkie, F. (1977). Stress, disease, aging and behavior. In J. E. Birren & K. W. Schaie (Eds.), *Handbook of the psychology of aging* (pp. 251-275). New York: Van Nostrand Reinhold.

Erikson, E. H. (1980). *Identity and the life cycle*. New York: Norton.

Erikson, E. H. (1982). *The life cycle completed*. New York: Norton.

Farrell, M., & Rosenberg, S. D. (1981). *Men at midlife*. Boston: Auburn.

Fiske, M. (1979). *Middle age: The prime of life?* New York: Harper & Row.

Fiske, M. (1980). Changing hierarchies of commitment in adulthood. In N. J. Smelser & E. H. Erikson (Eds.), *Themes of love and work in adulthood* (pp. 238-264). Cambridge, MA: Harvard University Press.

Fiske, M., & Chiriboga, D. A. (1985). The interweave of societal and personal change in adulthood. In J. Munichs, P. Mussen, E. Olbrich, & P. G. Coleman (Eds.), *Life-span and change in a gerontological perspective* (pp. 177-209). New York: Academic Press.

Golan, N. (1986). *The perilous bridge: Helping clients through mid-life transitions*. New York: Free Press.

Gutmann, D. (1964). An exploration of ego configurations in middle and later life. In B. Neugarten (Ed.), *Personality in middle and later life* (pp. 114-148). New York: Atherton.

Gutmann, D. (1975). Parenting: A key to the comparative study of the life cycle. In N. Datan & L. H. Ginsberg (Eds.), *Life-span developmental psychology: Normative life crises* (pp. 167-184). New York: Academic Press.

Gutmann, D. (1977). The cross-cultural perspective: Notes towards a comparative psychology of aging. In J. E. Birren & K. W. Schaie (Eds.), *Handbook of the psychology of aging* (pp. 302-326). New York: Van Nostrand Reinhold.

Gutmann, D. (1985). The parental imperative revisited. In J. Meacham (Ed.), *Family and individual development* (pp. 31-60). Basel: Karger.

Havighurst, R. J. (1952). *Developmental tasks and education*. New York: McKay.

Havighurst, R. J. (1957). The social competence of middle aged people. *Genetic Monographs, 56*, 297-375.

Hirsch, B. J. (1980). Natural support systems and coping with major life crises. *American Journal of Community Psychology, 8*, 159-172.

Hirsch, B. J. (1981). Coping and adaptation in high-risk populations: Toward an integrative model. *Schizophrenia Bulletin, 7*, 164-172.

Holmes, T., & Rahe, R. (1967). The social readjustment rating scale. *Journal of Psychosomatic Research, 11*, 213-218.

Horowitz, M. J. (1976). *Stress response syndromes*. New York: Jason Aronson.

Horowitz, M. J., & Wilner, N. (1980). Life events, stress and coping. In L. Poon (Ed.), *Aging in the 1980s: Psychological issues* (pp. 365-374). Washington, DC: American Psychological Association.

Jackson, S. E., & Maslach, C. (1982). After-effects of job-related stress: Families as victims. *Journal of Occupational Behavior, 3*, 63-77.

Jung, C. G. (1953). On the psychology of the unconscious. In *Collected works: Vol. 7. Two essays on analytical psychology*. New York: Pantheon.

Jung, C. G. (1954). Marriage as a psychological relationship. In *Collected works: Vol. 17. The development of personality*. New York: Pantheon.

Jung, C. G. (1960). The stages of life. In *Collected works: Vol. 8. The structure and dynamics of the psyche*. New York: Pantheon.

Kasl, S. V. (1979). Changes in mental health status associated with job loss and retirement. In J. E. Barrett, R. M. Rose, & G. L. Klerman (Eds.), *Stress and mental disorder* (pp. 179-200). New York: Raven.

Krystal, S., & Chiriboga, D. A. (1979). The empty nest process in midlife men and women. *Maturitas, 1*, 215-222.

Kubler-Ross, E. (1969). *On death and dying*. New York: Macmillan.

Lazarus, R. S., & Folkman, S. (1984). *Stress, appraisal, and coping*. New York: Springer.

Levinson, D. J. (1986). A conception of adult development. *American Psychologist, 41*(1), 3-13.

Levinson, D. J., with Darrow, C., Klein, E., Levinson, M., & McKee, B. (1978). *The seasons of a man's life*. New York: Knopf.

Lieberman, M. A. (1982). The effects of social supports on response to stress. In L. Goldberger & S. Breznitz (Eds.), *Handbook of stress* (pp. 764-783). New York: Free Press.

Lifton, R. J. (1979). *The broken connection: On death and the continuity of life*. New York: Simon & Schuster.

Lowenthal, M. F., & Chiriboga, D. (1972). Transition to the empty nest. *Archives of General Psychiatry, 26*, 8-14.

Lowenthal, M. F., & Chiriboga, D. (1973). Social stress and adaptation: Toward a lifecourse perspective. In C. Eisdorfer & M. P. Lawton (Eds.), *The psychology of adult development and aging* (pp. 281-310). Washington, DC: American Psychological Association.

Lowenthal, M. F., Thurnher, M., & Chiriboga, D. (1975). *Four stages of life: A comparative study of women and men facing transitions*. San Francisco: Jossey-Bass.

McCrae, R. R., & Costa, P. T., Jr. (1984). *Enduring lives, enduring dispositions: Personality in adulthood*. Boston: Little, Brown.

McGill, M. E. (1980). *The 40 to 60 year old male*. New York: Simon & Schuster.

McKinney, J. C. (1987). *The medicalization of aging*. Paper presented at the 1st International Conference on the Future of Adult Life, Noordwijkerhout, the Netherlands.

Michels, R. (1984). Psychoanalytic perspectives on normality. In D. Offer & M. Sabshin (Eds.), *Normality and the life cycle: A critical integration* (pp. 289-301). New York: Basic Books.

Neugarten, B. L. (1964). Summary and implications. In B. Neugarten & Associates (Eds.), *Personality in middle and late life* (pp. 198-199). New York: Atherton.

Neugarten, B. L. (1968). The awareness of middle age. In B. L. Neugarten (Ed.), *Middle age and aging* (pp. 93-98). Chicago: University of Chicago Press.

Neugarten, B. L. (1977). Personality and aging. In J. E. Birren & K. W. Schaie (Eds.), *Handbook of the psychology of aging* (pp. 626-649). New York: Van Nostrand Reinhold.

Nissel, M. (1984). The family costs of looking after handicapped elderly relatives. *Aging and Society, 4*(2), 185-204.

Offer, D., & Sabshin, M. (1984). Patterns of normal development. In D. Offer & M. Sabshin (Eds.), *Normality and the life cycle: A critical integration* (pp. 393-425). New York: Basic Books.

Pan American Health Organization. (1986). *Health conditions in the Americas, 1981-1984* (Vol. 1, Scientific publication no. 500). Washington, DC: World Health Organization.

Pearlin, L. I., Menaghan, E. G., Lieberman, M. A., & Mullan, J. T. (1981). The stress process. *Journal of Health and Social Behavior, 22,* 337-356.

Pineo, P. C. (1961). Disenchantment in the later years of marriage. *Marriage and Family Living, 23,* 3-11.

Robinson, B., & Thurnher, M. (1979). Taking care of aged parents: A family cycle transition. *Gerontologist, 19,* 586-593.

Schaefer, C., Coyne, J., & Lazarus, R. (1981). The health related functions of social support. *Journal of Behavioral Medicine, 4,* 381-406.

Schlossberg, N. K. (1987). Taking the mystery out of change. *Psychology Today, 21*(5), 74-75.

Schneider, E., & Brody, J. (1983). Aging, natural death, and the compression of morbidity: Another view. *New England Journal of Medicine, 309,* 854-855.

Schulz, R., & Rau, M. T. (1985). Social support through the life course. In S. Cohen & S. L. Syme (Eds.), *Social support and health* (pp. 127-147). Orlando, FL: Academic Press.

Sherman, E. (1982, April). *Comparative adjustment and coping strategies of men and women in relation to mid-life family crises.* Paper presented at the 59th Annual Meeting of the American Orthopsychiatric Association.

Spanier, G., Lewis, R., & Cole, C. (1975). Marital adjustment over the life cycle: The issue of curvilinearity. *Journal of Marriage and the Family, 37,* 263-275.

Springer, D., & Brubaker, T. H. (1984). *Family caregivers and dependent elderly: Managing stress and maximizing independence.* Beverly Hills, CA: Sage.

Tamir, L. M. (1982). *Men in their forties: The transition to middle age.* New York: Springer.

Thoits, P. (1982). Conceptual, methodological and theoretical problems in studying social supports as buffers against stress. *Journal of Health and Social Behavior, 23,* 145-159.

Troll, L. E., Miller, S. J., & Atchley, R. C. (1979). *Families in later life.* Belmont, CA: Wadsworth.

U.S. Bureau of the Census. (1986). *Statistical abstracts of the United States: 107.* Washington, DC: Government Printing Office.

U.S. Department of Health and Human Services, National Center for Health Statistics. (1985). *Vital Statistics of the United States: Vol. 2. Mortality, Part A, 1950-84.* Washington, DC: Government Printing Office.

U.S. Department of Health and Human Services, National Center for Health Statistics. (1986). DHHS publication no. (PHS) 87-1232. Washington, DC: Government Printing Office.

Wallerstein, J. S. (1986). Women after divorce: Preliminary report from a ten year follow-up. *American Journal of Orthopsychiatry, 56,* 65-77.

Wan, T. H. (1982). *Stressful life events, social support networks and gerontological health.* Lexington, MA: D. C. Heath.

Zarit, S. H., Orr, N. K., & Zarit, J. M. (1985). *The hidden victims of Alzheimer's disease: Families under stress.* New York: New York University Press.

6

Personality at Midlife

Norma Haan

As reassuring to readers as definitive conclusions about personality at midlife might be, prudence as well as honesty about the progress of research
demands qualifications and equivocations. There are three major reasons for
caution: First, even though people's everyday communication is not seriously confused about the meaning of the word *personality,* theorists and
researchers propose varying and contradictory definitions of personality.
Readers, therefore, need to know which of the many possible aspects of
personality researchers are considering.

Second, even when the meaning of a particular aspect of personality
seems clear and straightforward, many scientifically based descriptions of
the midlife personality result from researchers' comparing middle-aged
people with other people of older or younger ages. Thus identification of the
strands of personal continuity and change that distinguish midlife can only
be assumed, rather than known factually. Results may be due to inherent,
age-insensitive differences in particular samples' personality that would
appear no matter what the samples' ages were at the time of comparison.

Third, several current formulations of the midlife personality wholly
depend on subjects' retrospective descriptions of themselves in comparison
with their views of their present status. These are then brought into line with
researcher-theorists' schemes that encompass their own ways of viewing the
life course. Thus the subjects' stories are simplified and gain coherent
comprehensiveness and an implication of generality that may or may not
hold for other subjects. It could be said that the myths of researchers,
investigators and subjects merge.

This chapter begins with a discussion of these three reasons for a degree
of equivocation in assessing conclusions about midlife personality, and in
each instance presents the remedies that were attempted in the research that
is later described in detail. The deficiencies and sufficiencies of these
remedies are also evaluated. This investigation was conducted on the life

course of two samples of people who were intensively studied over a 50-year span by the staff of the Institute of Human Development, University of California, Berkeley (see, for example, Eichorn, Clausen, Haan, Honzik, & Mussen, 1981).

What Is Personality?

To illustrate how different definitions of personality shape views of the middle-age personality, I turn first to psychoanalytic theory. Of course, Freud (1923/1953) was the parent of modern, formal theories of personality, which he described dynamically and in depth. For him, personality was constituted by three structures: an Id that continuously threatened to erupt with all its instinctual energies; the Ego, nearer to the surface, that continuously and vigilantly defended against the Id; and a third structure, the conscience-driven Superego. Because the Id was thought to be biological energy, its pressure, according to Freud as well as the views of his time, could only be regarded as perverse (no good would come to rational humans from an animalistic source). Still its urgency and perversity were expected to diminish as people aged—as biological energy declined and the coerciveness of social pressure became more effective through increased power of the Ego and Superego. The main life issue for this theory was that of gaining control. Life expectancy was much shorter during Freud's life than today, so that the period we now call midlife could readily be seen as a time of accumulated certainty, comfort, and even stodginess. More sanguine, but still reflecting the view that comfortable socialization and diminished Id pressures constitute the optimal midlife state, is Erik Erikson's (1950) proposal that well-functioning older people reach or should reach a stage of generativity toward young people.

More recently, however, as life expectancy has been extended and observation and investigation of midlife have become more comprehensive and accurate, views of midlife have changed. On one hand, sociologically minded scholars, impressed with the advantaged social and economic position of the middle-aged, have focused on the social aspects of personality. The middle-aged have been called the "command generation," that is, in economic American society they are often at the top of their work careers and, therefore, have more wealth and consequent power than either younger or older generations (Neugarten & Datan, 1973). On the other hand, they are said by some lay and professional writers to undergo "a midlife crisis," a state beset by questions as to the worth and meaning of their lives at this point in the face of the remaining time they have to achieve greater or deeper meaning and satisfaction. These views are not easily reconciled with Freudian views. Instead they portray the middle-aged as either forceful or restive and still asking, "What can I be and what can I achieve?"

This lack of fit illustrates the selectivity of theoretical definition and how theory can shift with changing historical circumstances. In other words, mythologies of a time and place tend to ensnare researcher and citizen alike. A serious question is posed, then, for contemporary investigation: How can personality be described so that it is less vulnerable to shifting historical fashions and conditions and less selectively bent by parochial theory? The research that is described in this chapter was not based on a highly formalized, explicit theory but rather on a large variety of descriptive variables that people commonly use to characterize one another—variables that are identified by words like *straightforward, self-confident, dependable, rebellious, submissive,* and so forth. This approach was not innocent of theory but the theory was an informed folk formulation—a conglomeration of popular descriptions that people and clinicians frequently use when they talk about themselves and other people. This brand of theory did not predetermine what aspects of personality should characterize middle age.

Finding Out About
Personality by Comparing
Groups of Different Ages

To do justice to the complexity of personality means that it cannot be easily measured. For example, personality has many facets that are brought into play in accordance with the demands of particular situations. For example, a woman who is submissive with colleagues at work can be highly assertive with her own family. Because measurement of personality is difficult, it is expensive. Most investigations of the life course, therefore, are based on comparatively small numbers of people in different age groups. These age groups are then compared one with another so that the distinctive features of a particular age group can be determined. When samples are small, however, the peculiar aspects of a particular sample can color results. To learn about the distinctive features of middle-aged people in this way, the comparison groups of other ages should be identical to the middle-aged group in all ways that are age-insensitive and only differ in ways that are age-sensitive. For instance, the groups of different ages that are compared should be of the same sex and geographic location—surely two characteristics that are age-insensitive but vary in whatever features of personality that are sensitive to their difference in age. This standard is difficult to meet because no one is clear about the age-insensitive aspects of personality that should be identical or the age-sensitive ways that might differ.

For these reasons, successfully repeated measurements of the same people over long periods of time should provide more definitive answers about personality at particular times in life. This is true because the procedure makes the subjects their own control—their age-insensitive attributes will presumably not change from one time to another. The personality of a whole generation, however, may be affected at a certain time in their life by a commonly experienced, critical event like a war, economic depression, starvation, or unusual opportunity (as was allowed to ex-military personnel by the GI Bill of Rights after World War II). Longitudinal research, then, can also be biased, but in its own way. For example, it may confuse the effects of dramatic events with age-sensitive changes. Some scholars (Baltes, Reese, & Nesselroade, 1977) have proposed complex research designs that include both longitudinal and cross-age groups that then allow statistical control of the biases inherent in both approaches. The expense of this approach, however, when applied to the laborious and complex measurement of personality, makes it unfeasible, so it is not further considered here.

The research presented here is a description of the personalities of approximately 100 people in two samples; the first studied from the age of 5 through 55 and the second from the age of 11 through 62. The samples were different ages when critical nationwide events occurred—the younger sample were toddlers and the older were teenagers during the Great Depression; the younger participated in the Korean War while the older served in World War II.

Observation or Self-Description?

Recently several popularized accounts—for instance, Gail Sheehy's (1976) *Passages* and Daniel Levinson et al.'s (1978) *The Seasons of a Man's Life*—portrayed adult life as a series of stages with midlife being especially characterized as a time of crisis. These accounts draw their themes from life stories told retrospectively by people who were willing to cooperate with the authors and who, like all human beings, were undoubtedly pleased with the opportunity to relate their experiences to an interested and expert listener. This approach has a certain value because the free flow of expression can bring aspects of self and living to the fore that a researcher might overlook. But it is also limited by everyone's proclivity to experience his or her own life as a drama. These stories are propelled by individuals' self-convictions and fictions of how they have doggedly persisted or courageously adapted despite the outrageous onslaughts or opportunities of fortune. To have been stressed and survived is a badge of courage.

People usually have no difficulty admitting experiences of severe stress that could be change-producing, but they are notably inaccurate and even self-deceptive in reporting or gauging the effects of stress. Marked individual differences occur. Some people minimize but others dramatize its effects. When life-span stress is broadly defined as any kind of internal or external event that implies change—as presented here—many individuals' accounts of themselves at midlife, and especially those people who cooperate and talk with researchers, may not provide accurate information about the past.

There is probably no reason for people to change their personality unless conditions extraneous to their personality have changed—for example, their biological status (menarche to menopause, health to illness) or social status (employee to employer, wife to widow). The question of concern here is whether the advent of midlife includes conditions of such standardization and importance that personality changes in specifiable, similar ways for all or most individuals. If this is the case, then it is reasonable to speak of the "midlife personality."

For these reasons, observations by impartial, trained observers probably provide more accurate information than retrospective self-descriptions. Sets of observations, made by different sets of observers at different times in the subjects' life spans, provide the most certain basis for determining how people have changed, in what ways they have remained the same, and the distinctive features of any life period. This procedure still introduces a degree of error—"observer error"—because the professionals who make these observations, for example, psychologists and social workers, have their own selectivities and biases. Nevertheless, if there are many observers and different sets of observers for each period in the life span, then this kind of error is fairly well randomized and whatever results ensue from comparisons of age groups can probably be regarded as nearer to the "truth."

Personality of Midlife

The research findings presented here are based on work that involved longitudinal observations of the same people over a 50-year span by essentially different sets of psychologists and social workers (Haan, Millsap, & Hartka, 1986). The time span was segmented as early and late childhood (modally 6 and 8 years), early and late adolescence (modally 14 and 17 years), and early, middle, and late adulthood (modally about 35, 45, and 55 years). Approximately 50 professionals made observations and judgments of participants at these seven points in time on 73 variables. For the adult years, these evaluations were based on intensive clinical interviews that lasted two or more hours, whereas earlier observations were variously based on interviews, observations of behavior, test scores, and so forth. Although this large number of variables was originally assessed, statistical clustering reduced their number to the following six: (a) self-confident/victimized, (b) assertive/submissive, (c) cognitively committed, (d) outgoing/aloof, (e) dependable, and (f) warm/hostile.

The first variable, called *self-confident/victimized*, is defined as comfort with one's own self (e.g., satisfied with self, calm, and straightforward) and certainty of acceptance by others (cheerful, arouses liking, turned to for advice). The negative items present an opposite and neurotic sense of self (feels victimized, self-defeating, ruminative) along with expectancies that others are harmful.

The positive items defining the second variable, called *assertive/submissive*, describe an ascendant, direct, and vigorously aggressive approach to living (assertive, independent, rebellious), whereas the negative items describe a withdrawing, controlled, rule-dependent approach (submissive, conventional).

The third variable, *cognitively committed*, represents an intellectual, achievement orientation accompanied by a degree of innovativeness (introspective, wide interests, interesting, and nonconventional). The negative pole seems not to reflect intellectual lack but rather emotionally driven passivity and lack of certainty (uncomfortable with uncertainty, withdraws when frustrated). The variable cognitively committed is associated with IQ, but they are by no means synonymous, especially after early adolescence. On either the Stanford-Binet or the Wechsler tests, IQs, concurrent with scores for cognitively committed, had the following associations: early childhood, .53; late childhood, .67; early adolescence, .65; late adolescence, .45; middle adulthood, .41; and late adulthood, .24 (all p's $< .001$).

The items for *outgoing/aloof*, the fourth variable, are almost all interpersonal in nature, with the positive items reflecting social responsiveness and enjoyment of others (cheerful, warm, gregarious), whereas the negative items reflect reserved, cautious reactions to others (aloof, distrustful, bland).

The positive side of *dependable*, the fifth variable, represents dependable, controlled productivity, while the negative side has no distinctiveness other than suggesting lack of dependability (rebellious, undercontrolled, self-defeating).

Finally, the positive side of the sixth variable, called *warm/hostile*, conveys a tender theme of interpersonal giving and support (sympathetic, giving, protective). It is similar to outgoing/aloof. Both dimensions share three positive items (warm, arouses liking, and straightforward), but they clearly differ in negative items. Aggressive, open hostility is indicated by the negative pole for warm/hostile, whereas cool, withdrawn caution characterizes the negative pole of outgoing/aloof.

All together these six variables represent aspects of personality that are often studied—cognitive investment, dependability, self-confidence versus self-degradation, and three modes of interpersonal exchange in which the self is outgoing or aloof, warm or hostile, assertive or submissive.

Needless to say, high standards for reliability of judgments were exerted. The technical details of this research are not given here; instead, the implications about personality at midlife are presented. Details of the data and their analyses are presented elsewhere (Haan, Hartka, & Millsap, 1985; Haan, Millsap, & Hartka, 1986).

Continuities and Changes
Across Transitions

One statistic that reflects whether particular features of personality are age-sensitive or insensitive is the correlation of the dimensions between adjacent time periods, for instance, between early and middle adulthood. Notice, however, that correlations only represent shifts within a sample; they reveal nothing about the extent or amount of change. Overall analyses of these longitudinal data showed that the continuity or stability within these samples of the six personality dimensions—arbitrarily based on correlations of .50 *(p < .001)*—was the greatest during the following three intervals: from early to late childhood (94% of the correlations were greater than .50), late childhood to early adolescence (83% were greater than .50), and early to late adolescence (78% were greater than .50). The transition between late adolescence and early adulthood was the time of least stability within the sample (22%); and across the early to middle and middle to late adult intervals, only modest stability occurred (both 56%). Thus the adolescence to adulthood and, more surprising, the adult intervals were actually less stable (or more age-sensitive) than the childhood and adolescent years. *This pattern of findings is exactly opposite to what is usually expected, and most particularly expected by psychoanalytic theory*. Clearly this pattern needs elucidation. My colleagues, Roger Millsap and Elizabeth Hartka, and I came to a possible understanding of this surprising finding after we questioned conventional thinking about the nature of personality. Personality may be more fluid, adaptive, and innovative than is usually thought. Furthermore, because even infants are said to have distinctive personalities, personality development cannot be considered a matter of accumulating "more" or even a matter of possessing qualitatively different characteristics. These considerations suggest that personality development may be different from cognitive development. According to Haan et al. (1986, p. 230):

> Because the velocity of physical and cognitive growth and acquisition of knowledge of children and adolescents is obviously greater than for adults, personality development concepts have understandably been based on the parallel supposition that early, rapid, and unidirectional acceleration also characterizes personality. These results imply the contrary. In fact, substantial changes still seem to be occurring up to late maturity, especially for the women. If personality is fluid, innovative, and adaptive, then it logically follows that changes should occur when people confront definitive experiences of clear, unalterable consequence. *Because society and adults protect the young, experiences of serious consequence do not generally or regularly occur during childhood, and usually not during adolescence.* (emphasis added)

The two adult intervals from early to middle and middle to late adult years were times of stability for both women and men in the degree of their assertiveness, outgoingness, and dependability. All three dimensions, however, had been notably unstable and discontinuous during the adolescent to adult transition when people must position themselves vis-à-vis the adult world. These findings suggest, then, that these are characterological attributes that become age-insensitive—or ingrained—by adulthood. Thus the pattern reveals nothing distinctive about personality at midlife compared with other adult periods. In contrast, both sexes' self-confidence and warmth were strikingly unstable during the two adult intervals. The men particularly registered marked discontinuity in their warmth and self-confidence from early to middle adulthood, perhaps in response to the pressures of their careers and the degree of their success. The women's discontinuity came later, during their transition from middle to late adulthood. They registered discontinuity at this time in their lives, not only in their self-confidence and warmth but also in the extent of their cognitive commitment and, marginally, for their dependability. During this last adult period about one-half of the women began a new line of work, about one-third had experienced major illnesses, another one-third the deaths of close friends, and about one-fifth had experienced major illnesses in their immediate families (Haan et al., 1986).

Extent of Change:
Lifetime Trends

Correlations do not reveal whether the amount of change in personality was superficial or significant. Two other kinds of statistics provide this information: analyses of lifetime averaged trends and *t*-tests of the samples' averages between adjacent time periods, such as early to middle adulthood. The former is considered first.

From early childhood to late maturity, all six dimensions markedly changed in the sense of gaining importance in the personality of the participants. Their accumulated experiences of living were accompanied by steadily growing skill in living—they became more self-confident, assertive, cognitively committed, outgoing, dependable, and warm.

Midlife was a time, moreover, when three of these dimensions—assertive, cognitively committed, and outgoing—registered their highest point, followed by drops at late adulthood. This pattern was most salient for the women. At midlife both sexes were more assertive and cognitively committed and the women more outgoing than they had ever been before or were afterward. The midlife personality of the participants was consistent with the power and prestige of their station in life. Future work will determine whether these positively flavored aspects of personality will continue as these people reach old age.

The extent of change revealed by *t*-tests of sample averages for each dimension and between time periods is now considered. In these analyses a salient fact becomes clear: the women registered significant changes more than twice as often as the men ($p < .01$) on various dimensions (12 significant changes for women and 5 for men). It is likely that women's multiple, conflicting, and shifting role commitments from motherhood to empty nest to paid work contributed to these changes.

By midlife the women were distinctively more self-confident, cognitively committed, and outgoing than they had been as young adults. During the same interval the men became only more outgoing. But by late maturity both sexes had become warmer than they had been at midlife, while the women became less assertive. Thus a move away from *la force de l'age* of the middle years (de Beauvoir, 1960) seemed to occur.

Descriptions of Midlife
Personality: Conclusions

The analyses of these data, generously supplied over the years by the samples, who were mostly White, middle-class Northern Californians, provide "facts" about *their* midlife personality. To the extent that these individuals do not represent all middle-aged people, the findings, although true of them, may still represent a fiction. The value of this study lies in its attempt to describe the midlife personality for a group of individuals over a 50-year period. The measures of personality were not bent by a parochial theory but based on personality as it is commonly conceived. And the measures were based on observers' judgments instead of the participants' perceptions about themselves. Most important, midlife descriptions were drawn from participants' responses both before they reached midlife and after this period in their lives.

The following conclusions are drawn from this study:

(1) At midlife the participants were functioning more comfortably than at any time before, so there is little evidence to support the contention that midlife is a time torn by crisis.

(2) The move to midlife, and from midlife to later maturity, was accompanied by moderate shifts in personality dimensions within the samples. The midlife status of individual participants was only modestly predicted, compared to the high degree of predictability that was possible across the childhood and adolescent intervals and compared to the low degree of predictability and high degree of instability that typified the transition from adolescence to adulthood. The findings, therefore, give no support for another common myth that personality is set early in life and becomes all but impossible to change by middle age. Older dogs evidently do learn new tricks.

(3) By the adult years three attributes—assertive, outgoing, and dependable— were again age-insensitive, as they had been during childhood and adolescence. We assume that this age-insensitivity is *not* programmed biologically but is rather due to the timing of critical life events that necessitate change. The correlations for assertive, outgoing, and dependable indicated that the status of individual sample members changed very little during the adult years. The three other variables—self-confidence, warmth, and cognitive commitment—were age-sensitive, but the sexes differed in the timing of their reactivity. For men these changes occurred from early to middle adulthood in their gains in self-confidence and warmth; for women gains occurred from middle to late adulthood in their self-confidence and warmth and also in cognitive commitment. Events of consequence probably occurred at different times for the sexes—for the men after they established their career and adapted to its particular demands; for the women after they completed the tasks of motherhood and turned to other occupations, which frequently meant paid work. The results also suggest that some aspects of personality may be ingrained, that is, not changing for a time, while other aspects are more viable and fluid at middle age. Because this appears to be the case, it seems erroneous to speak of the midlife personality as a holistic structure.

(4) Three dimensions that seemed to represent vigor, self-certainty, and efficient problem solving peaked at midlife and then began to drop, although not always to a significant degree. Both men and women were more assertive and cognitively committed, and the women were more outgoing at midlife than ever before or afterward. We do not yet know whether these moves downward represent trends that will continue through late maturity to old age, but they clearly reflect *la force de l'age* (de Beauvoir, 1960) expected of the middle aged. Moves away from this commanding position are suggested by the specific findings that the women were significantly less assertive at late maturity than they were at midlife and that both sexes were significantly more warm.

Implications for Human Services

The results reported here are trends for groups of people, not for individual persons who are the clients of professionals in human services. The findings depend on statistics of probability that indicate that the personalities of *most* members of these samples changed at midlife or stayed the same in the ways described. Professional practitioners, therefore, need to regard these results only as rough guides; any one middle-aged person can be quite different from what this research describes.

These results do not support—in fact, they contradict—two prevalent myths about middle age: the midlife crisis and middle-aged immutability and stodginess. Helping professionals may do middle-aged clients a disservice by expecting them to be either crisis-ridden or unable to adopt new ways of living and coping.

The results further imply that personalities may change most markedly when life conditions change. The investigation reported here does not comprehensively or directly establish this connection because the timing and nature of the participants' life events were not thoroughly analyzed in relationship to their changes in personality. Although future work will focus on this possibility, it seems reasonable to assume that the marked personality shifts that typified the adolescent to adult transition and the sex-differentiated timing of the shifts during the last two adult intervals—men changing from early to middle adulthood and women from middle to later adulthood—parallel shifts in life status and conditions that regularly occur at these times in life. If this line of reasoning has truth, then professional practitioners may find it necessary to focus more on the life circumstances of clients, if they want to effect client change, rather than using individual counseling or psychotherapy.

References

Baltes, P. B., Reese, H. W., & Nesselroade, J. R. (1977). *Life-span developmental psychology: Introduction to research methods.* Monterey, CA: Brooks/Cole.

de Beauvoir, S. (1960). *La force de l'age.* Paris: Gallimard.

Eichorn, D. H., Clausen, J. A., Haan, N., Honzik, M. P., & Mussen, P. H. (Eds.). (1981). *Present and past in middle life.* New York: Academic Press.

Erikson, E. (1950). *Childhood and society.* New York: Norton.

Freud, S. (1953). The ego and the id (J. Strachey, Trans.). In J. Strachey (Ed.), *Standard edition of the complete psychological works of Sigmund Freud* (Vol. 19, pp. 3-66). London: Hogarth Press. (Original work published 1923)

Haan, N., Hartka, E., & Millsap, R. (1985, August). Development and stress-related change in personality. Paper presented at the Development in Adulthood Symposium, American Psychological Association meeting, Los Angeles.

Haan, N., Millsap, R., & Hartka, E. (1986). As time goes by: Change and stability in personality over fifty years. *Psychology and Aging, 1*(3), 220-232.

Levinson, D. J., with Darrow, C. M., Klein, E. B., Levinson, M. H., & McKee, B. (1978). *The seasons of a man's life.* New York: Knopf.

Neugarten, B. L., & Datan, N. (1973). Sociological perspectives on the life cycle. In P. Baltes & K. W. Schaie (Eds.), *Life-span developmental psychology: Personality and socialization* (pp. 53-71). New York: Academic Press.

Sheehy, G. (1976). *Passages: Predictable crisis of adult life.* New York: Dutton.

7

Modern Myths About Men at Midlife: An Assessment

Lois M. Tamir

Men, their wives and associates, as well as those in the helping professions, have pondered the myth of a male midlife crisis. If the man at age 45 is happy, well-adjusted, and fulfilled in the realms of work, family, and community, he wonders if it all is tentative, if suffering is around the bend, or if the theorists are mistaken. If, on the other hand, the man at 37 is undergoing a debilitating depression and alcoholic addiction, he wonders if this is a midlife crisis or perhaps a basic personality flaw.

To pin a label upon a psychological phenomenon, such as midlife blues, can be deceiving to both the individual and to those with whom he is in contact. The issues of personality, individual history, familial constellation, cohort membership, historical moment, and socioeconomic culture all play a part in the continuing individuation of the man as he undergoes middle age. There are consistencies in the research literature, and there is a tenable theory of adult development that underlies the research findings. This chapter will discuss those predictable themes emerging in middle age that are consistent with a life-span approach, such as alterations in one's life perspective at the midpoint of one's work and family careers. Along with this are the inconsistencies in the literature that confuse us, and the research populations that refuse to conform to predictable expectations at middle age.

This chapter attempts to integrate both the consistencies and the inconsistencies from the perspective of developmental psychology. Foremost in this examination is a recognition that, throughout adulthood, the individual male can and does change, ever adapting to the new demands brought on by age and an evolving social environment. Second, there is a strong acknowledgment of the influences of social class on developmental phenomena. The life courses of working-class and upper-middle-class men are often not parallel, but divergent. This is a function of formative social forces that influence daily routine, economic stability, interpersonal relations, and philosophy of life.

What Age Is Middle Age?

Individual differences aside, and even though vague generalizations plague our assessments of midlife men, it is possible to identify the turning point from young adulthood to middle age. Examination of the research literature indicates a reasonable age range for the transition to middle age: 40 to 49, give or take several years at each end.

Qualitatively, the life-style and life demands of young adulthood differ from those of middle adulthood. Haan (1981, p. 175) aptly described the period of young adulthood as one of "accommodation." Young adults are paving their way through society and attempting to develop a niche for themselves simultaneously in work, family, and community. They must accommodate to all the roles before them in order to become successful. Home demands are at a peak with emotional and financial responsibilities for small children and spouse, and communities require some demonstration of support in order to grace the young man with social recognition. Men, especially, must exert themselves at work in order to catch a place on the fast track. In total, young adulthood comprises a whirlwind of activity, with little concrete time for self-reflection. Haan (1981, p. 175), in her comparison of young adults to middle-aged adults, described the young adults as "reactive and adaptive," less self-expressive and less self-aware.

At some point, presumably in his forties, the man achieves an acceptable level of status and, it is hoped, respite, so that he can examine the products of his efforts. This period of time is what merits the label "transition to middle age." According to Jung (1933) it constitutes entry into the "afternoon of life," where "serious attention" is diverted from the demands of society and its prescribed role behaviors to one's inner self, which has remained to this point unexpressed in the search for a socially sanctioned identity. Jung acknowledged this turning point over 50 years ago in his pioneering literature on adult development. Research to date has confirmed the forties as transitional for contemporary men over the past ten to twenty years. Levinson (1978), who collected extensive biographical interview data from 40 middle-aged men, discussed the forties as a time in which his research subjects entered a period of self-appraisal, having to that point subjected themselves to extensive social pressure for affirmation and advancement. Vaillant (1977), who longitudinally followed Ivy League graduates, also found that, during their forties, his men, and particularly his most well-adjusted men, became less inhibited, more honest with themselves, and more concerned with inner exploration. Similarly, studies eliciting retrospective accounts of older men (ranging from 60 to 85 years) found that the men identified the forties, on average, as the onset of middle age (Drevenstedt, 1976; Jackson, 1974). In the Jackson study, men aged 75-85 defined middle age as a qualitatively different time than young adulthood, a time of maximum accomplishment and serious decision making in an effort to organize life's final direction.

A cautionary note on this transitional age range is critical, however. Social-class differences clearly divide the lower and working classes from the upper-middle classes for age of onset and format of the transition to middle age. Taking into account rather loose definitions of social class by varying authors, the literature nearly always reveals different life patterns and coping strategies for men at the lower and higher ends of the socioeconomic scales. Neugarten and Datan (1974) highlighted the idea that blue-collar men, presumably at the lower rungs, age more quickly than business executives and professionals, who comfortably reside within the upper-middle class. By age 40 the blue-collar worker often considers himself to be middle-aged, simply holding on to what he has achieved to that point. For the upper-middle-class man, however, often the apex is not reached until the early fifties, which he will designate as entry to middle age. The lower-middle classes, consequently, fall somewhere between these two extremes. Giele (1980) concluded that adult development is experienced more positively by the educationally and occupationally advantaged. Our ideals of individual stagelike growth and the rewards of enhanced self-awareness with age often correspond to the elite classes of our society. Fiske (1980) longitudinally followed a sample of middle- to lower-middle-class adults, most of whom had not completed a college education, thereby eliminating them from the higher socioeconomic levels (Lowenthal, Thurnher, & Chiriboga, 1977). Based upon her research of this sample, she suggested using a paradigm of changing commitment strategies as opposed to one of continued growth through adulthood. Not all men emanate enhanced mental health in the transition through middle age. The less advantaged may simply alter their commitments midway through life without the benefit of personal growth.

The polarization of the classes is most clearly demonstrated by Farrell and Rosenberg (1981), who collected interview and instrument data from 300 men aged 38-48 years. They followed up, with more extensive interviews, 20 of these men and their families. Farrell and Rosenberg found that men from the lowest socioeconomic rungs of their sample were the most alienated from society, work, self, and others. In a linear fashion the researchers demonstrated that, as social status increases, alienation decreases within the middle-aged group. Interestingly, these researchers did not find significant socioeconomic differences in alienation in a younger sample of 200 men aged 20-30 years. Indeed, the onset of middle age may, in some areas of personal functioning, serve to demarcate more radically the differences between the classes in our society.

Why Study Only Men?

To extend the above subtitle a bit further, the question should read: Why not study men and women together? The answer is that the life courses of men and women are so divergent, their approaches to self and interpersonal relations so polarized, and the social constraints upon men and women so often reversed, that to average the two together would yield meaningless conclusions. Certainly both men and women are capable of a developmental transition at middle age, self-assessment, and personal growth. The reason a man or woman may change, and the form this change may take, however, are likely to differ.

Women, even career-oriented women, especially of the cohort that today is middle-aged and older, organize their lives according to the life course of the family—more precisely, the age of the children. Relinquishing the familiar maternal role upon launching young adult or late adolescent children from the home will often lead a woman to redirect the course of her life. For men, as significant a change as launching may be, they are more often likely to examine their lives in accord with the progress they are making at work. At the middle-age transition, the man will have a fairly clear picture of how much further he is capable or even willing to proceed at work and from that point will make significant midlife choices. Hence, the life course perspectives for men and women differ immensely (Neugarten, 1968). Family life course changes are far more variable for women than expectations of the work environment for men. While a woman may launch her firstborn at age 36 or 56, and henceforth alter her life course, a man at age 45, across the board, is appraised by self and others regarding the parameters of his career expectations. For this reason it is perhaps even easier for the researcher to study men from the perspective of age. Age expectations are more clearly demarcated both in the work environment and in the social setting for men. Women display a far more mixed bag of life course possibilities, which vary as a function of marital status, age of children, and extent of employment.

An additional critical difference between men and women that affects a midlife transition is emotional and interpersonal expressivity (Lowenthal & Robinson, 1976). Traditional socialization has rendered women more expressive of individual and interpersonal emotions. Articulating and confronting powerful feelings is not likely to be a new experience for a woman at 45. Men, however, have been socialized as instrumental beings, strong enough to control any sign of weakness or emotional vulnerability. If self-awareness and assessment is deemed a task of middle age, it may constitute a significantly new and potentially stressful experience for the man who has been so self-contained. Perhaps for this reason we have heard so much about the "male midlife crisis" and not the "female midlife crisis" in lay and professional literature.

Is There a Male Midlife Crisis?

The premise of this chapter is that, in his forties, the man experiences a transition to middle age. This may encompass changing commitments or recommitments to self and others, and an altered perspective of one's life line, namely, in Neugarten's (1968) words, a view of one's life in terms of "time left to live" instead of "time since birth." Crisis is optional.

Most men at transition to midlife, as determined by interview and survey studies, do not directly indicate that they are in crisis in their forties (e.g., Bray & Howard, 1983; Farrell & Rosenberg, 1981; Lowenthal et al., 1977). Indirect measures (for example, depression scales), symptomatic behaviors (for example, alcoholism), or projective measures (for example, the Thematic Apperception Test), however, indicate that this transitional group is unique, and may be plagued, more so than at other ages, with deep-seated self-doubts or confusion, (e.g., Boyd & Weissman, 1981; Campbell, Converse, & Rodgers, 1976; Lowenthal et al., 1977; Mirkin & Meyer, 1981; Tamir, 1982). This is not to say that these men in transition are immobilized, bemoaning their plight in life, but the evidence suggests that this is a turning point. For the man to avoid examining the issues at hand, namely, that life is half-way through, and that the future must be delineated, is only to put off the inevitable. Self-examination is hard and can be personally draining whether or not one chooses to label this activity as a crisis. Levinson (1978) is the researcher who most forcefully makes the case that if the man at middle age does not practice self-assessment in some manner, a full-blown crisis is likely to emerge at a later time in his life.

Defending against self-examination is a not unpopular (although unproductive) choice among men in this age range. Farrell and Rosenberg's

(1981) study isolated four major personality approaches among the 200 men they studied, aged 38-48 years. These four types were organized into a 2 x 2 matrix: satisfied/dissatisfied x denies stress/confronts stress. Among the men openly confronting stress are the *antihero* and the *transcendent-generative*. Among the men who deny stress are the *pseudodeveloped* and the *punitive-disenchanted*.

The *antihero* type constituted only 12% of the Farrell and Rosenberg middle-age subject sample. The antihero was notably in crisis: dissatisfied, stressed, and alienated. Most antiheroes appeared to express regrets over the past, wishing to start anew, particularly in the work arena. Family relations appeared for the most part satisfactory whereas activity in the wider social environment was stifled. These men were likely to admit to anxiety and self-doubts, were free of bigotry, and displayed psychosomatic symptoms. One wonders whether once these men get over the crisis they can clear the path for a more fulfilling life in the future.

The *transcendent-generative* type of man constituted the highest percentage within Farrell and Rosenberg's four quadrants at 32%. Transcendents did not deny that stresses may have entered their lives, but they were the most satisfied. These men appeared to have it all: satisfaction in work and family, freedom from anxiety and stress-related symptoms, open-mindedness, self-assurance, and a history of successfully coping with adversity. They displayed no evidence of having undergone a midlife crisis or anticipating one, but seemed to sail through each phase of life with increasing self-improvement and maturity. This group was largely from the upper rungs of the socioeconomic ladder.

The *pseudodeveloped* type constituted 26% of the middle-age sample. This group denied stress and reported high levels of satisfaction in a self-deceptive manner. Pseudodeveloped types, middle or working class, desperately attempted to appear perfect to the naked eye, denying problems in work and family, and expressing high levels of mental health. More probing measures, both in survey-type and in projective questionnaire items, as well as in interview data with the men and their families, revealed the depth of their self-deception, the rigidity of their personalities, and the bigotry they maintained against others. The pseudodeveloped displaced badness from within to without.

Finally, Farrell and Rosenberg identified the *punitive-disenchanted*, at 30%. Largely from the working classes, this group of men denied stress but were the most severely dissatisfied with life. They were truly in crisis: depressed, alienated, and likely to experience problems in work and family. Although the punitive-disenchanted man wanted to maintain an image that was socially acceptable, he failed to do so, blaming his miserable familial, social, and societal circumstances for his misfortunes. These men were the most bigoted of the middle-age sample and probably displayed the poorest prognosis for a more fulfilling life because of a lack of introspection.

In sum, according to Farrell and Rosenberg's study, entry into middle age does not doom the man to crisis. Their study highlighted the class differences portrayed by the extremes of the punitive-disenchanted (largely working class) and transcendent-generative (largely middle to upper-middle class) in coping with midlife entry. Their analysis also illuminates the idea of individual coping patterns as opposed to a universal and natural developmental crisis at midlife that must be confronted, as Levinson's (1978) study suggested.

The major drawback of Farrell and Rosenberg's research may be viewed from the perspective of the age range they studied, 38-48 years, and the cross-sectional nature of their study. Given class differences in self-perception of aging, it is probably unrealistic to clump working- and upper-middle-class men within these age boundaries in order to examine the midlife transition. A midlife transition for the working classes will likely range around the early forties, the transition for upper-middle-class men around late forties to early fifties. Hence, although Farrell and Rosenberg's age limits are not entirely off target, it is likely that a 42-year-old upper-middle-class man may appear as a lifelong transcendent-generative, but in reality will undergo an extended period of introspection several years down the line. It is also possible that a working-class 47-year-old may be resigned to a pseudodeveloped personality style, perhaps having undergone more manifest crisis at an earlier time. Such speculations, naturally, cannot take the place of a well-constructed longitudinal analysis.

There are definite indicators (described in the following paragraphs), loosely around the forties, that the man is in transition, however. It may be a privilege of the upper classes to enjoy and benefit from the introspection their educational background and leisure time permits. Working-class men, on the other hand, appear to be socialized into a mode of coping where verbally expressed emotions are repressed. Rubin (1976), who spent extensive time interviewing husbands and wives of working-class families, described the men as often having amorphous feelings and yearnings that were unacknowledged. In the working classes there are few models of male emotional expressivity and no partners (aside from one's wife) with whom to share concerns that are exclusively male. Rigid defenses, such as those described by Farrell and Rosenberg, may result.

Yet entry to middle age does require a certain degree of self-analysis and decision making. The issues at hand include mortality, reaching one's peak, and consideration of leaving a legacy. Let us consider each in turn.

The issue of mortality was first brought to life by the landmark Jaques (1965) article titled "Death and the Mid-Life Crisis." Although placing this "crisis" somewhat earlier than the forties, Jaques discussed the impact of realizing that one's life is half complete, and that one's future years no longer outnumber those past. His analysis is developmental. Acceptance of mortality encompasses a serious period of introspection and of coming to terms with oneself and others. Glowingly, Jaques described the benefits of this phenomenon: one ultimately comes to accept one's own and others' imperfections and the contradictions that so well characterize our world.

This identical theme is reiterated time and again by theorists and researchers of life-span development. Neugarten (e.g., 1976) used the term *interiority* to describe the natural process of turning inward in one's forties in order to self-assess. Vaillant (1977), who followed Ivy League graduates through their middle age, described their process of exploring the world within. Gould (1972) documented the upsurge of existential questioning that characterizes middle age, and Lowenthal et al. (1977) found a peak at middle age in the individual's active reconstruction of the past, in particular, in the man's examination of his formative career choices. Levinson (1978) strongly made a case for this active review as the means by which to maintain subsequent mental health. The positive outcomes of this review, in accord with Jaques, include an integration of life's contradictions and polarities within oneself and greater self-understanding, acceptance, and maturity.

In surveying these research interpretations, it becomes clear that the process of self-assessment and its positive outcome is likely a benefit of upper-class status. Members of the middle to upper-middle classes, especially those who are willing to be interviewed for 10-20 hours (for example, in Levinson's 1978 study), simply in the course of being probed about their lives may come to these harmonious conclusions. It sounds like a process Farrell and Rosenberg's (1981) "transcendent-generative" men successfully underwent. But this is not to say that each man does undergo this process. Over one-half of Farrell and Rosenberg's (1981) sample (especially of the lower classes) did not come to terms with imperfection, but instead become neurotically entrenched within a bigoted and authoritarian frame of mind. Presumably those were the men Levinson alluded to when he discussed the necessity for self-review.

Another issue pertaining to the midlife transition involves coming to terms with reaching one's peak in life. Midlife men are accorded the highest respect of all age groups precisely because they are at their peak and because they are the generation in between: responsible for youth and responsible for an aging parental generation (e.g., Borland, 1978; Cameron, 1970; Neugarten, 1968). The man at middle age not only must guide and often finance the upcoming generation of his children but is usually put in a position of authority vis-à-vis his aging, and often ailing, parents. Whether or not he is performing caretaking tasks for his parents, much of their decision making and financial assessments fall upon his shoulders (Horowitz, 1985). This delegates the highest amount of influence to the middle-aged man simply by virtue of his age. Correspondingly, a study by Bourque and Back (1969), which asked a wide age range of adults to rate their lives prospectively and projectively with regard to happiness, found the highest-ranked period to range from about 40 to 60 years. This period of time was ranked even higher by younger adults in anticipation of middle age than by the middle-aged adults themselves.

Aside from the issue of mortality, it may be that the recognition that one is at a peak period may stimulate the man toward self-assessment. In Lowenthal et al.'s (1977) sample, as mentioned previously, serious review of one's job history among lower-middle-class subjects may have been a direct result of viewing one's work future as more limited than ever. The man must come to terms with this state of affairs in order to proceed realistically with his life.

As prestigious as a peak may be in our competitive, capitalistic society, the man at midlife may begin to compare his peak with others. In young adulthood the sky is the limit. By middle age the man's limits are staring him in the eye. For this reason, he must examine his options. The man may accept his lot with recommitment, work harder toward new goals, or wallow in self-pity. We have seen how these options may be played out by Farrell and Rosenberg's (1981) personality types. The point remains that reaching the apex has both its rewards and its setbacks.

The final issue that affects a midlife transition was first highlighted by Erik Erikson (1950) in his description of the theme of middle age: generativity versus stagnation. The man at middle age, to progress through this developmental period successfully, must leave a legacy to others, be it upcoming generations in his immediate family or a wider social environment. Levinson (1978) emphasized this theme of generativity by discussing the successful negotiation of middle age by those men who become mentors to younger men at work, putting aside their own immediate ambitions to help a younger man develop a fruitful career. Neugarten (1968) described how "self-utilization," as opposed to advancing oneself by using others, becomes a more dominant drive at middle age. Yet again, there may be a strong class bias in the direction of greater generativity among the more privileged. Farrell and Rosenberg (1981), for example, found higher generativity scores among the upper- as opposed to lower-class middle-aged men of their sample, the former having access to a greater number of organizations in which they could make a contribution.

The issue of generativity ties in with the acceptance of mortality and recognition that one is at one's peak of influence. Failure at midlife to accept mortality, to come to terms with one's level of functioning, or to guide the next generation theoretically can result in personal crisis, in alcoholism, in depression, in symptomatic behavior (e.g., Levinson, 1978; Vaillant, 1977). As already stated, however, a full-blown crisis is not inevitable. Some men confront the issues of middle age with little or no trauma, some men struggle, and some men deny. Denial, however, appears to be the most detrimental approach, according to Farrell and Rosenberg's (1981) analysis.

The Myths

Aside from these more global developmental issues of middle age that permeate the academic literature, there are some common stereotypes of middle-aged men that merit scrutiny. These involve our caricatures of the over-the-hill middle-aged man who is striving to regain some remnant of his youthfulness. In work and family relations the man at middle age is considered in current lore to be floundering, as represented by some form of the two following myths, often encountered in the media, in conversation, and in gossip:

(1) Men at middle age are obsolete at work. They have neither sufficient education nor updated technical training to compete with younger, more educated workers.

(2) Men at middle age leave (or at least want to leave) their wives for young blond women, and drive off in fancy sports cars wearing trendy clothes and shiny jewelry.

Let us consider each of these myths.

Men at Work: Myth 1

Obsolescence at work, in particular for the middle- to upper-middle-class segment of midlife men, could not be further from the truth. Executive cognitive capacity is at a peak at middle age. Schaie (1977-1978) described the ability of the adult man, in his forties, to visualize the "big picture" instead of focusing on details that can be delegated to a younger, eager man or woman. Other research similarly has documented the enhanced judgmental skills of the middle-aged man: his ability to delegate, make efficient decisions, manage contradiction, and conceptualize wide issues (e.g., Birren, 1970; Borland, 1978; Neugarten, 1968). In a longitudinal study of middle management conducted at AT&T by Bray and Howard (1983), actual gains in mental ability were observed among both college- and non-college-educated men over the time period they were studied (from 1956-1976). Assuming the enhanced decision-making and managerial skills of the 45-year-old man, the technical details and scrupulous number-crunching may be left to the younger adult who is anxious to make initial headway up the ladder of success.

In addition to improved cognitive capacities at work, the majority of research studies have indicated that men at middle age are the most highly satisfied with their jobs (e.g., Bray & Howard, 1983; Farrell & Rosenberg, 1981; Tamir, 1982). They are at or nearest to their highest earning power and level of prestige and are least likely to make a job or career change by this age (Jaffe, 1971; Tamir, 1982). High job satisfaction by middle age is the end product of a gradual increase in job satisfaction from young adulthood to the middle years. The dynamics involved in high job satisfaction are different between those men who are successful, versus moderately successful, and analogously between the college- and the non-college-educated men.

Bray and Howard (1983; see also Howard & Bray, 1980) documented this process in their 20-year analysis of middle managers who were observed from their mid-to late twenties to their mid- to late forties. Their initial sample of 422 men (which was reduced to 266 by 1976) was stratified into two groups slated for management: college- and non-college-educated men. As it turned out, the non-college men gradually advanced only to the lower to middle rungs of management, whereas a more sizable proportion of the college-educated rose to the upper-middle to higher management slots. Over this time period, the men's career aspirations began to correspond more accurately to their actual advancement. Consequently, they tended over time to become more and more satisfied with their management level. Jaffe (1971), in a review article about men's work published about 10 years earlier, identified the identical process: men with more schooling moved up the occupational scale faster and higher, yet most men eventually adjusted to their achieved level by middle age and, at minimum, self-reported high job satisfaction.

Bray and Howard (1983) brought forth the critical point that, regardless of occupational level, challenge at work and a stimulating agenda were highly coveted by all the men they studied. The continued desire to do challenging work through middle age indicates that the man in his forties is not ordinarily deadweight around the office, but continues to be a potentially vital and contributing member of an organization. The research literature, however, suggests that men at middle age begin to disengage from the work place as a source of emotional fulfillment. Research has shown that, for middle-aged men, work satisfaction has little or no bearing upon emotional well-being. A national survey study by Tamir (1982) that cross-sectionally compared men in their forties with men aged 25-39 and 50-69 years found a correlation of .04 between life satisfaction and job satisfaction for men in their forties (at other ages the correlation was significant). Similarly, there was a correlation of -.02 between self-esteem and satisfaction derived from work for this age group (again compared with the other age groups). The Bray and Howard (1983) study found the insignificant correlation of .10 between happiness and management level for their longitudinal sample when they reached their forties.

Disengagement from work on an emotional level may be a reality for men at this life stage. This is not to say that men are not performing well at work or that all men handle their time and attention to work in an identical manner. Individual coping differences based upon job history, personality, social class, and the historical time frame (a point to be covered shortly) affect the man's attitude toward and practice of his work. Clinical and research literature has revealed two major patterns of working at middle age that characterize men at this transition: the workaholics and the mellowed.

There are indeed a significant number of men at middle age who appear to be workaholics. This includes men of both blue-collar and white-collar occupations. For those men who neither have achieved their occupational dreams nor cherish their work activities, a frenzy of job activity may still persist in a last-ditch effort to attain financial security prior to retirement. This may be particularly true for non-college-educated men, as in the Lowenthal et al. (1977) study, where financial security was foremost among the middle-aged men's concerns, as well as in the Tamir (1982) study, where more non-college-, as opposed to college-educated, men in their forties chose financial security as a major value in their lives.

A second form of workaholism, more characteristic of high-level professionals, is described by Cooper (1981). Many men at middle age have achieved high levels of management authority and responsibility, and they may be unable to relinquish them voluntarily in a single blow. Often the man at this level is bombarded with responsibilities to manage people, direct meetings, meet deadlines, and remain accountable. Should a man in this predicament decide to take it a bit easier, the system itself would be hard put to let him go. He keeps on working, and working hard.

The Howard and Bray (1980) longitudinal study described a sizable group of men in their forties who appeared well-adjusted and continued to strive toward further advancement and recognizable achievement. These were the college-educated men who had already reached the near-highest rungs of management but who also had realistic opportunities to advance even higher. The most successful (as measured by management level) men of the AT&T study still saw work as their primary source of satisfaction, enjoyed leading others, and were more aggressive and less nurturant than the remainder of the sample. Bardwick (1978) studied a similar sample of successful men aged 33-49, who placed work foremost in their lives. Everything else was muted. Bardwick noted that such immersion in work enables one to avoid any form of concerted introspection. Given that the ages of the AT&T successful managers only averaged 44.6 years at the 20-year follow-up, one wonders whether a midlife assessment period awaits in the future when that final promotion will be achieved.

Another segment of middle-aged men have mellowed with regard to individual work achievement. As noted earlier, men by middle age often make peace with their level of achievement to that point. The best adjusted within this group do not feel a sense of failure, but rather a sense of relaxation. Bray and Howard (1983) described these men as satisfied with their careers, happier, less cynical, less selfish, and steadier in temperament than their more successful counterparts. Emotional disengagement from work and pressure to advance is not limited to white-collar workers and professionals. A study by Harlan (1983) of blue-collar and nonmanagement employees found that, with age, the men tended to become increasingly disengaged from work, neither wanting nor expecting promotion within five years. Howard and Bray (1980) found men at middle age resistant to promotions for reasons such as not wanting to relocate, not wanting additional aggravations and responsibilities, and not wanting to play politics. Similarly, Clausen (1976), who studied the nearly lifelong longitudinal samples of men from the Oakland Growth Study in California, reported that at age 38 more than one-half of the men expected promotion. By age 50, less than one-fifth had similar expectations. Nevertheless, most of the subjects felt that the years had treated them kindly.

Regardless of ostensible success, nearly all men at midlife desire challenge at work. Social relations at work appear to take on new meaning at this time, however. Most notably, men get more satisfaction from interpersonal contact and appear to thrive in a mentor-protégé relationship. Levinson (1978) highlighted the act of mentoring as an ideal means for achieving generativity at middle age, remaining connected to youthful vitality, and committing an act of altruism. Howard and Bray (1980) found that both their most successful men and their best-adjusted men enjoyed leading others. Mentoring was similarly suggested in the Tamir (1982) survey study, where there was a highly significant correlation between opportunities to talk with others at work and job satisfaction for college-educated men in their forties.

Returning to myth 1, men at middle age are not obsolete at work. For some, concern for financial security keeps them functioning at maximum levels throughout the middle years. For others, advancement remains a possibility, and they too function at optimal capacities. For all, challenge remains a potent motivator at work, regardless of level achieved. And for those middle-aged men who have the opportunity to implement the "big picture" processes, the detailed technical know-how can be delegated to younger men or women.

Men at Home: Myth 2

Myth 2 asserts that middle-aged men contemplate leaving their wives. Actual data prove otherwise. There is no upsurge in divorce at middle age. Any increase in middle-age divorce that has appeared over the decades is basically a function of an increase in divorce at all age levels. In fact, about one-half of all divorces occur within the first several years of marriage, with a decline in the divorce rate thereafter with age (Turner, 1980). Perhaps the reason why middle-age divorce appears to the naked eye as rampant is precisely because it is anomalous, or contrary to our expectations, to observe a couple breaking up after nearly a lifetime together. We remember succinctly each incident of middle-age divorce, summing them up in our minds and concluding that the problem is widespread, rather than atypical. Friedman (1981) found that most marriages continue through middle age even if the partners are dissatisfied with their relationship, because of the fear of resuming courtship and of admitting that the marriage might have been a mistake.

Given that most marriages survive the midlife transition, this is not to say that the dynamics of the husband-wife relationship do not change at this time. Research suggests that the husband and wife begin to interact at a new level because of both individual and familial transformations at middle age.

From the perspective of the man, emotional development at middle age, whether consciously appraised or subconsciously present, affects his marital feelings. This emotional development involves a shift in sources of well-being from the world of work achievement to more interpersonal strivings. It is important to reiterate that the man may not be entirely aware of this development. For example, in Lowenthal et al.'s (1977) lower-middle-class sample, most men at middle age described a typical day as one in which they went to work and came home again. Financial security was of great conscious concern to them. In projective TAT assessments, however, conjugal concerns were prominent, and needs for affiliation and reciprocal nurturance were expressed in this indirect way. Fiske (1980) believed that this middle-age shift in men, from the desire for instrumental mastery to interpersonal dependency, may be more innately developmental and not a function of economic class or status.

Studies document this midlife development, whereby the individual acquires, or allows to emerge, traits that were previously without expression (e.g., Cytrynbaum, Blum, Patrick, Stein, Wadner, & Wilk, 1980; Gutmann, 1975; Levinson, 1978). Men, usually over 40, begin to appear more androgynous (Hyde & Phillis, 1979). They do not simply relinquish the instrumental talents acquired to this point, but the best-adjusted integrate them with the more feminine characteristics of interpersonal gratification and sensitivity. Farrell and Rosenberg (1981, p. 207) observed that, for their sample, the man at the midlife transition displayed a "heightened emotional investment" in his family, and in particular, in his wife. This occurred even for the men whose family relationships were dysfunctional because the man in this age range began to regard his identity as linked with his family relations.

Heightened interpersonal strivings for the man at middle age are likely to render him even more highly invested within the marital relationship than previously. Levinson (1978) described how the man in midlife was more likely to acknowledge his responsibility in contributing to marital dissatisfaction. The man at a younger age was more likely to blame the wife for marital problems. Yet, Levinson noted, at middle age it is the wife who initiates marital reappraisal in many cases.

Although the man undergoes some form of personal reintegration, the woman at the middle-age stage often undergoes rapid self-development, usually stimulated by the anticipation of emptying her nest. This is described for women in terms of acquiring more masculine traits, such as ambitiousness, assertiveness, and aggressiveness. In a recent study attempting to assess Levinson's developmental schema for women, it was found that as women ended their thirties they were better able to see themselves in a broader context, taking on more leadership roles and authority within the community (Roberts & Newton, 1987). Cooper and Gutmann (1987) found that when the female nest is emptied the woman displays many more masculine traits, as assessed by interview and TAT techniques. Hence, it may be the woman who expresses greater marital dissatisfaction than the man during the middle-age transition. Lowenthal et al. (1977) found that women about to empty the nest were the most critical of their husbands from among the four life-stage groups they studied. Conversely, the husbands emphasized their wives' virtues and their own inadequacies in meeting their wives' expectations.

A key point in this phenomenon of sex-role reversal at middle age relates precisely to family life stage. Pre- and post-empty-nest marital functioning is likely to differ simply because the presence of children constitutes such a powerful influence. The classic research study by Rollins and Cannon (1974) documented the curvilinear relationship between marital satisfaction and family life stage. Most relevant here is that portion of the graph that demonstrates a notable upswing in marital satisfaction once the nest is emptied. Feldman, Biringen, and Nash (1981) found that the largest sex differences between men and women occurred during the active parenting stages, whereas empty-nest adults of both sexes described themselves more similarly in terms of sex-related self-attributions. Hence, the problem point in midlife marriage may come at the time when teenagers roam the house, allowing the parents neither sufficient time nor energy to appreciate each other, or to indulge in positive self-development (see Rollins, Chapter 8, this volume).

Deutscher (1968) highlighted the effects of the empty-nest transition in a landmark study published over 20 years ago. The majority of his "postparental" sample of husbands and wives reported a positive aftermath to launching, including an improved relationship with one another. Part of this improvement involved moving the relationship from a mom-dad focus back to husband-wife, and using this time together in a positive, companionable way. Deutscher found, however, social-class differences postparenthood. Upper-middle-class spouses displayed a more positive outlook on postparental life than did the lower-middle-class couples.

Presumably, class differences relate to sex-role flexibility. The lower class, more firmly entrenched in traditional sex-role ideology, has a more difficult time relinquishing the mom-dad role and searching for self and interpersonal fulfillment along more androgynous avenues. Lowenthal et al.'s (1977) more lower-middle-class sample appears to display precisely this sex-role rigidity. The empty-nesting women were the most depressed of the sample, fearing the impending loss of their maternal role. The men of this stage, although internally feeling strong dependency needs, externally saw their family role in economic terms: provider and protector. Farrell and Rosenberg's (1981) study similarly illustrated the greater rigidity of the lower- to lower-middle-class men, who more often fell into the quadrants characterized by authoritarianism, rigidity, and covert or overt depression.

On the other end of the spectrum are those men who achieve interpersonal fulfillment within the context of marriage at middle age. Most often this happy state of affairs is characteristic of the middle- to upper-middle-class segments of society. Nearly all studies that look at marriage at middle age concur on this point. Among Farrell and Rosenberg's (1981) transcendent-generative men, 80% saw their marriages as rewarding. On the other hand, among the punitive-disenchanted, a full 45% saw their marriages as *un*-rewarding. In his study of Ivy League graduates, Vaillant (1977, p. 320) stated that no single longitudinal variable "predicted mental health as clearly as a man's capacity to remain happily married over time." Additionally, the man's self-perceived happiness in his forties was highly related to his marital happiness. Strikingly similar are the results of the Tamir (1982) national survey study, which found that marital happiness was most highly correlated with general happiness (.50), life satisfaction (.46), and self-esteem (.56) for college-educated men in their forties. Clearly, for men in transition to middle age, and in particular well-educated middle-class men, marital bliss, as opposed to occupational achievement, is becoming the primary correlate of well-being.

The transition to middle age does not necessarily result in marital unfaithfulness. Optimal functioning men with good mental health tend to have good marriages at middle age. There are pressure points upon the marriage, however. One such point is the stressful period of parenting adolescent children, although most couples survive this chapter of their lives in anticipation of the freedom of an empty nest. Rodeheaver and Datan (1981) referred to this life chapter not as pre-empty nest, but as the "crowded nest." A second pressure point in middle-age marriage is when the nest is emptied. If the spouses cannot treat one another as husband and wife again, but instead mourn the loss of mom and dad roles without replacement, problems are likely to surface. Marital discord at this time is not likely to be the result of a newly emerging problem, but rather a long-standing problem that had been diverted by the presence of and attention to children. Without such diversion, denial of these problems is no longer tenable. A final pressure point upon the marriage, unique to middle age, pertains to individual personality development. If the woman is becoming more assertive, aggressive, and geared toward mastery in the external world, she may be, perhaps for the first time in her life, insensitive or unable to fulfill her husband's developing interpersonal desires for dependency and nurturance. A strong marriage will survive and benefit from these individual developments. A poor marriage may disintegrate under the strain. Many discordant marriages will persist, with a nagging sense of resignation, dissatisfaction, and mutual distancing between a husband and wife unwilling to break up after all those years (Friedman, 1981).

With regard to the young blond and sports car of midlife myth 2: If in fact the middle-aged man is unhappy with his marriage, his emerging dependency needs are highly likely to drive him into the arms of another woman. Often marriage or remarriage is the only way in which a man can satisfy his intimacy needs (Lowenthal & Robinson, 1976); hence, once divorced, the man will tend to find a new mate and remarry immediately. For the upper-middle-class man at the height of financial earning power, a fancy sports car can readily be purchased. Will it fill a void in his life more than temporarily? Probably not. The lower-middle-class man, worried about achieving financial security prior to retirement, would be foolish to consider such an extravagant purchase. Finally, there is no research to date on whether men at middle age clothe themselves to a significant extent in trendy outfits and jewelry as stated in myth 2. The stereotype may remain until research scientists prove otherwise.

Conclusions

Each man makes his transition to middle age in his own unique way. Adult developmental theory posits a sequence of personality changes that lead a man to greater psychological insight, self-utilization, and a more well-rounded personality that contribute to his growing sense of maturity and wisdom. This is the ideal model of development, most characteristic of the well-educated upper-middle-class man. Not all men search their souls, grapple with existential questions, or develop the skills to cope with contradiction, however. Some tune out of the rat race of work while others sprint to the finish line. More consistent is the personality reorganization whereby men, consciously or not, develop a greater desire for interpersonal dependency. Farrell and Rosenberg's (1981) study is the most illustrative to date of the diversity in coping patterns for men in their forties: patterns that correlate with social class, societal integration, and educational background.

An issue of great importance in examining the developmental changes with age is cohort membership and succession. Each cohort or generation of adults experiences the social and historical environment unique to the particular moment they entered the world. Each cohort develops its own personality based upon the formative influences of history and its contemporary social forces. The Great Depression cohort survived a childhood of economic deprivation. The baby boom cohort faces an environment of intense competition for jobs, promotions, and economic rewards.

The middle-aged men researched in the literature cited in this chapter belong most often to the cohort sandwiched between the depression and the baby boom. Those men, who were about 40 in the 1970s (born either during or on the tail end of the depression era) gave birth to the baby boom cohort. We have developed our theories of adult development from their behaviors and insights. Jung's (1933) seminal work suggested in the 1930s that middle age brings on mortality concerns and personal reintegration. For the most part, the cohorts we have researched have confirmed this assumption. The baby boom cohort, however, may or may not differ.

There are some major differences between the baby boom cohort (born 1946-1964) and preceding generations in terms of historical environment. As children of the 1960s, baby boomers became more cynical of government and conventional models of achievement. Nesselroade and Baltes (1974) uncovered this phenomenon in their sequential study of teens in the early 1970s, who decreased in superego strength, achievement, and even IQ, uniformly from 1970 to 1972. Correspondingly, in a second wave of their longitudinal study of middle management, Bray and Howard (1983) found that the young adults who were in their twenties in 1977 displayed lower motivation to conform to authority and regulations than their original sample, who were in their forties. The baby boom cohort, not quite middle-aged, is a more cynical and individualized cohort than its predecessors. This cohort has also benefited from more liberal sex-role attitudes, allowing women to indulge in achievement and mastery needs prior to and during childbearing years, whereas men of this cohort have been encouraged to express interpersonal needs (although the extent of their expression is unclear and can only be assessed in hindsight). The impact upon their middle age is yet to be seen. A more androgynous cohort to begin with, it will be interesting to observe the nature of a middle-age sex-role crossover for this group. Presumably, even more individualized patterns will emerge.

An additional powerful impact upon this cohort involves the sheer number of its members. Economics commentator Jane Bryant Quinn (1982) noted that the presence of too many people and too few high-level jobs is causing a bottleneck at the middle management levels of corporate hierarchies. Well-educated, ambitious men are topping out earlier in their careers than men of the previous cohort, leading to a "stalled career" problem (Quinn, 1982, p. 19B). It is unclear as of yet whether this phenomenon will precipitate a period of premature midlife blues or psychological reassessment for the stalled middle-management executive. Studies of previous cohorts indicate that most men make peace with their achievements by middle age. The current cohort may be more restless. Naisbitt (1982) in his book *Megatrends* also recognized this emerging problem, and suggested that a transformation from a hierarchic structure to a networking structure will become a trend in corporate and bureaucratic settings of the near future. Again, changing the nature of a man's work progression is likely to affect his adult development.

Similarly, the apparent transformation from idealistic "hippie" to materialistic "yuppie" in our baby boom stereotype is likely to be a function of scarcer commodities to be shared with more people. Hence, a hustle for material security overlays a strong background of idealism and search for personal fulfillment (LaBier, 1986). This too will probably have an impact on the aging of this cohort as it enters a midlife period of self-assessment, or perhaps as it seeks to avoid such assessment in continued pursuit of material wealth.

The issue of cohort has been raised to focus on the population currently entering a midlife transition, and the population next in line to seek counseling for problems at midlife. The research cited that has studied the preceding generation concludes that enhanced self-knowledge and the opportunity to continue challenging work, to guide others, and to fulfill interpersonal needs are the hallmarks of mental health at middle age. Counseling may be geared toward achieving these goals. Discussion of personal and interpersonal assessments and goals, however, might not be as appealing to a lower-class or lower-middle-class individual as to the more educated upper-middle-class individual.

A constructive therapeutic approach with men at midlife involves a positive attitude about middle age and recognition that the mythology has little foundation in fact. Middle age can be a fruitful and fulfilling episode of the life course, embellished by enhanced self-understanding, accomplishments, love, and pleasant anticipation of the second half of life. Mann (1980) stated that often the middle-aged client would prefer to set goals for therapy in terms of time allotted and outcome, and, most important, that the client may benefit more from relating to the therapist as an equal rather than from a dependent posture. The man at middle age has developed the cognitive skills and has accumulated a sizable repertoire of experiences to take an active role in the task of emotional healing and self-development in the course of individual therapy. It is the job of the therapist to facilitate the process with a clear understanding of the multiple benefits middle-age status has to offer, and a healthy respect for the wisdom of the client, despite the emotional and practical pressures that bring him to the counseling setting. The middle-aged man certainly should be allotted the dignity of his age as he pursues the task of gaining insight into himself and his place in society.

References

Bardwick, J. M. (1978). Middle-age and a sense of future. *Merrill-Palmer Quarterly, 24,* 129-138.

Birren, J. E. (1970). Toward an experimental psychology of aging. *American Psychologist, 25,* 124-135.

Borland, D. C. (1978). Research on middle-age: An assessment. *Gerontologist, 18,* 379-386.

Bourque, L. B., & Back, K. W. (1969). The middle years seen through the life graph. *Sociological Symposium, 3,* 19-29.

Boyd, J. H., & Weissman, M. M. (1981). The epidemiology of psychiatric disorders of middle-age: Depression, alcoholism, & suicide. In J. G. Howells (Ed.), *Modern perspectives in the psychiatry of middle-age* (pp. 201-221). New York: Brunner/Mazel.

Bray, D. W., & Howard, A. (1983). The AT&T longitudinal study of managers. In K. W. Schaie (Ed.), *Longitudinal studies of adult psychological development* (pp. 266-312). New York: Guilford.

Cameron, P. (1970). The generation gap: Which generation is believed powerful versus generational members' self-appraisals of power. *Developmental Psychology, 3,* 403-404.

Campbell, A., Converse, P. E., & Rodgers, W. L. (1976). *The quality of American life.* New York: Russell Sage.

Clausen, J. A. (1976). Glimpses into the social world of middle-age. *International Journal of Aging and Human Development, 7,* 99-106.

Cooper, C. L. (1981). Middle-aged men and the pressures of work. In J. G. Howells (Ed.), *Modern perspectives in the psychiatry of middle-age* (pp. 90-102). New York: Brunner/Mazel.

Cooper, K. L., & Gutmann, D. L. (1987). Gender identity and ego mastery style in middle-aged pre- and post-empty nest women. *Gerontologist, 27,* 347-352.

Cytrynbaum, S., Blum, L., Patrick, R., Stein, J., Wadner, D., & Wilk, C. (1980). Midlife development: A personality and social systems perspective. In L. W. Poon (Ed.), *Aging in the 1980s* (pp. 463-474). Washington, DC: American Psychological Association.

Deutscher, I. (1968). The quality of post-parental life. In B. L. Neugarten (Ed.), *Middle-age and aging* (pp. 263-268). Chicago: University of Chicago Press.

Drevenstedt, J. (1976). Perceptions of onsets of young adulthood, middle-age, and old-age. *Journal of Gerontology, 31,* 53-57.

Erikson, E. H. (1950). *Childhood and society.* New York: Norton.

Farrell, M. P., & Rosenberg, S. D. (1981). *Men at midlife.* Dover, MA: Auburn House.

Feldman, S. S., Biringen, Z. C., & Nash, S. C. (1981). Fluctuations in sex-related self-attributions as a function of stage of family life cycle. *Developmental Psychology, 17,* 24-35.

Fiske, M. (1980). Changing hierarchies of commitment in adulthood. In N. J. Smelser & E. H. Erikson (Eds.), *Themes of work and love in adulthood* (pp. 238-264). Cambridge, MA: Harvard University Press.

Friedman, H. J. (1981). The divorced in middle-age. In J. G. Howells (Ed.), *Modern perspectives in the psychiatry of middle-age* (pp. 103-115). New York: Brunner/Mazel.

Giele, J. Z. (1980). Adulthood as transcendence of age and sex. In N. J. Smelser & E. H. Erikson (Eds.), *Themes of work and love in adulthood* (pp. 151-173). Cambridge, MA: Harvard University Press.

Gould, R. L. (1972). The phases of adult life: A study in developmental psychology. *American Journal of Psychiatry, 129*, 521-531.

Gutmann, D. (1975). Parenthood: A key to the comparative study of the life cycle. In N. Datan & L. H. Ginsberg (Eds.), *Life-span developmental psychology: Normative life crises* (pp. 167-184). New York: Academic Press.

Haan, N. (1981). Adolescents and young adults as producers of their development. In R. M. Lerner & N. A. Busch-Rossnagel (Eds.), *Individuals as producers of their own development* (pp.155-182). New York: Academic Press.

Harlan, S. L. (1983). *Opportunity and anomie: Attitudes toward job advancement in a manufacturing firm* (Working paper no. 108). Wellesley, MA: Wellesley College Center for Research on Women.

Horowitz, A. (1985). Sons and daughters as caregivers to older parents: Differences in role performance and consequences. *Gerontologist, 25*, 612-617.

Howard, A., & Bray, D. W. (1980). *Career motivation in midlife managers.* Paper presented at the annual meeting of the American Psychological Association, Montreal, Canada.

Hyde, J. S., & Phillis, D. E. (1979). Androgyny across the life span. *Developmental Psychology, 15*, 334-336.

Jackson, D. W. (1974). Advanced aged adults' reflections of middle-age. *Gerontologist, 14*, 255-257.

Jaffe, A. J. (Ed.). (1971). The middle years: Neither too young nor too old [Special issue]. *Industrial Gerontology.* (Washington, DC: National Council on the Aging)

Jaques, E. (1965). Death and the midlife crisis. *International Journal of Psychoanalysis, 46*, 502-514.

Jung, C. G. (1933). *Modern man in search of a soul.* New York: Harcourt Brace Jovanovich.

LaBier, D. (1986). *Modern madness.* Reading, MA: Addison-Wesley.

Levinson, D. J. (1978). *The seasons of a man's life.* New York: Knopf.

Lowenthal, M. F., & Robinson, B. (1976). Social networks and isolation. In R. H. Binstock & E. Shanas (Eds.), *Handbook of aging and the social sciences* (pp. 432-456). New York: Van Nostrand Reinhold.

Lowenthal, M. F., Thurnher, M., & Chiriboga, D. (1977). *Four stages of life.* San Francisco: Jossey-Bass.

Mann, C. H. (1980). Mid-life and the family: Strains, challenges and options of the middle years. In W. H. Norman & T.J. Scaramella (Eds.), *Mid-life: Developmental and clinical issues* (pp. 128-148). New York: Brunner/Mazel.

Mirkin, P. M., & Meyer, R. E. (1981). Alcoholism in middle-age. In J. G. Howells (Ed.), *Modern perspectives in the psychiatry of middle-age* (pp. 251-365). New York: Brunner/Mazel.

Naisbitt, J. (1982). *Megatrends.* New York: Warner Books.

Nesselroade, J. R., & Baltes, P. B. (1974). Adolescent personality development and historical change: 1970-1972. *Monographs of the Society for Research in Child Development, 39* (Serial No. 154).

Neugarten, B. L. (1968). The awareness of middle-age. In B. L. Neugarten (Ed.), *Middle-age and aging* (pp. 93-98). Chicago: University of Chicago Press.

Neugarten, B. L. (1976). Adaptation and the life cycle. *The Counseling Psychologist, 6,* 16-20.

Neugarten, B. L., & Datan, N. (1974). The middle years. In S. Arieti (Ed.), *American handbook of psychiatry* (pp. 592-608). New York: Basic Books.

Quinn, J. B. (1982, November 29). The stalled career. *Newsweek,* pp. 19B-19E.

Roberts, P., & Newton, P. M. (1987). Levinsonian studies of women's adult development. *Psychology and Aging, 2,* 154-163.

Rodeheaver, D., & Datan, N. (1981). Making it: The dialectics of middle-age. In R. M. Lerner & N. A. Busch-Rossnagel (Eds.), *Individuals as producers of their development* (pp. 183-196). New York: Academic Press.

Rollins, B. C., & Cannon, K. L. (1974). Marital satisfaction over the family life cycle: A reevaluation. *Journal of Marriage and the Family, 36,* 271-282.

Rubin, L. B. (1976). *Worlds of pain.* New York: Basic Books.

Schaie, K. W. (1977-1978). Toward a stage theory of adult cognitive development. *International Journal of Aging and Human Development, 8,* 129-138.

Tamir, L. M. (1982). *Men in their forties.* New York: Springer.

Turner, N. W. (1980). Divorce in mid-life: Clinical implications and applications. In H. Norman & T. J. Scaramella (Eds.), *Midlife: Developmental and clinical issues* (pp. 149-177). New York: Brunner/Mazel.

Vaillant, G. E. (1977). *Adaptation to Life.* Boston: Little, Brown.

Part IV
The Social Context: Marriage and Family

The three chapters in Part IV address the topics of marital quality, dual-career families, and intergenerational relationships. In Chapter 8, Rollins compares the stability and satisfaction of marriage at midlife with marriage at earlier and later stages. He reports that divorce is more common among those in their teens and twenties than among those at midlife or older ages. Although the divorce rates are lower at midlife, marital satisfaction seems to be at a low point. Perhaps, as Rollins suggests, the alternatives to married status are worse than a poor-quality marriage.

In examining the literature on marital quality over the career of the family, Rollins observes that the quality of marriage declines when children enter the home, gradually declines further until children start leaving home, and increases again after they depart. Rollins presents the argument that, under the stress of what he calls "roles overload," married persons with dependent children at home neglect marital roles to meet the needs of children, and that neglect has a negative impact on marital satisfaction. He also discusses other stressors at midlife such as family life in general and career.

Rollins suggests that when "roles overload" occurs in the family roles of married adults, marital communication and companionship are sacrificed to meet the role demands of child caregiving. Professional helpers can be alert to marital problems of their clients at midlife that are related to poor communication and lack of companionship. For example, couples with limited financial resources or large numbers of children may find that the demands of roles accumulation can compel them to neglect each other's desires for conversation and companionship.

Rollins indicates that lack of adequate preparation for parenthood can also create family difficulties at midlife. He suggests that more education and assistance, in terms of anticipatory socialization, be given to parents before the first child is born. Professional helpers interested in prevention can facilitate the availability of community education classes and other media as a way to aid prospective parents. Rollins also suggests that family planning and child spacing goals can help couples achieve a high-quality marriage.

A major implication of this chapter is that if couples will be patient with decline in marital satisfaction during midlife, their marriages will eventually get better as the pressures of child rearing subside and as communication and companionship increase. Counselors and therapists can encourage their clients to be patient and to learn how to handle their children more effectively, as well as to give proper attention to their partner's interests and concerns.

In Chapter 9, Gilbert and Davidson identify the stresses and satisfactions experienced by families with dual-career couples at midlife. They discuss personal, relational, and environmental factors that influence how work and family are combined. The authors also identify three types of coping strategies used by the couples: cognitive restructuring, increased role behavior, and role redefinition.

The major issue for dual-career couples is how to combine occupational and family roles. The authors describe three ways in which spouses handle this situation in patterns called the traditional dual-career family, the role-sharing dual-career family, and the participant dual-career family. Gilbert and Davidson conclude that a satisfying and fulfilling dual-career marriage requires both spouses to struggle with the difficulties of integrating career and family despite societal pressures to conform to sex-typed roles and behaviors. Personal resources, family resources, and societal resources are employed by the couples to sustain their marriages.

Counselors, therapists, and educators can help dual-career couples examine the stresses related to their roles, and to use appropriate coping strategies and resources to deal with their circumstances. They can also encourage the couples to be patient in grappling with their difficulties in combining work and family, which may take time and experience to achieve a harmonious balance for each partner.

In Chapter 10, Troll examines myths of midlife intergenerational relationships, focusing on a cluster of beliefs about parent-child relationships. For example, there is a popular belief that parents and their adult children are estranged from each other. This is countered, however, by surveys showing that most adult children and their parents share similar beliefs and values, keep in close touch, live fairly close to each other, and visit frequently or talk on the telephone. The ideal of independence is strong, however, and both generations try to maintain separate households unless there is economic necessity or extreme physical disability. Another myth that research findings challenge is that middle-aged men and women, because they are selfish and narcissistic, abandon their aging parents. Troll identifies other intergenerational myths and compares them with research findings. She concludes that most middle-aged men and women are committed to both their children and their parents throughout their lives and help in times of need.

Some of the research findings that Troll presents may differ for certain ethnic groups such as Hispanics or Blacks, or might vary according to social class. Future research needs to be done with these groups. Counselors and therapists can help families identify conflicts between the norm of self-realization and that of filial obligation, in order to clarify and work out their responsibilities and desires for both.

8

Marital Quality at Midlife

Boyd C. Rollins

The status of being married is popular in the United States. Though in comparison to the 1950s, young adults today are postponing marriage, and increasing numbers are "living together" with someone of the opposite sex without the benefit of marriage, the vast majority still end up in the status of being married. Cherlin (1981) estimated that 90% of the present cohort of young adults will eventually marry. Even the magnitude of divorce in the United States (more than 1 million per year since 1974) is not an argument against the popularity of being married. The percentage of divorced men and women who remarried increased from 1960 to 1977 (U.S. Department of Commerce, 1980). Also, although 3.4% of the married women in the United States in 1977 obtained a divorce (1,125,000 divorces), 8.4% of the divorced women in the United States in 1977 were remarried (675,000 remarriages) that year.

From a social exchange perspective (Nye, 1979), the social status of being married must be rewarding to individuals or one would expect them either to avoid marriage in the first place or to divorce and not remarry. With the high popularity of being married, one would assume that most people either experience a reasonable amount of personal satisfaction in their marital relationships or they hope to at some future time. Of specific concern in this chapter is the quality and meaning of marriage for individuals at middle adulthood or midlife, which will be considered here as approximately age 30-60. Although this age range is somewhat arbitrary as a parameter of midlife, it is used in the human development literature (Peterson, 1984). Subjectively, some individuals would undoubtedly place themselves at midlife before age 30 and out of midlife before age 60, whereas for others it would start after age 30 and end after age 60.

To evaluate marriage at midlife, a comparative analysis among marriages at various stages of the life career will be used rather than a focus only on married persons at this stage of development. Specifically, divorce rates and marital satisfaction at various stages of the life career of individuals will be used as a basis for describing the experience and meaning of marriage for individuals at midlife. This, along with information on other sources of unique stressor events and sources of life satisfaction at this stage of life, will be used to construct a description and evaluation of marriage at midlife.

A basic question addressed is this: What is the stability and satisfaction of marriage at midlife compared to the stability and satisfaction of marriage at earlier and later stages? Further, if marital satisfaction is lower at midlife than at earlier and/or later stages, three corollary questions are: (1) What is an explanation for the differences? (2) What hope do married persons have that they can avoid losses in marital satisfaction at midlife or cope in such a way as to minimize the meaning of such losses? (3) What hope do they have that marital quality will improve later in life?

Divorce During the Life Career

There is consistent evidence in the United States that divorce is correlated with age of the individual at the time of divorce and with length of time married. Age-specific divorce rates indicate that divorce is more common among those in their teens and twenties than among those at midlife or older (England & Kunz, 1975). For example, in 1970 in the United States, divorces obtained that year per 1,000 married women aged 14-19 ranged from 33.7 for the youngest to 24.2 for the oldest. Among married women aged 30-59, the rate of divorce that year ranged from 17.6 to 3.7 per thousand. The divorce rate was even lower for those women aged 60 or more. This is a substantial difference in divorce rate in terms of age.

In terms of the timing of divorce, the data clearly indicate that divorce is much less likely to occur at midlife than earlier in life. If one considers the ratio of currently divorced persons to currently married persons by life course categories, however, there is clearly a higher ratio from midlife than earlier (Levitan & Belous, 1981). That is so because persons who divorce before age 30 and do not remarry accumulate in the category of the currently divorced. Therefore, midlife is a time when divorce is less likely to occur, although the total proportion of ever-married persons who are divorced is relatively high.

Divorce rates have also been evaluated in terms of length of time married rather than by age of married persons. The results are congruent. One-half of the divorces that occur in the United States are among those married seven years or less (Collins, 1985) and include husbands who are age 31 or less and wives who are age 29 or less. These two types of data about divorce indicate that divorce is much more likely for married persons who are at teenage and young adult stages of the life career than those in middle adulthood.

What does a lower divorce rate at midlife suggest about the quality of marriage at midlife? If married couples are more likely to stay together at this stage, does that signify that the quality of the marriage is relatively high and produces sufficient rewards to maintain it?

Midlife, for most married adults who have children, coincides with stages of the family career when dependent children are residing in the household requiring caregiving and primary socialization from adults. The oldest children are school age or teenage. Further, at this stage of the family career, midlife stress occurs simultaneously with adolescent stress, so that "two generational transitions exist together—often feeding on each other—with the potential for at least a mild amount of stress" (Kidwell, Fischer, Dunham, & Baranowski, 1983, p. 82). Olson and McCubbin (1983) found that stressor events in families tended to "pile up" during the child-rearing stages, reaching an apex when children are teenage. The number of stressor events declined as children were launched from the home.

It seems somewhat puzzling that divorce rates are much lower for married adults at midlife than in early adulthood while the pileup of stressors that might lead to family crisis is greater. One might surmise that either other aspects of family life at midlife are sufficiently rewarding to adults to maintain the marriage (Nye, 1979), or alternatives to married status at this time in their lives are sufficiently poor that they hang on under poor-quality conditions of family life (Levinger, 1965; Spanier & Lewis, 1980).

Marital Quality During the
Career of the Family

Since the landmark study of Pineo (1961) and the literature review and empirical study of Rollins and Feldman (1970), a substantial body of literature has focused on some aspect of marital quality (particularly marital satisfaction) during the life career of the family. This literature has generally presented empirical data congruent with the declaration of Rollins and Feldman (1970) that marital satisfaction follows a U-shaped pattern over the family career. Particularly well established is the evidence of decline from early marriage through the childbearing and child-rearing years. Such support comes from longitudinal studies over the early stages (Meyerowitz & Feldman, 1966; Paris & Luckey, 1966; Pineo, 1961). Support has also come from cross-sectional studies comparing couples at various stages of the family career from newly married couples through various developmental stages when dependent children are in the home to the "empty-nest" stages including retirement (Bradburn & Caplovitz, 1965; Burr, 1970; Campbell, Converse, & Rodgers, 1976; Figley, 1973; Olson & McCubbin, 1983; Orthner, 1975; Rollins & Cannon, 1974; Smart & Smart, 1975; Spanier, Lewis, & Cole, 1975). A third body of support comes from cross-sectional studies of couples at the later stages of the family career as children are launched from the home and retirement ensues (Axelson, 1960; Deutscher, 1964; Miller, 1976). Collectively these studies suggest that the quality of marriage declines when children enter the home, that it gradually declines further until children start leaving home, and that it increases again after they are gone.

The literature on marital quality over the family career has been severely critiqued and a substantial caution has emerged in the interpretation that the stress of children depresses the quality of the marriage. Many textbooks present the U-shaped curve as descending sharply and deeply before increasing again. Rollins and Cannon (1974) cautioned that, though their data demonstrated the reliability of the curve, the curve was actually shallow and accounted for only a small amount of the variation from couple to couple in marital satisfaction. Others, such as Spanier, Lewis, and Cole (1975), have raised numerous methodological issues about the supporting studies, especially the cross-sectional studies showing an increase over the later stages. Methodological artifacts such as the selective elimination of couples who had divorced before their children left home could account for higher average scores of couples still married in the "empty-nest" stages. Such arguments are compelling. The shallow curve might indicate that some people are more satisfied with their marriage during child-rearing stages, some do not change, some are less satisfied, and it all averages out in favor of the less satisfied.

Nevertheless, combined with the literature suggesting that the attainment of parenthood instigates new stressor events in the lives of married persons (LaRossa & LaRossa, 1981; Miller & Myers-Walls, 1983), the data indicating lower levels of marital satisfaction during the child-rearing years is still worthy of serious attention. Glick and Norton (1977) reported that for the last 50 years one-half of all divorces have occurred by the seventh year of marriage. The cross-sectional studies indicate an average decline in marital satisfaction from the initial marriage through the childbearing and child-rearing years (approximately 20-25 years of marriage). This is so irrespective of the great likelihood that the earlier stages contained some married couples that would likely be divorced before they are in the middle stages. Thus the actual decline from the newly married stage to the teenage child-rearing stage is likely much sharper than the cross-sectional data suggest. Such a view is supported by the few studies that actually followed the same couples over the first 15-20 years of their marriage (Pineo, 1961).

If children are the basis for increased pressure on parents in terms of their time, financial, physical, and emotional resources, then it seems logical that the presence of dependent children in the home could lower the quality of marriage of the parents. This would seem especially so if the parents were not socialized in advance for the experience of parenthood (LeMasters, 1957), if they had children when they did not want them, or if they had more children than they desired (Christensen, 1968).

As the data suggest that marital satisfaction is lower at midlife for most married persons than at earlier or later stages, Rollins and Galligan (1978) presented a rationale to explain why this would be expected. The logic of this argument is as follows:

(1) As children enter a family and proceed through stages of developmental dependency, family roles of adults accumulate until a roles overload exists (as children mature and leave home, the family roles of adults decline to a more manageable number).

(2) Roles overload leads to role strain (subjectively felt difficulty in the performance of a role) unless some coping mechanism is used to avoid role strain for a particular salient role.

(3) Role strain results in poor quality of role enactment by an individual.

(4) Poor quality of role enactment of a salient marital role by one's spouse negatively affects the marital satisfaction of a married person.

If we assume that under the stress of roles overload most married persons with dependent children at home would neglect marital roles to meet the needs of children, then salient marital roles would be neglected, having a negative impact on the marital satisfaction of one's spouse.

If high levels of marital satisfaction at midlife can be dismissed as an explanation for relatively low divorce rates during this stage of life, then what is a reasonable explanation? As Spanier and Lewis (1980) explained, marital satisfaction is a poor predictor of marital stability, because some unhappily married persons remain married. The costs of divorce are too great and alternatives to the continuation of the marriage are poor (for example, an affluent middle-class, midlife, wife-mother considering the option of divorce decides that she has a good chance of living close to the poverty level and remaining a single parent, as her chances of remarriage are slim).

Another explanation is that marriages at midlife have a high probability of remaining intact because of anticipated future rewards such as an improved quality of marriage after the stress of child rearing is over. Before pursuing further the meaning of marriage at midlife, let us look at some of the other stressors that married persons at midlife face aside from the likelihood of roles strain resulting from roles overload from expanded child caregiving demands.

Other Stressors at Midlife

Middle adulthood is considered quite stressful in areas such as occupational career (Levinson, Darrow, Klein, Levinson, & McKee, 1978), personal adjustment (Bigner, 1985; Kidwell et al., 1983), and family life in general (Olson & McCubbin, 1983). Collectively these stresses are sometimes referred to as "midlife crisis" (Skolnick, 1987). These, along with lowered marital satisfaction at midlife, present a gloomy picture of the meaning of marriage at midlife.

Levinson et al. (1978) described two phases of transition in midlife between periods of relative stability. These transition phases are at approximately age 28 to 33 (oldest child of school age) and age 40 to 45 (oldest child a teenager). These transition years are assumed to be marked by turmoil, confusion, and the reoccurrence of unresolved issues from earlier years. According to Sheehy (1976), as their children reach out to an expanding world of experiences and opportunities, adults start to evaluate their own dreams and ambitions to determine what they have accomplished. Frustrated with unobtained personal goals, they often resolve to strive even harder to succeed. A basic dilemma they face is that they are already overloaded with family demands. This is an obvious stress-producing situation that requires substantial personal resources for coping or a new and realistic definition of goals in order to avoid a crisis situation (McCubbin & Patterson, 1983).

The other transition period for adults at age 40 to 45 coincides with the adolescent stage of life of the oldest child in the family. According to Sheehy (1976) adults perceive this period as the opportunity for a last-ditch effort to realize their dreams and make the most of their personal lives. Women are likely to make the commitment to pursue a career or intensify their efforts for career advancement. Men also respond to the situation with a sense of "now or never" to reach the top of one's profession (foreman, full professor, company vice-president, or senior member of a law firm). Also, questions about one's sexual appeal are raised and both husbands and wives are more likely to explore sexual liaisons outside of marriage.

According to Kidwell et al. (1983), the parallel stressors for adolescent children and their parents of going through a transitional phase of their lives greatly complicates the problem. A son might optimistically be considering a vocational career while his father, wistfully looking on, realizes his own unmet dreams. A daughter might be emerging into the realm of the sexually attractive while the mother is concerned about her dwindling sex appeal. The opportunities of youth, and their idealistic dreams of who they might become, could be ghostly reminders to their parents that they have fallen short of the mark they set early in their lives.

The stressors of developmental transitions in the individual lives of husbands, wives, and teenage children are systemically intertwined. As a consequence they are likely to show up in various types of family problems. Not only did Olson and McCubbin (1983) find a pileup of stressor events in families with parents at midlife, the dominant stressors were interpersonal relationship and financial strains. Decision-making processes were apparently more difficult than when children were younger, and more conflict existed concerning economic resources in the family. Thus it seems that at the very time in life when married persons experience great challenges in other aspects of their personal lives, they experience greater stress in their families and less satisfaction in their marriages.

We have not resolved the dilemma as to why married persons are not divorcing in greater numbers during midlife, when marital quality appears lower than at other times and family and personal stressor events are higher. Perhaps the other stressor events are associated with gender at this stage of life. Females have less bargaining power in the potential marriage market if divorce were to occur. As mentioned above, lack of viable alternative might be an explanation of relatively low divorce rates for those at midlife. Another, more optimistic view of the meaning of marriage at midlife is presented below.

Hope for the Married at Midlife

A somewhat gloomy scenario of marriage at midlife was painted above. It should be recalled, however, that differences among group averages in marital satisfaction at all stages of the family career are not substantial. Perhaps only a small portion of marriages decline in quality during the phases of married life when parents are burdened with child-care responsibilities. Perhaps many others use coping strategies to arrest or prevent deterioration of marital quality. The empirically based theory of marital quality of Spanier and Lewis (1980) posited two social interaction processes as primarily responsible for the level of marital satisfaction of a married person. They are (a) effective communication and (b) companionship. Perhaps if married couples make a conscious effort to maintain effective communication and companionship throughout the marriage, decrements in marital satisfaction associated with the stressors of parenthood would be avoided.

Rollins and Feldman (1970) demonstrated that marital satisfaction of husbands and wives declines during childbearing and child-rearing years, to return after children are launched from the home. Using the same data set, Rollins (1981) found the same pattern for amount of marital communication and amount of marital companionship. Perhaps when roles overload occurs in the family roles of married adults, marital communication and marital companionship are sacrificed to meet the role demands of child caregiving. Following this lead, Rollins (1981) reanalyzed the Rollins and Feldman data, controlling for the amount of marital companionship in the individual marriages. The result was that, with the amount of companionship held at a constant level, there were no differences in marital satisfaction of married men or women at different stages of the family career.

The above findings suggest that some couples have probably avoided negative consequences of roles overload from compelling demands of children because they gave high priority to enhancing effective spousal communication and spousal companionship. The salience of companionship as a marital role of American married couples was clearly demonstrated by Blood and Wolfe (1960) nearly three decades ago. Thus hope exists for married couples to maintain a high quality of marriage during the most stressful years of midlife and avoid drops in marital satisfaction. Such hope carries a price tag of discipline, sacrifice, and great effort to maintain the marriage relationship. There is evidence that the quality of marriage will improve at the stage of life when the demands of dependent children are reduced and greater time resources are available for maintaining the marriage relationship. This requires the discipline of delayed gratification.

Perhaps for some, especially for those with limited financial resources and/or large numbers of children, the demands of roles accumulation are so great that they feel compelled to ignore important marital roles. For them, the hope is offered that marital quality can improve after the demands of extensive child caregiving have subsided. Also, as experienced by grandparents worldwide, grandchildren are a delight without the responsibility of constant care (usually they are the primary responsibility of someone else). A heritage of grandchildren might be viewed by some as compensation for losses in marital quality.

Perhaps part of the stress of parenting children that affects marital quality is a lack of adequate preparation for the status of parenthood. In terms of the initial transition to parenthood, for example, parents could more easily cope if they were realistically prepared through anticipatory socialization before the first child is born. Similar preparation would also be beneficial with older children. Books, community education classes, and hands-on experience with infants and young children can help couples learn about the needs and characteristics of children. Discussions with others who have experienced and effectively coped with their children without compromising the marriage could help provide a promising perspective.

The impact of children on the quality of marriage is in part a function of the congruence between when parents desire children, and how many, and when and how many children actually join their family (Christensen, 1968). This finding suggests that adults should carefully and thoughtfully engage in family planning to maximize the attainment of their family size and child-spacing goals.

Hope for a high-quality marriage at midlife comes with a price tag. This is likely the case for most things in life that are highly valued. Because most Americans seem to value a high-quality marriage, it will more likely be attained by those who put forth constructive effort and search for help from couples who are satisfied with both their marriages and their children.

References

Axelson, L. J. (1960). Personal adjustment in the postparental period. *Marriage and Family Living*, 22, 66-68.

Bigner, J. J. (1985). *Parent-child relationships*. New York: Macmillan.

Blood, R. O., & Wolfe, D. M. (1960). *Husbands and wives: The dynamics of married living.* Glencoe, IL: Free Press.

Bradburn, N. M., & Caplovitz, D. (1965). *Reports on happiness*. Chicago: Aldine.

Burr, W. R. (1970). Satisfaction with various aspects of marriage over the life cycle: A random middle class sample. *Journal of Marriage and the Family, 32*, 29-37.

Campbell, A., Converse, P. E., & Rodgers, W. L. (1976). *The quality of life: Perceptions, evaluations and satisfactions*. New York: Russell Sage.

Cherlin, A. (1981). *Marriage, divorce, remarriage.* Cambridge, MA: Harvard University Press.

Christensen, H. T. (1968). Children in the family: Relationship of number and spacing to marital success. *Journal of Marriage and the Family, 30*, 283-289.

Collins, R. (1985). *Sociology of marriage and the family.* Chicago: Nelson-Hall.

Deutscher, I. (1964). The quality of postparental life. *Journal of Marriage and the Family, 26*, 52-60.

England, J. L., & Kunz, P. R. (1975). The application of age-specific rate to divorce. *Journal of Marriage and the Family, 37,* 40-48.

Figley, C. R. (1973). Child density and the marital relationship. *Journal of Marriage and the Family, 35,* 272-282.

Glick, P. C., & Norton, A. J. (1977). Marrying, divorcing, and living together in the U.S. today. *Population Bulletin, 32,* 1-39.

Kidwell, J., Fischer, J. L., Dunham, R. M., & Baranowski, M. (1983). Parents and adolescents: Push and pull of change. In H. I. McCubbin & C. R. Figley (Eds.), *Stress and the family: Vol. 1. Coping with normative transitions* (pp. 74-89). New York: Brunner/Mazel.

LaRossa, R., & LaRossa, M. M. (1981). *Transition to parenthood: How infants change families.* Beverly Hills, CA: Sage.

LeMasters, E. E. (1957). Parenthood as crisis. *Marriage and Family Living, 19,* 352-355.

Levinger, G. (1965). Marital cohesiveness and dissolution: An integrative review. *Journal of Marriage and the Family, 27,* 19-28.

Levinson, D., Darrow, C. N., Klein, E. B., Levinson, M. H., & McKee, B. (1978). *The seasons of a man's life.* New York: Knopf.

Levitan, S. A., & Belous, R. S. (1981). *What's happening to the American family?* Baltimore: Johns Hopkins University Press.

McCubbin, H. I., & Patterson, J. M. (1983). Family transitions: Adaptation to stress. In H. I. McCubbin & C. R. Figley (Eds.), *Stress and the family: Vol. 1. Coping with normative transitions* (pp. 5-25). New York: Brunner/Mazel.

Meyerowitz, J. H., & Feldman, H. (1966). Transition to parenthood. *Psychiatric Research Report, 20,* 78-84.

Miller, B. C. (1976). A multivariate developmental model of marital satisfaction. *Journal of Marriage and the Family, 38,* 345-347.

Miller, B. C., & Myers-Walls, J. A. (1983). Parenthood: Stresses and coping strategies. In H. I. McCubbin & C. R. Figley (Eds.), *Stress and the family: Vol. 1. Coping with normative transitions* (pp. 54-73). New York: Brunner/Mazel.

Nye, F. I. (1979). Choice, exchange, and the family. In W. R. Burr, R. Hill, F. I. Nye, & I. L. Reiss (Eds.), *Contemporary theories about the family* (Vol. 2, pp. 1-41). New York: Free Press.

Olson, D. E., & McCubbin, H. I.. (1983). *Families: What makes them work.* Beverly Hills, CA: Sage.

Orthner, D. K. (1975). Leisure activity patterns and marital satisfaction over the marital career. *Journal of Marriage and the Family, 37,* 91-104.

Paris, B. L., & Luckey, E. B. (1966). A longitudinal study of marital satisfaction. *Sociology and Social Research, 50,* 212-223.

Peterson, O. C. (1984). *Looking forward through the life span: Developmental psychology.* Sydney, Australia: Prentice-Hall.

Pineo, P. O. (1961). Disenchantment in the later years of marriage. *Marriage and Family Living, 23,* 3-11.

Rollins, B. C. (1981). *Companionship in marriage as a mediating variable in the family life cycle and marital satisfaction relationship.* Unpublished manuscript, Brigham Young University, Provo, UT.

Rollins, B. C., & Cannon, K. L. (1974). Marital satisfaction over the family life cycle: A reevaluation. *Journal of Marriage and the Family, 36,* 271-282.

Rollins, B. C., & Feldman, H. (1970). Marital satisfaction over the family life cycle. *Journal of Marriage and Family, 32,* 20-28.

Rollins, B. C., & Galligan, R. (1978). The developing child and marital satisfaction of parents. In R. M. Lerner & G. B. Spanier (Eds.), *Child influences on marital and family interaction* (pp. 71-106). New York: Academic Press.

Sheehy, G. (1976). *Passages: Predictable crises of adult life.* New York: Dutton.

Skolnick, A. S. (1987). *The intimate environment: Exploring marriage and the family.* Boston: Little, Brown.

Smart, M. S., & Smart, R. C. (1975). Recalled, present and predicted satisfaction in states of the family life cycle in New Zealand. *Journal of Marriage and the Family, 37,* 408-415.

Spanier, G. B., & Lewis, R. A. (1980). Marital quality: A review of the seventies. *Journal of Marriage and the Family, 42,* 825-840.

Spanier, G. B., Lewis, R. R., & Cole, C. L. (1975). Marital adjustment over the family life cycle: The issue of curvilinearity. *Journal of Marriage and the Family, 37,* 262-276.

U.S. Department of Commerce. (1980). *American families and living arrangements* (Series P-23). Washington, DC: Government Printing Office.

9

Dual-Career Families at Midlife

Lucia Albino Gilbert
Sherwin Davidson

In our society, fortieth and fiftieth birthdays generate special celebrations and good-natured sympathy. There is a shared folk wisdom about the stress associated with these passages and a unique poignancy about the irreversible realities of aging. Yet for individuals in dual-career families, these bittersweet celebrations of midlife are likely to occur in a context that differs considerably from members of their cohort who have chosen more traditional life-styles. In 1969, when individuals now at midlife were young adults, social scientists first used the term *dual-career family* to describe a variation of the nuclear family that represented "social change" (Rapoport & Rapoport, 1969). This variation of the nuclear family replaced the traditional view of men as providers and women as housewives and mothers with the view that both women and men can pursue careers and at the same time maintain a family life together.

Many of these individuals, who as young adults entered dual-career families in the 1960s, did not intend to be models of social change. Rather, the change was more a function of societal circumstances than of personal desires. More career opportunities for women, made possible by the feminist movement and by changing social and economic conditions, increased women's career choices. Women worked, but often it was with the understanding that any occupational work was in addition to attending to the needs of their husbands and children. Thus the impact on women's roles in the family in most cases was minor. As Bernard (1975, p. 188) noted, "It was easier [for women] to be for equal pay than for equality vis-à-vis husbands." Times continued to change, and during the period from the 1960s to the 1980s, the women's movement broadened its focus to embrace equitable roles with men in the worlds of work *and* family.

This chapter concerns individuals at midlife who entered dual-career marriages during these changing times. The purpose is to provide an understanding of men and women in dual-career families at this life stage—the obstacles, the opportunities, the dilemmas, and the myths. It will also provide human service professionals with knowledge of the unique aspects of dual-career marriages at midlife and what makes these marriages work. The material presented is based on pertinent research and clinical reports. Only selective references are included for practical purposes. Studies in this area are for the most part based on self-reports from wives, husbands, or both partners, which were gathered on paper and pencil measures or through interviews.

Dual-Career Families in
Societal Perspective

As Neugarten (1968) noted, men and women at midlife are more likely to look to context than to age as a way of locating themselves. Thus the lives of dual-career couples must be viewed within the context of the times.

More women are in the paid work force than ever before—53% of all women were employed in 1982 as compared with 35% in 1980 (Tausky, 1984). Of all married women with children under the age of 6, 53.5% were employed outside the home in 1985, up from 32% in 1970 and 19% in 1960; the percentage of employed, married women with children between the ages of 6 and 17 was 69.9% in 1985 (U.S. Bureau of Labor Statistics, 1986). Moreover, women now constitute nearly 39% of the professional labor force, compared with 26% in 1960; the large majority of these women are married and most have children. Not all these employed women live in dual-career families but an increasingly significant proportion do. In contrast to women in the larger category of dual-earner families who typically work out of economic necessity, women in careers, similar to men, view what they do outside the home as important to their life goals and sense of self.

Other important changes are accompanying this increase in dual-career and dual-earner families. Foremost among these are the greater psychological expectation that wives will work and the greater significance attributed to work and career as a source of primary identity for women (Giele, 1982). Also noteworthy is the change in sex-role definitions, which Giele (1982, p. 128) described as a crossover—"that both women and men can usefully perform many tasks that once were assigned to the opposite sex." The broadening of sex-role definitions, however, which is increasingly apparent in the public realm, is more a popular notion than an actual reality in the private realm of home and family. "Custom and male prerogative are not easily changed" (Gilbert, 1985, p. 11). Men are reluctant to perform "women's work," although greater changes in this area are being demanded of men.

Unfortunately, these modifications in labor force demographics and sex-role definitions, which reflect profound changes in the lives of individual women and men, have not significantly altered the traditional structure of the workplace. Although there have been some changes in employee benefits (Nieva, 1985; Walker, Rozee-Koker, & Wallston, 1987), innovations such as on-site child care, parental leave (as opposed to maternal leave), and flex-time are still far from the norm. This workplace intransigence, coupled with the "new breed worker" who values work along with other kinds of opportunities for self-expression (Yankelovich, 1979), presents difficulties, and at times insurmountable dilemmas, for spouses in dual-career families.

Moreover, today's dual-career families are living in a changing world economy with a downsizing of such mainstays of the American economy as telecommunications, mining, and auto manufacturing. This kind of corporate shrinkage, which creates the feeling of being at risk for economic failure, coexists with what Yankelovich (1982) called the psychology of affluence—the expectation of acquiring more nice things and the entitlement to greater personal freedoms. In addition, as the 1950s baby boom swells the ranks of adulthood, the sheer numbers of people who enter corporations with a definition of upward mobility as their standard of success are increasing. There is an inevitable crunch as individual career ideals meet the hierarchical structure of corporations, where only 1% ever reach that "top ring" (Bardwick, 1986). It is within this larger social context that dual-career couples at midlife are now considered.

What We Know About Dual-Career Families

Contrary to popular beliefs, two high-power careers in the same family are not representative of dual-career families. Many combinations are possible from two family-oriented spouses to two career-oriented spouses. The distinctive features of the dual-career family are that both spouses are committed to occupational work and to a family life together, and that they support each other's desire to combine roles that traditionally were viewed as incompatible. These goals not only are out of step with traditional views of work and marriage but also are inconsistent with how many women and men, now at midlife, as teenagers and young adults thought they would live their lives.

Satisfactions and Rewards

There are stresses unique to the dual-career family at midlife as well as benefits. The benefits for the female partner are readily identified. They include the opportunity to develop professionally and to establish a sense of self separate from a man and children, economic independence, and greater intellectual companionship and contentment. Because these women have both their careers and family relationships to use in defining their adult lives, the typical midlife transition from active child rearing to the proverbial empty nest is qualitatively different. Rossi (1980), for example, noted that, unlike what was true for women twenty years ago, cohorts of middle-aged women show no elevation of stress compared with men their age. She speculated that this difference is due to the predictability of women's continuing continuous employment. Similarly, Baruch, Barnett, and Rivers (1983) concluded that women, especially those in middle adulthood, are feeling better off because they are able to develop the "doing" side of themselves and to enhance their sense of mastery and independence.

The benefits of dual-career marriage for men at midlife are less dramatic and perhaps less evident than those for women; men have experienced less constraints from their traditional roles and have not asked for change. As one man said, "Sometimes I think, 'My father didn't do it that way, my friends don't do it that way, why should I?' But then I realize that those rules aren't in effect and it turns things from black and white to gray" (Gilbert, 1985, p. 114).

Historically, the successful man provided well economically for his dependent wife and children but had little involvement in the home. Thus one clear benefit for the male partner at midlife is freedom from the burden of total economic responsibility for his spouse and family. Wives' incomes, for example, allow husbands to shift careers, go back to school, or work fewer hours. A second important benefit to the man at midlife is the chance to have been and still be involved with his child or children and to express his human needs to nurture and bond.

As a couple, there is a sense of having struggled through difficult battles about male prerogative and female nurturance and having survived. There is also a sense of pride in each other's having been able to make the necessary changes in a world that was not particularly hospitable to their personal goals.

Finally, their children benefit by being involved with both parents. They also are exposed to less-sex-role stereotypic behavior in the home. One young man said, "The main advantage to me was seeing my mother and, therefore, other women as my equal and learning that I was just as responsible for doing work around the house" (Knaub, 1986, p. 435).

Common Stressors

At the same time, stress is inevitable. Although dual-career couples at midlife are similar in many ways to their cohort of traditional families, the demands of two careers in the same family provide a unique overlay of complexity (Nadelson & Nadelson, 1980), which in turn results in a different life and family pattern or gestalt. The formation of this gestalt comes about because of underlying aspects of career, marriage, family, and personal development (O'Neil, Fishman, & Kinsella-Shaw, 1987), and because of specific conflicts inherent in the dual-career life-style (Gilbert, 1988)..

Implicit in the professional career patterns of our society is the promise of some kind of reward for the hard work required in the early years. The expectation of reward varies among individuals but typically takes the form of status, money, autonomy, or a sense of having made an impact or difference. As aspiring young careerists, each partner in the dual-career couple has a particular definition of success, and a personal or societally imposed timetable that results in a prescription, often implicit, for where each should be when. How closely spouses' expectations approximate reality has a great deal to do with the career mood of the couple at midlife. That two people are possibly reviewing and coming to terms with where they stand with regard to these kinds of career issues, and that they must then deal, as interdependent equals, with the results of their review, gives a distinctive quality to the dual-career couple's gestalt. Midlife reassessment of career is also likely to stimulate self-examination because in our society the meaning of work is so closely tied to the definition of self. Pertinent to this process at midlife are concerns about physical decline, awareness of mortality, a sense of the fewer years remaining rather than those behind, a recognition of personal limitations in contrast to earlier dreams, and existential reflection about the meaning of life (McIlroy, 1984).

Moreover, family and career issues interact in a particular way at midlife. Whatever the decision made with regard to children—to have them early, to have them late, not to have them at all—at midlife the consequences of the decision are often reviewed against the backdrop of career for both partners and of how each combined their occupational and family roles. For women and men in dual-career families with children reaching maturity, there is the prospect of what might have been achieved had it not been for the family demands. For those who delayed childbearing, there is the challenge of dealing with adolescents or even toddlers while still struggling to preserve the career ground that has been gained. For those who decided not to have a child, midlife represents a finalizing of the decision.

It is within this broader context that certain troublesome areas, unique to individuals in dual-career families, are now considered.

Combining Work and Family

"I feel a split loyalty. This is an important time in my career, and teenagers act far more independent than they often really are." (A highly ambitious woman in her mid-forties who is close to her teenaged daughter and who is on an upward trajectory in her career)

How to combine occupational and family roles can be a thorny and continuing source of stress for both women and men in dual-career families at most phases of the life and career cycles. Neither gender has role models for doing so, and neither gets much encouragement or assistance from their professional world to do so. The traditional societal norm has not changed—the family is still expected to accommodate to work demands.

Generally speaking, men and women at midlife may settle the family issue differently. Men's traditional role legitimizes their prioritizing career over family, and ignores or hides possible costs in their relationships with children. For the male spouse, children's departure from the home brings an awareness of what he as a father may have missed. Women's traditional role, in contrast, legitimizes their prioritizing family over career and ignores or hides possible costs to their personal development and fulfillment. Many women, for example, worry that giving too much emphasis to their careers will endanger relationships with their husband and children and, at the same time, also worry that giving too high a priority to their family will jeopardize progress in their careers. For them, the departure of children may bring a relief from role conflict and permission to involve themselves in their careers as much as they would like.

In an in-depth study of men in dual-career families, Gilbert (1985) found three basic ways in which spouses handle this situation. In the first, which she called the *traditional dual-career family*, the responsibility for family work is retained by the woman, who adds the work role to her traditionally held family role. In these families, the man believes that work within the home is women's work. The woman in these families generally accepts and acts upon the same premise. A husband in his early forties, for example, described his wife "as the best of the old and the best of the new. She does everything around the house because she enjoys it." Far more professionally

TABLE 9.1.
Factors That Influence How Couples Combine Work and Family Roles

Personal factors

Personality (e.g., how important is it for a person to have an intimate relationship, to be emotionally close with children, to be number one in her or his field?)

Attitudes and values (e.g., what are a person's beliefs about who should rear a child, who should be breadwinners?)

Interests and abilities (e.g., how committed is a person to his or her work, how satisfying is it to them, how successful are they at what they do?)

Stages in the career and life cycles (e.g., is one spouse peaking career-wise and the other opting for early retirement?)

Concept of self as a man, woman (e.g., does being feminine mean being the primary nurturer and taking the back seat career-wise?)

Relationship factors

Sources of power in the relationship (e.g., who decides on major purchases? Who has the final say?)

Tasks that need to be done to maintain the family (e.g., who does the grocery shopping? Who pays the bills?)

Concepts of equity (e.g., what seems fair and do the spouses agree on this?)

Spouse support (e.g., to what degree can one spouse, particularly the husband, put his or her needs aside and support the other spouse?)

Shared values/expectations (e.g., to what degree do spouses share life goals, views of men and women?)

Environmental factors

The work situation (e.g., how flexible are work hours? Can one work at home if a child is sick?)

Employers' views (e.g., if a parent leaves at 5:00 to watch a child perform, will she or he be viewed as not ambitious enough?)

Societal norms and attitudes (e.g., is quality child care readily available? Do employers offer paid paternity leave?)

Support systems (e.g., are there friends or relatives to help out with parenting? Are colleagues supportive?)

---

ambitious than their wives, the men in these families typically earn significantly more than their wives and see their wives as highly successful in combining their careers with family life.

At the other extreme, and approaching the ideal image of the dual-career family, is the second type—the *role-sharing dual-career family*. In these families both spouses are actively involved in both household duties and parenting. The role-sharing dual-career family is clearly the most egalitarian of the three types and best represents the pattern for which many couples strive. Spouses' salaries tend to be comparable and so is their involvement in child-rearing and household chores. The men in these families are not simply "helping out" and are what some people call "the modern male." There seems to be an implicit assumption that neither spouse is more responsible for home responsibilities: "When one of us gets busy, the other takes over more responsibility."

The third type, called the *participant dual-career family*, may be a transitional one. Here, as in the role-sharing dual-career family, parenting is shared by the spouses. The woman, however, retains primary responsibility for maintaining the home and doing such tasks as cleaning, cooking, and shopping. Thus husbands in these families are involved in the day-to-day rearing of their children; but, for them, housework is another story. "It's totally unfair and unreasonable," said one husband, "but she does everything around the house." Another commented, "Intellectually I think the old values are unnecessary and wrong but in practice she has more responsibility than I do." Typically these men show little motivation to change and seem content to live with a somewhat ambivalent situation.

How do these ways of combining work and family come about and what is the result? It is not surprising that the pattern couples choose or find themselves in depends on a number of factors. Categories helpful in understanding possible influences are *personal factors*, *relationship factors*, and *environmental factors*. These are summarized in Table 9.1 and discussed in more detail later.

Job Placement and
Occupational Mobility

"I wouldn't mind following her for her career. She has as much of a right to work elsewhere as I do, but I feel there are relatively few places that I would consider." (A man in his late forties married to a woman he views as much more ambitious and occupationally committed than himself)

Finding two equally attractive job offers within reasonable geographic proximity in a desired locale is no small feat and indeed may prove to be impossible. In fact, finding a job of choice or moving from a current position may very well be the most difficult issue for members of dual-career families. And there is no ready or easy solution.

Couples often wish to give equal weight to the interests of both partners. The reality, however, is that locations or relocations based on the husband's needs are still the norm. Husbands are usually older than wives and have more years in their profession. Also, men still generally command higher salaries than women. Job offers for either spouse are likely to be more stressful when one or both want to stay in their present situation because of the climate, their children, their family roots, or their positions (Gilbert, 1985).

A man's own sense of entitlement may come to the fore when decisions about relocation must be made. As one man remarked, "It is difficult for the man in the family—me—to put my career at the mercy of my wife's. In the starkest psychological terms, I would be following her and abdicating my role as a man" (Mott, 1985, p. 58). Another man, who left his university position so that his wife could seize a career opportunity with her company, described his mixture of pride and anger. He felt genuine pleasure at her success, "and yet," he said, "I was unable to quell my resentment at her. I felt that because of her, nobody knew who I was."

Whether to Parent

"We haven't decided not to have children but we wonder whether our desire to have children warrants the sacrifices that would be involved." (A couple in their early forties who love their work)

When dual-career couples consider whether to have children, they also face the additional question of who will care for them. Parenting is usually equated with mothering and this typically is still the case even among dual-career families (Gilbert & Rachlin, 1987). Moreover, given current employment benefits and policies, women are better able than men to ask for and receive the accommodations necessary for combining work and family responsibilities (e.g., maternity leaves, flexible schedules). As Congresswoman Pat Schroeder (1985, p. 16) noted, "If the father would want to take off [to stay home with a newborn infant], if he even mentions it, it's like he has lace on his jockey shorts. You don't do that in America."

Perhaps most crucial to stress in this area is the importance of a child, and a close emotional relationship with a child, to each spouse's self-concept and life goals. Should this importance differ markedly between the spouses, the stress associated with a decision of whether to have a child could be considerable, depending on which spouse wanted a child more. It is easier for the man to admit a low desire to be involved in child rearing, and then actually to remain relatively uninvolved, than it is for the woman. The decision to have a child is also made more stressful when one spouse feels she (or he) will have to do all the accommodating. Particularly relevant here is the couple's concept of synchrony or the degree to which they are on-schedule with regard to normative social time lines (Neugarten & Neugarten, 1987) and how they are affected by being off time. If a dual-career couple at midlife changes their decision to be childless and begins a family, they confront not only society's judgments of propriety, but also the effect of parenting on two careers that have likely become more complex with the years.

Finally, the psychological cost involved in deciding to have a child at midlife can be lowered. Typically this is done by limiting the number of children to one, by a commitment on the husband's part to be involved in parenting, and by redefining traditional ideas that a child should be reared full-time by the mother.

Career Cycle and
Career Expectation Differences

"I always knew my wife was far more ambitious than I, but I thought by midlife it would play itself out and we would have more time together." (A 50-year-old man in a role-sharing marriage)

The degree to which career expectations and career reality match for each individual partner, and between partners, is a potential source of stress. If both partners have a high degree of match, or relative comfort with their career accomplishments, there is unlikely to be any issue. If, however, one or both are disappointed, then it is likely that the disappointment will take the form of a midlife sense of regret or, at the very least, career reevaluation, and perhaps even career change. Although one of the potential benefits of the dual-career family is the flexibility for career change, such a change by either spouse, particularly if it involves relocation, can affect the marital relationship as well as the other spouse's career.

Conversely, if one has achieved a personal nadir, he or she may be ready to reap the rewards described earlier, and to let up a little, or to enjoy greater flexibility. Differences in the pace with which each spouse pursues individual definitions of success, however, can create an imbalance, and in some cases what appears to be an impossible gulf. These differences can generate reactions ranging from jealousy and resentment, on one hand, to support, on the other. Differences of this kind are most likely to occur when a woman at midlife enters or returns to a career. A case in point is a physician in his late forties whose wife had devoted herself to parenting, the home, and community volunteer work. He now sees himself as "facing a situation where my wife is totally immersed in her graduate studies and in plans for a demanding career." She is struggling to find a balance between the roles she has always filled and the new roles she is creating. He is struggling with unselfishly supporting her while at the same time being pushed at midlife into changes in personal values and life goals that he did not envision or invite.

What Makes Dual-Career Marriages Work?

"We are both determined to make it work and take the time to make it work. We love each other very much and we are a good fit. Our roles are not real strongly defined. Among some of our friends the husband expected the wife to work all day and come home and serve him coffee. They are now divorced." (A role-sharing couple in their late fifties)

A satisfying, fulfilling dual-career marriage depends on many things. Most important is the spouses' willingness to struggle with the difficulties of integrating career and family despite societal pressures to conform to sex-typed roles and behaviors. The resources needed to weather these difficulties, dilemmas, and stresses effectively are conceptually similar to the factors shown in Table 9.1—personal factors, relationship factors, and environment factors.

Personal Resources

Most crucial among the personal resources for dealing with stressors are material or financial assets, education, physical health, and sociopsychological characteristics. Sociopsychological resources are especially important in dual-career couples, particularly one's personality and one's beliefs and attitudes about love, work, and how men and women should live their lives. For example, when asked, "Why is your marriage making it?," the most frequently noted reasons are personalities and values (Gilbert, 1985). Men and women in successful dual-career families typically hold relatively liberal attitudes about sex roles, are supportive of their spouses' career efforts, and value strengths in their spouses. When it comes to coping, strategies that reflect redefinition, compromise, realistic expectation, and commitment are most effective. As one couple noted, "Both of us are accommodating people. If an expectation is not met, that is not cause for walking out." Coping strategies are important for both short-term (e.g., whether to take a different job) and ongoing conflicts (e.g., providing quality parenting for a child).

Three general types of coping strategies can be identified in examining research on the various stress and coping models (e.g., Elman & Gilbert, 1984; Gilbert, 1988; Gilbert & Holahan, 1982; Lazarus & Launier, 1978):

(1)   strategies that focus on understanding of the problem,
(2)   strategies that serve to manage the stress and are not directed to the problem itself, and
(3)   strategies that require an action that would alter or change the source of stress.

Cognitive restructuring, an example of a type 1 strategy, requires changes in attitudes, which in turn change the meaning the conflict situation has for the individual involved. If a person used this strategy in dealing with conflicts between professional and parental roles, he or she might think, "It could be a lot worse" or "This is a natural feeling/reaction for working parents."

A common strategy illustrative of type 2 is *increased role behavior*. Individuals who use this strategy try to meet all existing demands; they work more efficiently and plan their time more carefully with the idea of fitting everything in and "doing it all." People who mainly use this strategy are what we call "superwomen" or "supermen."

Role redefinition, in contrast, involves attempts to change the source of the stress and is an example of a type 3 strategy. This strategy is used when an individual arranges work schedules with an employer to allow time for certain parenting responsibilities, negotiates schedules with a spouse, or hires a part-time bookkeeper for family affairs. Other examples involve changes in definitions of life roles. For example, a person may view family or career as coming first, alter career or parenting aspirations temporarily, or change personal standards for home or work-related activities.

Typically, type 1 and type 2 strategies (e.g., cognitive restructuring and increased role behavior) are used more than type 3 strategies in the early stages of career and family (e.g., Elman & Gilbert, 1984; Gilbert & Holahan, 1982). In contrast, type 3 strategies, which require change, are more likely to be used at middle or later stages because these individuals often feel more established and secure as parent, spouse, and employee. How effective a particular strategy is also depends on other resources available at the time. Couples who have their first child when both partners have established careers, for example, are likely to feel less stress than do couples who have their first child when both partners are in the initial stages of demanding careers, regardless of which strategy they use.

Family Resources

The most essential family resource is spouse support—support by the husband for the wife's occupational work and support by the wife for the husband's involvement in parenting and housework. Stress is at a minimum when the husband has positive attitudes toward the wife's career and involves himself in housework and parenting. The husband is more involved in family work when the wife contributes more financially, and greater meaning and importance are attributed to her work by the family. Perhaps—and it would not be surprising—the smaller the difference between the husband's and the wife's income, the greater his involvement in the family and home (Barnett, 1983).

Even at midlife, spouses in a dual-career marriage may struggle with their own sex-role socialization. For example, men committed to role sharing may find it embarrassing to admit that their wives earn more of the family income than they do; their spouses, in contrast, may feel reluctant to put their career needs ahead of their husbands. Functioning as a dual-career couple may at times also require behaving in ways that counter societal expectations and risk peer disapproval. A man who "follows his wife," for example, might find that professional colleagues and friends cannot understand why he would risk his career for hers.

Finally, the sense of fairness or equity about the balance of family and occupational roles achieved by the spouses over time is crucial. Contrary to popular notions, equality of power is not the issue, but rather whether each partner, when considering the gestalt of their life together, feels fairness has prevailed.

Societal Resources

This is the category of resources over which individuals have the least control. It is also the resource that is most limited for dual-career couples. At the present time, spouses in dual-career families must cope individually with the stressors in their life-style. They negotiate stress-reducing changes and strategies on their own and in a "create as one goes" context. The long-term acceptance of the dual-career family as a feasible option for men and women, however, requires support from society as a whole. Flexible work hours, provision for adequate child care, rethinking of transfer and relocation policies by employers, and increased career opportunities for women are all social policy innovations that would make it significantly easier for dual-career families to thrive.

A case in point is conceptions of child care. Because spouses in dual-career families typically have children at a later age than their cohort groups, midlife often finds them with adolescent children. As one 45-year old mother of a 12- and 14-year-old noted, "I thought it would get easier as they got older. Instead, since they are in no one's care much of the time, I feel a greater pressure to be home and available—just in case." Typically society views child care as necessary for young children and freedom from child care is mistakenly anticipated as a midlife benefit. When children are school age, the responsibility for child care implicitly rests with the school and no explicit social policy seems necessary. At the same time, folk wisdom and daily reports from parents attest to the difficulties of the teenage years. If children in their teens show little interest in school, get involved in drugs, or feel little sense of direction, parents are likely to blame themselves, and perhaps their chosen life-style. Clearly this is a dilemma for parents in dual-career families and one for which social policy must provide greater assistance and support.

Implications for Practitioners

Although it is difficult to distill and summarize the factors important in the lives of midlife dual-career couples, an awareness of both the potential stresses and the potential satisfactions for men, for women, for couples, and for families can provide a relevant perspective for helping professionals. Within that perspective, an examination of the personal, relational, and environmental factors that influence how work and family are combined and that interact with career factors and parenting decisions provides a framework for identifying personal and family resources.

Dual-career couples at midlife are "myth-defying" both in their complexity and in their challenge to slowly changing societal norms. Attention to both the environmental pressures and the presence or absence of specific resources is an important part of helping each spouse deal with the personal role and career expectations that are woven into the gestalt they hold as a couple. An informed and shared identification of coping strategies is an essential focus if both individual and couple problem-solving capacities are to be enhanced.

References

Bardwick, J. (1986). *The plateauing trap*. New York: American Management Association.
Barnett, R. (1983, August). *Determinants of father participation in child care*. Paper presented at the annual meeting of the American Psychological Association, Anaheim, CA.
Baruch, G., Barnett, R., & Rivers, C. (1983). *Lifeprints: New patterns of love and work for today's women*. New York: McGraw-Hill.
Bernard, J. (1975). *Women, wives, and mothers*. Chicago, IL: Aldine.

Elman, M., & Gilbert, L. A. (1984). Coping strategies for role conflict in married professional women with children. *Family Relations: Journal of Applied Family and Child Studies, 33,* 317-327.

Giele, J. Z. (1982). Women's work and family roles. In J. Z. Giele (Ed.), *Women in the middle years* (pp. 115-150). New York: John Wiley.

Gilbert, L. A. (1985). *Men in dual-career families: Current realities and future prospects.* Hillsdale, NJ: Lawrence Erlbaum.

Gilbert, L. A., (1988). *Sharing it all: The rewards and struggles of two career families.* New York: Plenum.

Gilbert, L. A., & Holahan, C. K. (1982). Conflicts between student/professional, parental, and self-development roles: A comparison of high and low effective copers. *Human Relations, 35,* 635-648.

Gilbert, L. A., & Rachlin, Y. (1987). Mental health and psychological functioning of dual-career families. *The Counseling Psychologist, 15,* 7-49.

Knaub, P. K. (1986). Growing up in a dual-career family. *Family Relations: Journal of Applied Family and Child Studies, 35,* 431-437.

Lazarus, R. S., & Launier, R. (1978). Stress-related transactions between person and environment. In L. A. Pervin & M. Lewis (Eds.), *Perspectives in interactional psychology* (pp. 287-327). New York: Plenum.

McIlroy, J. H. (1984). Midlife in the 1980's: Philosophy, economy, and psychology. *Personnel and Guidance Journal, 62,* 623-627.

Mott, G. (1985, April 14). Following a wife's move. *New York Times Magazine,* p. 58.

Nadelson, C. C., & Nadelson, T. (1980). Dual-career marriages: Benefits and costs. In F. Pepiton-Rockwell, (Ed.), *Dual-career couples* (pp. 91-110). Beverly Hills, CA: Sage.

Neugarten, B. L. (1968). The awareness of middle age. In B. L. Neugarten (Ed.), *Middle age and aging* (pp. 93-98). Chicago: University of Chicago Press.

Neugarten, B. L., & Neugarten, D. A. (1987). The meanings of age. *Psychology Today, 21,* 29-33.

Nieva, Y. F. (1985). Work and family linkages. In L. Larwood, A. Stromberg, & B. A. Gutek (Eds.), *Women and work* (pp. 165-190). Beverly Hills, CA: Sage.

O'Neil, J. M., Fishman, D. M., & Kinsella-Shaw, M. (1987). Dual-career couples' career transitions and normative dilemmas: A preliminary assessment model. *The Counseling Psychologist, 15,* 50-96.

Rapoport, R., & Rapoport, R. N. (1969). The dual-career family. *Human Relations, 22,* 3-30.

Rossi, A. S. (1980). Life-span theories and women's lives. *Signs: Journal of Women in Culture and Society, 6,* 4-32.

Schroeder, P. (1985, December 29). Should leaves for new parents be mandatory? *New York Times,* p. 16E.

Tausky, C. (1984). *Work and society.* Itasca, IL: F. E. Peacock.

U.S. Bureau of Labor Statistics. (1986). *Labor force statistics derived from the current population survey: A databook.* Washington, DC: Government Printing Office.

Walker, L. S., Rozee-Koker, P., & Wallston, B. S. (1987). Social policy and the dual-career family. *The Counseling Psychologist, 15,* 97-121.

Yankelovich, D. (1979). Work values and the new breed. In C. Kerr & J. M. Rosow (Eds.), *Work in America* (pp. 3-26). New York: Van Nostrand Reinhold.

Yankelovich, D. (1982). *New rules.* New York: Bantam.

10

Myths of Midlife Intergenerational Relationships

Lillian E. Troll

Although there may not be more myths about midlife than about other times of life, or more about intergenerational relationships at midlife than at other times of life, it certainly is easy to come up with a dozen or more without thinking hard. These are of two kinds: those about what exists and those about what is good or right—what should exist. These two kinds are often hard to separate because we see what we expect to see. If we believe it is bad for adults to be close to their parents, for example, we see what we label pathology wherever we see them close. In fact, some clinicians probably decide, when they see family problems, that the generations must be too close. They rarely inquire why the parents and children are so much in the picture. Is it because there are problems? Are they present to help rather than because they are causing the problems?

A basic difficulty in the study of midlife is its varying definition. Most assume a chronological age base, but even if they do, some define midlife as beginning at 35 (or even 30) years old and others as beginning at 50 (or even 55). Similarly, the top end can vary from 50 to 65. I prefer a contextual definition, related to family situation. Because we are considering intergenerational relationships here, it seems strategic to consider midlife people as those whose children have grown up—"empty-nesters" if you will—or, if they do not have children, those whose parents are old.

As shown in Table 10.1, at least 15 general myths exist about midlife parent-child relations, although these overlap and some of them have a number of submyths. There is a cluster of beliefs around the idea of a "generation gap," for instance, which says that, from adolescence on, adults move as far apart from each other as they can, prefer not to communicate or help each other, are indifferent to each other's welfare, and move off into different life-styles. Sometimes associated with this cluster is the idea of

TABLE 10.1.
Some Midlife Intergenerational Myths

1. Midlife men and women live as far apart from their children and their parents as they can.
2. Midlife men and women rarely visit or receive visits from their adult children or their parents.
3. Midlife men and women rarely phone (or get phone calls) or write (or receive letters) from their adult children or their parents.
4. Midlife men and women do not exchange help with either their adult children or their parents.
5. Midlife men and women do not feel emotionally close to either their adult children or their parents.
6. Midlife men and women are distraught when their children grow up and leave their homes.
7. Midlife men and women are narcissistic, dwelling only on their own needs and wants and unconcerned about those of their adult children or their parents.
8. Midlife men and women abandon their parents when they get old and sick.
9. Midlife parents and their adult children are more likely to stay in touch and feel close if they share values and personality.
10. The family is a dying institution.
11. Grandparents lose their grandchildren if their children divorce.
12. Grandparents are avid for close and frequent contact with their grandchildren.
13. Grandparents feel they know how to raise their grandchildren better than their children are doing and are eager to interfere.
14. Extensive extended family contact is deleterious to mental health.
15. Adults should not live with relatives other than their young children and spouses.

"narcissism"; that adults in our society think primarily of their own comfort and pleasure and are insensitive to the needs of others, particularly their parents. Also associated is the concept that only nuclear families are important, that once children have been reared past adolescence, family relations should terminate. There are even those who insist that the family is dying, citing employment of mothers, high divorce rates, and child-care facilities as evidence. Associated with divorce is the myth that grandparents lose contact with grandchildren in the process. Other grandparent myths are that they are feeble old parties who feel deprived if they do not have frequent contact with the young.

Ironically, there are some opposing myths in this same domain. One is that close contact between adult parents and their children is bad, that generations should be separated for good mental health and good marital and family functioning. Related to this is the view that caring for aging parents is an unmitigated and destructive burden. There are a few other myths. One is that only parents and children who are alike stay in touch. Another is that the "empty nest" spells disaster for mothers, and sometimes fathers. Finally, there is perhaps the most dangerous myth of all: that of universality, that we are all affected the same way by what are often called "major life events" or, alternatively, that we change at specified chronological ages.

Kinds of Relationships

Before we review research findings, we should note that there is more than one kind of intergenerational relationship in middle age. First, middle-aged people can be parents of young adults. (If they became parents late they are, from the perspective of this topic, not middle-aged until their children become young adults.) Second, middle-aged people can also be the children of aging parents. And, third, they can be grandparents (in some cases even grandchildren). It is not unusual for them to be great grandparents. Further, if we subdivide by gender—which we must for both structural and functional reasons—we have a proliferation of kinds of generational relationships in midlife. Mother-daughter relationships are different from mother-son and from father-daughter and father-son. Daughters of aging parents are different from sons of aging parents; the difference even depends on whether the aging parent is a father or a mother. And grandmothers are different from grandfathers. There are all kinds of affinal relationships, then, which should not be ignored. Midlife men and women have stronger or weaker links but certainly connections with sons-in-law and daughters-in-law, fathers-in-law and mothers-in-law, to mention the most obvious, although we should not ignore the parents-in-law and siblings-in-law of children when they marry. We have a lot more research data about some dyads than about others. We know most about the mother-daughter dyad. Finally, there are significant and important ethnic and social class and perhaps even regional variations in all these relationships. Above all, let us not forget individual differences.

What can we say, then, about what adult parent-child relationships are really like in the latter part of the twentieth century in North America? And what do we know about the consequences, or at least the concomitants, of these relationships? What is good and what is bad?

Generation Gap?

The term *generation gap* became popular during the 1960s. It was meant to describe and explain the youth movement of that era. Late adolescents and young adults were presumed to have nothing in common with their parents and other of society's elders (in fact, to have no use for them at all), and to be in the process of building a new human society. Margaret Mead (1970) was one of the exponents of this cataclysmic point of view; she attributed what she perceived to be the sharp cleavage between generations to the atom bomb, which provided the new generation with an experience of the world and of life so different from that of their parents that there could be no contact of minds.

Bengtson and Kuypers (1971) referred to three positions with regard to generation gaps: those who, like Margaret Mead, believe in a "great gap," those who take the opposite position of "nothing really new," and those in the middle who perceive "selective continuity." A review of existing research that actually compares the ideas and behaviors of young adults with those of their own parents (Troll & Bengtson, 1979, 1982) affirmed the validity of the middle position, "selective continuity"—similarity in some characteristics more than in others, as will be noted below.

What Exists?

Research findings about midlife intergenerational relationships deal with amount of contact, amount of help, amount of influence, and kinds of feelings or quality of relationships.

Contact

The myth that parents and their adult children are essentially estranged from each other in today's Western society is so widespread and persistent that it is difficult to convince the general public that it is untrue. Yet survey after survey finds that most adult children and their parents keep in close touch, live not too far from each other, and visit frequently. Or, if they live too far away for easy visiting, they talk on the telephone and aim for long visits at less frequent intervals. Not many live together. The norm of independence is so strong that both generations try to maintain separate households and only share a home in cases of economic necessity or extreme physical disability. The majority of midlife men live with a wife. If they lose one wife, they remarry. Midlife women who lose a husband, given the realities of age and sex demography, find chances of remarriage bleak. Most prefer to live in their own homes, albeit near at least one child (Shanas, 1979; Troll, Miller, & Atchley, 1979). Less than 10% of parents over the age of 65 live with their middle-aged children, although almost one-quarter of Americans between 18 and 25 years of age live with their middle-aged parents, particularly those young adults who are not married (Glick, 1975). These figures fluctuate with economic conditions. When times are good, more adults of all ages move into their own homes. When times are bad, families double and triple up. When people over 65 live with a child, that child is likely to be a daughter rather than a son, an unmarried daughter rather than a married one, and it is more often the parent who is the "head of household" than the child. Finally, these multigeneration households are more likely to be two-generation than three-generation. Only 8% have grandchildren and grandparents living together.

The "launching" of children is considered a major event of the middle years, particularly for women. It was once thought to lead to misery and distress. While some research (Bart, 1978) shows an association between midlife women's depression and the "empty nest," this seems to be primarily true for those women who "put all their eggs in one basket," a minority of women today. Many have said that they could hardly wait for their children to leave. In one study of rural Pennsylvania families, both mothers and fathers reported a mixture of loss and gain in launching their children (Barber, 1978). The mothers tended to be more extreme, some reporting more loss than did the men and some reporting more gain. The gain was an increased sense of personal freedom and relief from parental responsibilities. Where negative experiences occurred, loss of the children in the home was often exacerbated by concurrent biological changes (menopause for women) and career changes (reported more by men). Some men said that they were faced with the independence of their children just when they were ready to get close to them. These rural families, however, may not be typical. A national study (Borland, 1979) found no evidence for the empty nest being a crisis or even a time of loss. Other research (Hagestad & Snow, 1977) found that most of the parents they interviewed saw this event as a distinct gain. They gained freedom, and they also gained a new set of resource people: their children. This was true more for mothers and daughters than for other family dyads. On the other hand, many West Coast fathers (Nydegger & Mitteness, 1979, 1982) also talked about the gain of friendship with their grown children. These men described transformations of relationships with their grown children over time. First, they dropped their authority, then providing protection, and, last, counseling. Friendship was what remained.

To those who regret the disappearance of the "golden age" of the extended family, a time when all generations and perhaps even all siblings were presumed to reside cozily together in the prairie shack, a historian (Smith, 1979) demonstrated that the present percentage of three-generation households is not lower than in the 1900s but, in fact, higher. Partly because far fewer people lived to be old then, the number of three-generation households was more like 3% of all households rather than 8% (Dahlin, 1980). And, most likely, in those complex households, the middle generation then, as now, was not the pivot of the home, torn between obligation to children and to parents, but subordinate to their parents. Cross-cultural and historical data consistently find that economic systems are what really determine household composition (Beck & Beck, 1984; Sweetser, 1984). Generations stay together when they are all involved in the family farm, father and son working side by side and sharing in the profit or loss. Generations spread out more in urban societies when each has an opportunity to follow independent jobs or careers. The same is true if there is land or substantial property to hand down.

A survey of Americans (Harris & Associates, 1975) found that 87% of those between 18 and 64 had seen their children and 48% had seen their parents within the past day. Contact increases when there is trouble, either the children's trouble or the parents'. Illness rallies family members to each other, although some of this rallying may be temporary. When a crisis is over, families that are not usually persistent visitors return to their previous level of contact. For example, studies of the effect on family visiting of the birth of a baby (Belsky & Rovine, 1984) or of the death of a spouse (Morgan, 1984) show stability of interaction over time, and little variation with age (Leigh, 1982). Parents and children who visit a lot have always visited a lot and those who seldom see each other have almost always been distant. Morgan found that knowing how much contact parents and their adult children had in 1969 was the best predictor of contact six years later, even though many of the older generation had become widowed during that time.

Help

If a spouse is not available for caregiving in times of illness, a child or parent generally comes to the rescue (Troll, 1986). Help is usually a mutual process (Hill, Foote, Aldous, Carlson, & MacDonald, 1970). The grandparent generation gives services and money to their children (Cheal, 1983), and the middle generation gives emotional support, household help, and care during illness to both parents and children, more to children than parents. These separate donations can be counted as reciprocal over the lifetime, flowing more toward younger generations at first and shifting toward older generations as circumstances change. For every disabled person in a nursing home, two or more equally disabled are cared for by their families (U.S. Comptroller-General, 1977). Brody (1985) spoke of "women in the middle," burdened with the care of their aging parents at the same time that they are concerned with their young-adult children, with the health of their husbands, and with their own often recently resumed career or job—and yet these "women in the middle" do not usually consider abandoning anybody. They just cut back more on their own private time, often past the point where they can no longer manage.

Influence

A study of 148 Chicago-area families (Hagestad, 1985b) found that both men and women in the middle generation admitted that they attempted to influence both their young-adult children and their older parents. The majority said that more of their influencing went down to their children than up to their parents, although one-third said their attempts up and down were equal. Men concentrated more on the younger generation whereas women were more balanced by generation, but influencing their mothers more than their fathers. Parents were given practical advice such as where to live, how to manage their home, and uses of time and money. For their children, they were more likely to try to shape behavior and outlook on education, work, money, dress, and grooming. Both the young-adult children and the aging parents admitted that they also tried to influence the other generations. Offspring of both generations felt that their parents tried to influence them more than their children did. At the same time, they reported more attempts to influence their parents than their parents perceived. The only area of influence that crossed all generations was health: All generations tried to keep the others healthy by trying to get them to watch their diet, stop smoking, see the doctor, and take their medicine. What the youngest generation did for their parents—and also their grandparents—was to "keep them up with the times"; that is, keep them abreast of social issues and the uses of free time.

Similarity

The major component of the "generation gap" myth is that each generation today has different values, life-styles, and personalities from those before and after. To an important extent, it is true that each birth cohort—those born at the same time of history and thus sharing the same world in their growing up years, a different world from their parents and children—sees and experiences the world uniquely. This is what the German sociologist, Mannheim (1952), meant when he spoke of the "non-contemporaneity of the contemporaneous." Elder's (1974) study of the cohort that grew up during the 1930s economic depression, *Children of the Great*

Depression, showed the lasting influence in their future lives of this particular historical context. Yet, somehow, this gap seems to be more meaningful for studying generations in society than generations in the family. An analysis of the perceptions of generational difference of high school seniors and parents of high school seniors (Thurnher, Spence, & Lowenthal, 1974) showed a theme of continuity from parent to child on the part of both generations. The middle-aged men and women said of their parents: "I doubt my goals will be any different. . . . When they were my age they thought the same, only customs were a little different" (p. 314), and the comments of the high school seniors about their parents were remarkably similar. The middle generation, however, perceived more differences between their own goals and those of their teenage children. It seems easier to accept the values of one's parents as being much like one's own than to see the same kind of continuity in one's children, at least when the children are teenagers trying to express their individuality. When these teenagers become adults and find themselves in situations comparable to those of their parents, they move close to their parents' values. The most recent study of Middletown families (Caplow, Bahr, Chadwick, Hill, & Williamson, 1982) found parallel continuities, attributable in part to the essential stability in life conditions over the past 50 years. There was probably more difference between today's very old people and their immigrant parents who came from rural, preindustrial origins than there is between midlife Americans today and their parents and children.

A review of all the studies that actually looked at the values of both parents and their own children instead of the perceptions of each other's values (Troll & Bengtson, 1979, 1982) reinforces not only the theme of "selective continuity" but what Bengtson and Kuypers (1971) called the "developmental (or generational) stake." This stake refers to the tendency of the parental generation to exaggerate similarities with its offspring in order to feel that it has instilled parental values; whereas the offspring generation exaggerates differences in order to emphasize its distinctiveness and separate identity from parents. During the post-World War II era, when most of this research was done, similarity between youth and their parents was most evident in religious and political areas, and least in sex roles, life-style, and work orientation. Transmission of similarity is enhanced when social and historical forces encourage particular behaviors or values and reduced where social forces discourage them. This can be seen for particular characteristics that become "keynotes" of a new rising generation—like the rock music, long hair, and pot smoking of the youth of the 1960s—where there is more evident discontinuity between youth and their midlife parents than in more "basic" values like political and religious beliefs (Troll, 1972). Friends and peers may serve as a moderating influence on family transmission in some areas, such as recreation, sexual behavior, or use of drugs. Parents and children tend to be more like each other than like their age mates, however, in idealism/materialism, achievement orientation, and political orientation. In general, peer and parent influences appear complementary rather than oppositional. Children and adolescents seem to choose friends from families much like their own. Curiously, qualitative aspects of family relationships, such as "closeness," do not seem to affect transmission. Adults and parents who feel closer to each other or are fond of each other are not likely to share values any more than those who feel more distant or dislike each other.

In support of the "generational stake" hypothesis, middle-aged parents consistently overestimated the degree of similarity between themselves and their children, whereas their children overestimated the degree of difference. It is presumed that the parents are motivated by a desire to see their work of socialization having a lasting effect, that their children will "carry the torch" so to speak, whereas their children are motivated by a desire to show that they are unique unto themselves and not duplicates of their parents.

Feelings

The final submyth of the "generation gap" is that parents and their children seek to estrange themselves from each other and are in basic conflict with each other. Many developmental psychologists who focus primarily on the very early years of life speak of the gradual severing of the bonds of attachment as children mature. Yet the data reported above of living close, of communicating frequently, and of mutual helping belie these assumptions (see review in Troll, 1986). Adult parents and children, on the whole, seem to feel close to each other, even though, following the "generational stake" again, parents are more likely to report feeling close than are their children. Studies of college students, even those dedicated to changing the world (Troll, Neugarten, & Kraines, 1969), may show a generation gap in society as a whole, but rarely in their own families.

The importance of maintaining relationships is attested to by the maneuvers family members use in handling conflicts. They tend to restrict their fights to "trivial" matters (Troll, 1972) rather than serious ones, to hair length rather than decisions for the future. Hagestad (1981) used the term "demilitarized zone" to describe the way families try to avoid discussing sensitive issues that would endanger ongoing relationships. When we speak of attachment between family members, incidentally, we do not mean positive affect alone because where there is strong feeling, as there usually is between parents and children, that feeling encompasses both love and hate, both positive and negative feelings. These intense emotions, on the part of both parents and their adult children, can continue to swing back and forth, particularly if grown children continue to live at home. As Hess and Waring (1978, p. 251) concluded, "Although years of separate residence and greater self-knowledge may erase some of the minor difficulties and blunt the edge of some of the major ones, struggles for control, patterns of blaming, disappointments about achievement and such, may linger." Times of crisis can reawaken conflict. One might say there is a continual push and pull of attachments throughout life. Most middle-aged parents admit they prefer "intimacy at a distance"; their feelings of closeness carry with them a need for some separateness.

In one study (Lowenthal, Thurnher, & Chiriboga, 1975), most middle-aged parents felt good about their children. About half had only positive things to say about them and only 10% said anything negative. Yet similar parents in another study (Parent, 1978) put their children high on the list of sources of stress in their lives. There is no reason to believe that both feelings cannot be there. In fact, we do not tend to get upset about people we do not feel are important to us. Research on divorce shows that parents of divorcing couples are far from disinterested and uninvolved. Parents of divorcing daughters are more likely to be involved but parents of divorcing sons are not exempted, as will be discussed later.

Narcissism

A common myth in the realm of aging is that middle-aged men and women, because they are selfish and narcissistic, abandon their aging parents. These midlife offspring are usually compared unfavorably with those of earlier times or other cultures by columnists and politicians, who say that we are worse than the Eskimos, who are reputed to put their aged out on the ice to die—at least the Eskimos are supposed to be conserving scarce resources while we have plenty. There is, incidentally, little evidence that the Eskimos actually do this just as there is little evidence that Asians, who shame us by honoring their old, do so unless these old have money and power (Keith, 1985). Also, in spite of the fact that no more than 5% of people over 65 reside in nursing homes or other such institutions, and that those who do tend to be the neediest—older women whose husbands have died or who have never married, and the childless—we still hear about "dumping" of parents. About 80% of old people who need care get it from their families

(U.S. Comptroller-General, 1977). As Shanas (1980) noted, for every sick old person in an extended care facility, there are two others being cared for at home. Some are being cared for by a spouse—these are usually men, who are more likely to be married—but when a spouse is not available, the caretakers are children, usually daughters caring for women. Further, most families that find it necessary to place an aged parent in a nursing home find it to be a difficult, emotion-filled decision (Archbold, 1982).

Vast sex differences exist. Women tend to live longer than men. Men tend to marry younger women. Therefore, old men are much more likely to have a wife to take care of them than old women are to have a husband. If a first wife dies, men find many younger women are ready to fill in. If a first husband dies, women remain widows.

The persistence of this myth of abandonment in the face of evidence (Nydegger, 1983; Shanas, 1979) led Brody (1985) to speculate that even though daughters often exceed the limits of endurance to care for their aging mothers, they never feel that they can repay the care their mothers gave them in their childhood. Another aspect of this myth of narcissism and abandonment—maybe another myth—is the belief that parents want to live with their adult children. This myth persists in spite of the fact that almost all surveys indicate that most older Americans prefer to live apart from their children and do so if at all possible—if they have enough money and can manage to take care of themselves (see Troll, 1986). In fact, joint households may be considered an index of poverty and feeble health. Most midlife people, at least midlife women, are unjustly accused of neglecting and even abusing their older parents. If anything, the truth is the other way around. Studies of nursing home admissions have shown that it would usually have been better for the health and well-being of both children and parents if help had been sought sooner (Troll, Miller, & Atchley, 1979).

Nuclear Family

It is widely believed that the prevailing "normal" American family is a self-contained household composed of an employed husband, his wife who is not employed outside the home, and one or more young children. Although such a "normal" family is judged by most Americans to be right and good, it definitely does not describe what exists. Many current households are headed by employed single women and many more are surrounded by households of kin. Over 20 years ago, Litwak (1960a, 1960b) showed that there are so many connections among related nuclear family households that we should use the phrase "modified extended families." This is particularly true of post-child-rearing units, and particularly when families are studied over time. There may well be a period of years when adult children scatter in pursuit of careers and independence—particularly in the middle class (Adams, 1968)—but later many of these separated family pieces come together again, either through relocations of the younger generation or of the older after retirement.

Allied to the nuclear family theme is that of the "death of the family," described earlier. This is based upon a variety of indices: the proliferation of independent households, the employment of women outside the home, the high divorce rate, the smaller number of children per couple, the later age at marriage and birth of first child, and a value shift from familism to self-realization. Although many of these shifts have occurred, at least temporarily, they do not necessarily connote a disappearance of family ties, concerns, or even obligations. It is not often easy for women who are raising children also to earn a living, but there is little indication that such women are less concerned about their children, husband, or parents than the idealized women of the past who stayed home. At a later chronological age, it is not easy for women to earn a living, tend to their husband, help out their children who are parenting young children, and take care of their aging parents, but there is similarly no indication that they are not dedicated to helping all these family members and keeping their families together.

Grandparents

The fact that a majority of North Americans now become grandparents in middle age and have no young children of their own still at home (except for the growing number of men in their second marriages) has contributed to changing the image of grandparents from that of an ample lap in a rocking chair to a companion in fun and an active family member. Troll (1983) said that we should call grandparents "family watchdogs" because they often play an important part in family dynamics; however, they are customarily less central to those dynamics than parents, their behaviors are much more diverse than those of parents, and they seem to like it that way. Contrary to myths that portray grandparents as interfering and clutching, most prefer to be monitors on the sidelines, ready to jump into action if needed when something goes wrong, but hoping that nothing goes wrong and they can "play with their own friends" or pursue their own careers. Few grandparents wish to return to parenting with their grandchildren (Bengtson & Robertson, 1985). Grandmothers are now as likely to be employed as grandfathers. Evidence from studies of grandparents' role in divorce and teenage parenting has shown their beneficial influence in these situations, but their morale is consistently higher when they see more of their friends than their children and grandchildren (Troll, 1986). Because exclusive interactions with family would often stem from their need to help with problems, such findings are not surprising.

On the whole, how attached grandparents and their grandchildren are to each other depends on how the parents feel about their parents (Bengtson & Robertson, 1985; Troll, 1986). Those who are close to them and live near them encourage direct and meaningful personal interactions (Gilford & Black, 1972). Consistent with sex differences in most family relationships, grandmothers are more important in family interactions than grandfathers, with the possible exception of the paternal grandfather/grandson dyad (Hagestad, 1985b), although one videotaped study (Tinsley & Parke, 1984) showed all four grandparents equally involved with infants. Younger grandparents are more active than older grandparents, particularly with younger grandchildren.

Major Life Events

It is not clear how much major life events like marriage, starting work, birth of first child, empty nest, widowhood, or retirement affect adult inter-generational relations. Marriage of a daughter may decrease the amount of involvement with her mother (Haller, 1982; Walker & Thompson, 1983), at least temporarily, although the evidence is conflicting (Troll, 1986). There is no research on this topic for other parent-child dyads. The birth of the first child probably has more effect on the couple relationship than on the relationship between members of the couple and their parents. Fischer (1981) noted that new mothers moved closer to their own mothers at this time, and further from their mothers-in-law, and Baruch and Barnett (1983) and Bengtson and Black (1973) also found that a new baby enhanced mother-daughter relations. On the other hand, as noted above, both Walker and Thompson (1983) and Haller (1982) found the opposite. Widowhood in the older generation may decrease mother-son attachment (Adams, 1968); however, the marital status of mothers does not seem to be related to mother-daughter relations. For most parents and children, the "empty nest" or formal moving out of the children from the parental household is not as drastic an event as generally depicted. It is more gradual and less complete than supposed.

Myths and Our Value System

The proliferation of myths in this area points to strong beliefs about what is good, and what ought to be, in family relations. In general, prevailing beliefs are that good relations among adult parents and children should be distant, autonomous, and formal. The important ties should be between husband and wife and between actively child-rearing parents and their offspring, although these latter should also gradually weaken from infancy on so that they can form appropriate "peer relationships." Commitment to familism values is deemed old-fashioned and even harmful because it is likely to get in the way of individual fulfillment.

Three basic values or norms are in conflict here. The first is that of independence; it is good for all individuals to stand on their own two feet and not lean on others. The second is that of self-realization; each person should try to reach his or her highest potential. The third is that of filial obligation; one should not let one's relatives, especially one's parents and children, suffer without trying to help.

We in Western society believe strongly that adults should be independent. Adulthood begins, by definition, when individuals move out of their parent's homes, support themselves, and rely on themselves for decisions about love and work. This is not true in all human societies, but it is the theme song of ours. Adult children who live close to their parents, not to mention with them, apologize to interviewers and confess their shame and guilt. Middle-aged parents whose children live near them or with them apologize just as much or maybe even more; somehow they must not have brought them up right. Aging parents who need to rely upon their children for help may have even stronger feelings of failure; many have been known to move to nursing homes prematurely to keep from burdening their children. We also have a norm of filial obligation, not to mention parental obligation or general family obligation, but this secondary norm is often canceled out by the high value we place on independence and our abhorrence of dependence. Part of our national fear of growing old is associated with the fear of needing to be dependent on others for most of our daily activities. To some extent it does not matter so much whether we need to depend on those we love or on strangers, because the state of dependency is itself so dreadful. We celebrate the progressing independence of our children as they learn to walk so they do not have to be carried, to feed themselves, to dress themselves, to "stand on their own two feet."

Context of Family as a Whole

Up until now, we have focused upon dyadic relationships: those between a particular parent and a particular child. We have largely ignored the other members. More important, we have ignored the family as an interactional system. In 1959, Hess and Handel published *Family Worlds*, an examination of family themes and family cultures in child-rearing family units. As Troll (1980) noted, these ideas about family themes, which vary from family to family, are most useful in understanding intergenerational relations and intergenerational transmission. Why are some characteristics transmitted in certain families and other characteristics in other families? Why are youths in some families more susceptible to emergent "generation keynote themes" like those celebrated in the 1960s—pot smoking and rock music (Bengtson & Troll, 1978; Troll & Bengtson, 1979, 1982)—whereas youth in other families do not get caught up in them?

Hess and Handel (1959, p. 1) defined the family as a bounded universe whose members

> inhabit a world of their own making, a community of feeling and fantasy, action and precept. . . . In their mutual interaction, the family members develop more or less adequate understanding of one another, collaborating in the effort to establish consensus and to negotiate uncertainty. . . . Separateness and connectedness are the underlying conditions of a family's life.

As stated earlier, one of the most dangerous myths about intergenerational relationships is to assume that they are alike in all families. To understand the dynamics of such relationships, it is necessary to look at them in the family context. Seven areas can be studied to reveal the diversity of meanings. These are adapted from those suggested by Hinde (1979), a British psychologist, as follows:

(1) Content of interaction. What do family members of different generations actually do together? Do they share the details of daily life? Do they partake in family rituals on holidays, Friday night or Sunday noon gatherings, or birthday parties? Do they eat together, have special foods (Grandpa Smith's Thanksgiving turkey or the Jones's birthday fruitcake)? Do they visit and talk or sit silently and watch TV? Do they work together, clean house, shop, build a deck, plant a tomato bed? And how do they interpret these activities? Does the daughter who takes her mother shopping feel that she is a favored child, a good child, or an abused child relative to her

siblings? Each member of the family can be keeping a balance sheet of reciprocal services and feel guilt, shame, denial, or gloating. Does the daughter who takes her mother shopping once a week feel that she is performing as valuable a service as her brother who prepares her income tax return once a year or her sister who takes her to the doctor every six weeks? Does the mother feel that she is being repaid for past services or that she is a shamefully dependent family member? Past family history and present shared family values are all prominent parts of any interaction.

(2) Diversity of interaction. How many different things do family members do with each other? Are all the activities helping chores, or are there also fun outings? Do some get to do the chores and others the fun? Do intergenerational activities involving older members tend to be mostly chores and those involving younger members tend to be fun, like a picnic or amusement park trip?

(3) Quality of interactions. Are the interactions characterized by loving or hating, or are they just boring or neutral? Do they take a lot of effort? Are they mostly verbal or nonverbal—mostly talking or mostly gestures? Are they initiated mainly by one person or joint efforts?

(4) Patterning of interactions. Is there a pattern regarding who initiates and who rejects contact? Is it usually parents who initiate and children who reject? Do parents share aches and pains with one child and joys and triumphs with another?

(5) Reciprocity or complementarity. Does each person return the same behavior as he or she gets? Do some family members support others' positions and other members ask for support or reject support?

(6) Intimacy. Do family members hold each other at a distance or come close? Are they close physically, hugging and kissing? Do they share confidences? Do they smile at each other? Do they feel united?

(7) Interpersonal perceptions. How does each family member perceive the others and how do they perceive the family situation? Are younger men valued most and older women least? Do they feel proud of their family or disgusted with it?

While each family has its own unique themes and perceptions, it is also possible to find common roles related to the larger family context. In their study of three-generational families in Ontario, Marshall and Rosenthal (1982) observed the significant role older family members played as "kinkeepers" and "heads of the family." Troll's (1983) conclusions about grandparents' functions as "family watchdogs" was referred to above. It is usually older women who are the "kinkeepers," who spread the family news, who arrange for family get-togethers, who alert others of the need for help or the occasions for congratulations, and who jump into the gap when no other help is available. It is usually older men who are the "heads of the family," who give advice about investments and jobs, who help out with income tax preparation and housing decisions, and who jump into the gap when no other source of such help is available. There is understandable overlap between family watchdogging and kinkeeping or heading the family. Watchdogging could be said to be a kinkeeping function, as could much of the work of family heads. These roles are often, not always, the functions of the oldest generation, not necessarily those in midlife, although studies of caregiving where members of the oldest generation are failing indicate that midlife family members take on the roles when these roles can no longer be fulfilled by their parents (Troll, 1984).

Because a growing number of families now have four or five generations and intergenerational relationships have an unprecedented duration, new phases of family development and new kinds of family relationships have emerged. Hagestad (1985a, pp. 145-146) tied these to three dimensions of time: individual time, family time, and historical time, which she explained as follows:

> In individual time, parents and children mature and age, going through socially marked life transitions that produce shifting constellations of needs, physical abilities, and available resources. Families also have their course of development. . . . Nuclear families move through recognized phases . . . starting with early family building and child rearing and ending with the empty nest, retirement, and death of a spouse . . . family lineages have generational careers: Nuclear families and their individual members move across a series of generational locations or stations. . . . A set of parents and children may start out their relationship career as the fourth and fifth generations in a family lineage. Sixty years later, the parents may be the oldest of three generations, while the children find themselves in the middle generation. It seems reasonable to expect that the parent-child bonds change not only as a consequence of individual maturation on both sides of the relationship and the amount of time the two have spent together, but also as a consequence of their location in a generational structure. . . . What we have is a set of nested careers. . . . In the context of historical time, generational linkages connect families and individuals to the movement of history. . . . Families are unique meeting grounds for individuals with different historical backgrounds. . . . Historical changes are seen and interpreted through family lenses.

Mothers and Daughters

Families are linked together by women; in a sense, families are women's worlds. Mother-daughter relationships are complex from infancy on. Mothers seem to feel more comfortable with girl babies than with boys, perhaps because of shared femaleness or because girls tend to be more developed and thus more responsive (Troll, 1987). Little girls stay closer to their mothers than little boys, who are allowed to wander. Adult daughters tend to live closer to their mothers, to visit them more often, and to turn to them more readily in times of need. A New York City study (Haller, 1982) found that middle-aged mothers and their young-adult daughters were more attached to each other than middle-aged mothers and their young-adult sons. When old mothers need help, it is to their daughters that they turn.

Weishaus (1978) analyzed the course of mother-daughter relationships over 40 years and found generalized stability in the quality of these relationships, underscoring the cross-sectional findings of Cicirelli (1981) and others. Those who had been warm and close when the daughters were little girls remained warm and close when the daughters were mothers themselves; those who were not did not become any warmer or closer with time. Declining health seems to lead consistently to decline in the good feelings on the part of the daughters, however (Baruch & Barnett, 1983; see Johnson & Bursk, 1977). Weishaus noticed a change over the decade from when the daughters were aged 30 to the time they were reinterviewed at age 40. Many of the daughters became less positive about their mothers when the mothers presumably had more serious health problems.

Middle-aged women in one study (Lowenthal, Thurnher, & Chiriboga, 1975) expressed as much concern over their sons as over their daughters, but the middle-aged men were more concerned about their sons. Another study found the mother/daughter dyad more balanced or reciprocal than other dyads (Hagestad & Snow, 1977). The father/daughter dyad was the most imbalanced, with the daughter giving much more than receiving. The mothers and daughters also agreed about what their relationship was like. Their consensus was higher than it was in other dyads. They also felt that their children were sensitive to their feelings and moods. Mothers, however, were more likely to discuss personal problems with children than were fathers. On the other hand, middle-aged mothers expected a lot from their young-adult daughters, but usually gave them no credit when they fulfilled these expectations. The same group of women expected much less from their sons, but were lavish with praise when they did anything for them. The first group of women, those interviewed by Lowenthal and her colleagues, interestingly, were not as pleased with their mothers as with their fathers, a theme that also emerged in a study of gerontologists and their parents (Turner & Huyck, 1982).

Conclusion

Two general points emerge from the preceding discussion. The first is that most midlife men and women are involved with, concerned about, and committed to both their children and their parents. The launching of children removes most feelings of responsibility and authority from the relationship, but enhances feelings of pleasure and friendship. When there is need, the parental and grandparental "watchdog"—often mothers and grandmothers—jump in to help in any way needed. The aging of parents induces feelings of concern and distress, but does not lead to abandonment. Instead, when needed, children—mainly daughters—jump in to help. The second point is that midlife men and women are happiest when they do not need to help their children or their parents. In part, this means that they have done a good job raising their children to be independent. In part, it means that all is well for the people they love and they do not need to grieve over their pain or misfortune. In part, though, it means that they can be free to "do their own thing." Today's middle-aged Americans are happiest when following the norm of self-realization rather than that of filial obligation, even though one does not cancel out the other, and both may be followed simultaneously.

It was noted earlier that clinicians often start from an assumption that the presence of parents and grandparents in adult family life causes family malfunction and individual behavior problems; however, the thesis of this chapter is the opposite. The prominent presence of parents and grandparents may be signals of trouble, it is true; but they may be there to help, and practitioners and clinicians would do well to avail themselves of their help. Rather than opponents, they are allies. Healthy families enjoy intergenerational, extended kinship relations and are enriched by them. In other words, it is not the presence of relatives that goes together with trouble, but the absence of relatives. Isolated nuclear households seem to always have been with us, in all parts of the world, but isolated nuclear families are usually a sign that something is wrong.

References

Adams, B. N. (1968). *Kinship in an urban setting.* Chicago: Markham.

Archbold, P. G. (1982). All-consuming activity: The family as caregiver. *Generations, 7*(2), 12-13.

Barber, C. E. (1978, November). *Gender differences in experiencing the transition to the empty nest: Reports of middle-aged women and men.* Paper presented at the meeting of the Gerontological Society of America, Dallas, TX.

Bart, P. B. (1978). Mother Portnoy's complaints. *Transaction, 8*(1-2), 69-74.

Baruch, G., & Barnett, R. C. (1983). Adult daughters' relationships with their mothers. *Journal of Marriage and the Family, 45*(3), 601-606.

Beck, S. H., & Beck, R. W. (1984). The formation of extended family households during middle-age. *Journal of Marriage and the Family, 46*(2), 277-287.

Belsky, J., & Rovine, M. (1984). Social-network contact, family support, and the transition to parenthood. *Journal of Marriage and the Family, 46*(2), 455-462.

Bengtson, V. L., & Black, K. D. (1973, October). *Solidarity between parents and children.* Paper presented at the annual meeting of the National Council on Family Relations, Toronto, Canada.

Bengtson, V. L., & Kuypers, J. A. (1971). Generational difference and the developmental stake. *Aging and Human Development, 2,* 249-260.

Bengtson, V. L., & Robertson, J. (Eds.). (1985). *Grandparenthood.* Beverly Hills, CA: Sage.

Bengtson, V. L., & Troll, L. E. (1978). Youth and their parents: Feedback and intergenerational influence in socialization. In R. Lerner & G. Spanier (Eds.), *Child influences on marital and family interaction* (pp. 215-240). New York: Academic Press.

Borland, D. (1979). *An investigation of the empty nest syndrome among parents of different marital status categories: Evidence from national surveys.* Paper presented at the annual meeting of the Gerontological Society of America, Washington, DC.

Brody, E. (1985). Parent care as a normative family stress. *Gerontologist, 25*(1), 19-29.

Caplow, T., Bahr, H. M., Chadwick, B. A., Hill, A., & Williamson, M. H. (1982). *Middletown families: Fifty years of change and continuity.* Minneapolis: University of Minnesota Press.

Cheal, D. (1983). Intergenerational family transfers. *Journal of Marriage and the Family, 45*(4), 805-813.

Cicirelli, V. (1981). *Helping elderly parents: Role of adult children.* Boston: Auburn House.

Dahlin, M. (1980). Perspectives on family life of the elderly in 1900. *Gerontologist, 20*(1), 99-107.

Elder, G. (1974). *Children of the Great Depression.* Chicago: University of Chicago Press.

Fischer, L. R. (1981). Transitions in the mother-daughter relationship. *Journal of Marriage and the Family, 43*(3), 613-622.

Gilford, R., & Black, D. (1972). *The grandchild-grandparent dyad: Ritual or relationship?* Paper presented at the annual meeting of the Gerontological Society of America, San Juan, Puerto Rico.

Glick, P. C. (1975, April). *Living arrangements of children and young adults.* Paper presented at the meeting of the Population Association of America, Seattle, WA.

Hagestad, G. O. (1981). Late twentieth century parent-child relationships. In T. Field (Ed.), *Human Development* (pp. 485-499). New York: John Wiley.

Hagestad, G. O. (1985a). Continuity and connectedness. In V. L. Bengtson & J. Robertson (Eds.), *Grandparenthood* (pp. 31-48). Beverly Hills, CA: Sage.

Hagestad, G. O. (1985b). Vertical bonds: Intergenerational relationships. In N. Schlossberg, G. O. Hagestad, I. C. Siegler, & L. E. Troll (Eds.), *The adult years: Continuity and change* (pp. 133-166). College Park, MD: International University Consortium & Ohio University.

Hagestad, G. O., & Snow, R. (1977). *Young adult offspring as interpersonal resources in middle age.* Paper presented at the annual meeting of the Gerontological Society, San Francisco, CA.

Haller, O. (1982). *An investigation of the perceptions of attachment in the mother-adult child dyad.* Unpublished doctoral dissertation, New York University.

Harris, L., & Associates. (1975). *The myth and reality of aging in America.* Washington, DC: National Council on Aging.

Hess, B., & Waring, J. (1978). Parent and child in later life: Rethinking the relationship. In R. Lerner & G. Spanier (Eds.), *Child influences on marital and family interaction* (pp. 241-274). New York: Academic Press.

Hess, R., & Handel, G. (1959). *Family worlds.* Chicago: University of Chicago Press.

Hill, R., Foote, N., Aldous, J., Carlson, R., & MacDonald, R. (1970). *Family development in three generations.* Cambridge, MA: Schenkman.

Hinde, R. (1979). *Mother-young interaction: What primates can tell us.* Paper presented at the Parenting Conference, Rutgers University, New Brunswick, NJ.

Johnson, E. S., & Bursk, B. (1977). Relationships between the elderly and their adult children. *Gerontologist, 17*(1), 90-96.

Keith, J. (1985). Age in anthropological research. In R. H. Binstock & E. Shanas (Eds.), *Handbook of aging and the social sciences* (2nd ed., pp. 231-263). New York: Van Nostrand Reinhold.

Leigh, G. K. (1982). Kinship interaction over the family life span. *Journal of Marriage and the Family, 44*(1), 197-208.

Litwak, E. (1960a). Geographic mobility and extended family cohesion. *American Sociological Review, 25*, 385-394.

Litwak, E. (1960b). Occupational mobility and extended family cohesion. *American Sociological Review, 25*, 9-21.

Lowenthal, M. F., Thurnher, M. T., & Chiriboga, D. (1975). *Four stages of life.* San Francisco: Jossey-Bass.

Mannheim, K. (1952). The problem of generations. In K. Mannheim (Ed.), *Essays in the sociology of knowledge.* London: Routledge & Kegan Paul.

Marshall, V. W., & Rosenthal, C. J. (1982). Parental death: A lifecourse marker. *Generations, 7*(2), 30-31.

Mead, M. (1970). *Culture and commitment: A study of the generation gap.* New York: Basic Books.

Morgan, L. (1984). Changes in family interaction following widowhood. *Journal of Marriage and the Family, 46*(2), 323-331.

Nydegger, C. (1983). Family ties of the aged in cross-cultural perspective. *Gerontologist, 23*(1), 26-32.

Nydegger, C., & Mitteness, L. (1979). Transitions in fatherhood. *Generations, 4*(1), 14-15.

Nydegger, C., & Mitteness, L. (1982). Old fathers and aging children: Marriage is major source of strain. *Generations, 7*(2), 16-17.

Parent, M. (1978, November). *The nature of stress in middle age.* Paper presented at the annual meeting of the Gerontological Society of American, Dallas, TX.

Shanas, E. (1979). The family as a social support system in old age. *Gerontologist, 19*(2), 169-174.

Shanas, E. (1980). Older people and their families: The new pioneers. *Journal of Marriage and the Family, 42*(2), 9-15.

Smith, D. S. (1979). Historical change in the household structure of the elderly in economically developed societies. In R. W. Fogel, E. Hatfield, S. B. Kiesler, & E. Shanas (Eds.), *Aging: Stability and change in the family* (pp. 91-114). New York: Academic Press.

Sweetser, D. A. (1984). Love and work: Intergenerational household composition in the U.S. in 1900. *Journal of Marriage and the Family, 46*(2), 289-293.

Thurnher, M., Spence, D., & Lowenthal, M. F. (1974). Value confluence and behavioral conflict in intergenerational relations. *Journal of Marriage and the Family, 36*(2), 308-320.

Tinsley, B. R., & Parke, R. D. (1984). Grandparents as support and socialization agents. In M. W. Lewis (Ed.), *Beyond the dyad* (pp. 161-194). New York: Plenum.

Troll, L. E. (1972). Is parent-child conflict what we mean by the generation gap? *Family Coordinator, 21*, 347-349.

Troll, L. E. (1980). Intergenerational relations in later life: A family system approach. In N. Datan & N. Lohmann (Eds.), *Transitions of aging* (pp. 75-91). New York: Academic Press.

Troll, L. E. (1983). Grandparents: The family watchdogs. In T. Brubaker (Ed.), *Family relationships in later life* (pp. 63-74). Beverly Hills, CA: Sage.

Troll, L. E. (1984, November). *Old ways in new bodies: Handing down kinkeeping.* Paper presented at the annual meeting of the Gerontological Society of America, San Antonio, TX.

Troll, L. E. (Ed.). (1986). *Family issues in current gerontology.* New York: Springer.

Troll, L. E. (1987). Mother-daughter relationships through the life span. In S. Oskamp (Ed.), *Family processes and problems: Social psychological aspects* (Applied Social Psychology Annual 7, pp. 284-305). Newbury Park, CA: Sage.

Troll, L. E., & Bengtson, V. L. (1979). Generations in the family. In W. Burr, R. Hill, F. Nye, & I. Reiss (Eds.), *Contemporary theories about the family* (Vol. 1, pp. 127-161). New York: Free Press.

Troll, L. E., & Bengtson, V. L. (1982). Intergenerational relations throughout the life span. In B. Wolman (Ed.), *Handbook of developmental psychology* (pp. 890-911). Englewood Cliffs, NJ: Prentice-Hall.

Troll, L. E., Miller S., & Atchley, R. (1979). *Families of later life.* Belmont, CA: Wadsworth.

Troll, L. E., Neugarten, B. L., & Kraines, R. (1969). Similarities in values and other personality characteristics in college students and their parents. *Merrill-Palmer Quarterly, 15*, 323-336.

Turner, B., & Huyck, M. H. (1982). Gerontologists and their parents: It's not any easier. *Generations, 7*(2), 32-33.

U.S. Comptroller-General. (1977). *The need for a national policy to better provide for the elderly* (U.S. General Accounting Office HRD-78-19). Washington, DC: Government Printing Office.

Walker, A., & Thompson, L. (1983). Intimacy and intergenerational aid and contact among mothers and daughters. *Journal of Marriage and the Family, 45*(4), 841-850.

Weishaus, S. S. (1978). *Determinants of affect of middle-aged women towards their aging mothers.* Unpublished doctoral dissertation, University of Southern California.

Part V
Personal Development and Social Responsibility

The two chapters in this part address the topics of change, growth tasks, power, and social responsibility at midlife. In Chapter 11, Weick challenges the normative, linear view of human development that assumes most individuals develop in a predictable, sequential manner. The typical direction of change posited by such a model has been one of inevitable, downward decline from an ideal state. As an alternative, Weick proposes a "Growth Task Model" of development that conceptualizes growth as a cluster of developmental tasks forming cyclical themes in an individual's life. Growth is viewed as a natural process of change that is expressed in physical, emotional, intellectual, and spiritual dimensions. The growth process is catalyzed by the interaction of an inner life force with physical and social contexts.

Weick describes the five core growth tasks of intimacy, nurturance, productivity, creativity, and transcendence as channels through which each person's growth potential is challenged and exercised. In her Growth Task Model, the social and physical dimensions of the environment are examined to determine how a society, through its political, economic, and social opportunities, both supplies and restricts the opportunities for individuals to use their own personal power for growth.

The Growth Task Model questions certain beliefs about the role of the professional helper in the helping process. Weick believes that more attention should be given to helping people discover and develop their own power to grow and to change, rather than focusing on techniques to demonstrate the professional's power and ability. She suggests that the five growth task areas can serve as a framework for helping clients assess their own growth without being tied to the ways in which they perform their social roles. For example, in the area of nurturance, Weick's model proposes that nurturing can be extended beyond the care of one's own children to include a range of people of all ages who could benefit from nurturing. Another implication of Weick's model is that professional helpers can help their clients to think beyond the norms of societal expectations regarding certain social roles or life-styles, such as being middle-aged and unmarried.

In Chapter 12, Maas presents his thesis that in Western society there can be an expansion of involvements in socially responsible activities at middle age that can enrich the lives of both participants and beneficiaries. This is contrary to the popular belief that middle age is a time when the life course narrows and socially productive activities decline. According to the author, involvement in socially responsible interests at midlife depends on concurrent and previous environments or contexts, including opportunities for democratic social participation and personal development.

Maas presents his schema on social development, called the CDI approach, which identifies contexts that facilitate both social development and social responsibility. Through social development, capacities for social responsibility evolve, such as attachment, curiosity, empathy, caring, reciprocity, sense of competence, intimacy, sharing, collaboration, and cooperation. Another prerequisite associated with social responsibility is a sense of obligation and indebtedness toward the general welfare. Social responsibility requires that opportunities for its expression at various levels of society are available. Social workers and other helping professionals can foster social responsibility through influencing and designing social policies that create environments conducive to social development and thereby the development of capacities for social responsibility.

11

Patterns of Change and Processes of Power in Adulthood

Ann Weick

The process of change in adult life has received increasing attention, as researchers and academicians recognize that development is not the exclusive domain of the young. In the past 10 years, the area of adult development has flourished amidst a variety of attempts to plot the nature of adult developmental processes and interpret these findings for educators and clinicians. As a result of these activities, there is general acceptance of the vibrant, energetic character of human growth and change throughout the life course. The central issue that presents itself to interested inquirers is not whether adults change but how developmental change occurs. It is the process of change, then, that forms the most promising line of inquiry. By developing a model for the nature of change in adulthood, the foundation is set for careful consideration of the more subtle elements that constitute processes of adult change.

The formulation of a model of human development is fundamentally a philosophic matter. Although it is customary for researchers to approach the study of a phenomenon as though it could be addressed solely as a problem of methodology, underlying any investigation is a set of assumptions about the nature of the phenomenon being examined. In adult development literature, assumptions about the sequential nature of growth, the importance of age in identifying developmental stages, and changes in social roles as periods of crisis all represent a normative, linear view of human development (Weick, 1983). Certain changes are expected to occur at certain periods in much the same way that childhood maturation has been traditionally defined. There is, in these approaches, the assumption that normal human beings develop in a predictable, lockstep fashion and that this pattern of change can be charted to show an underlying universality to adult development. In contemporary language, these approaches represent a traditional ontogenetic paradigm (Dannefer, 1984), which counts as inherent in human beings characteristics that are far more socially shaped and idiosyncratically displayed than these approaches acknowledge.

Myth About Change

Attachment to developmental models based on assumptions of linearity, sequence, normativeness, and progress all reify a series of myths about adulthood that haunt and perhaps hinder the ability of people to welcome both anticipated and unanticipated change in their lives. The typical direction of change has been seen as one of inevitable, downward decline. After a youthful surge, where physical powers are at their peak, people begin to expect a gradual diminishment of their intellectual and physical well-being. The cult of youth makes even more poignant the predicted changes: loss of hair, loss of memory, loss of hearing, loss of sexual drive. Preoccupation with loss reinforces the belief that there is a state of perfection from which human beings fall.

The Platonic notion of an ideal state lingers in the background as a powerful image against which we measure ourselves. In spite of our experience in a irrevocably imperfect world, we cling to the belief that it is both possible and desirable to be perfect. Given our current preoccupation with physical perfection, we work to cover up or remove those aspects of our bodies that do not correspond to the cultural ideal. Appraisal of a midlife body, for example, might lead to trying to "repair" it through makeup, hair dye, exercise, diet, or plastic surgery (Colarusso & Nemiroff, 1981). The amount of energy and imagination devoted to these pursuits is a continuing indication of the power we grant to dreams of perfection.

There are numerous ironies in this view of human change, not least of which is the notion that perfection is intimately connected with the preference not for change but for stability. The perfection fantasy is as follows: If one can achieve, usually by hard work and some luck, a time in one's life where things seem to be as good as they'll ever get, then our most heartfelt wish is that nothing changes. In this sense, it is not that we will not accept change; we just want change to be of a certain kind. Simply put, change is acceptable when it matches our view of what is desirable and it is objectionable when it alters our set pattern of what life should be like.

Fear of death is the ultimate metaphoric representation of our fear of change (Becker, 1973). Westerners tend to treat death as the betrayal of their belief that they can reach and remain in a state of contented stability. The finality of death looms as a dreaded end to the dream of a better life. Neugarten (1968, p. 97) suggested that "the awareness that time is finite is a particularly conspicuous feature of middle age." Although we are beginning to see more important revisions in this view of death as gerontologists work to put death in the context of a natural process, we may not be able to change our cultural views about death until we change our cultural views about life.

What is implicit, but still unformed in much of the adult developmental literature, is a view of growth and change that breaks with the philosophic assumptions underlying the linear view of human change. Dannefer (1984) suggested an underlying logic in the current developmental paradigms that makes them all similar, in spite of their apparent differences. The roots of the paradigms are in a biological perspective that emphasizes predictable, sequential stages rather than more indeterminate, multidimensional patterns of change.

A Growth Task Model

An approach to human development that explicitly tries to take into account the social and the personal aspects of adult change is the Growth Task Model of development (Weick, 1983). In contrast to the normative character of adult developmental theories, the Growth Task Model conceptualizes growth as a cluster of developmental tasks that form cyclical themes in individuals' lives. The content of these themes is reflected in many models of human development, most notably the work of Erikson (1963), and includes the capacity for intimacy, the capacity to nurture, the opportunity to engage in productive activity, the opportunity to experience one's creativity, and the capacity to transcend personal concerns. Identifying the growth tasks is an important foundation for the model because the tasks form the *telos*, or goal, of human behavior. The model recognizes an array of capacities and talents that are to be engaged in the course of one's life and expressed to the fullest extent possible. In one way or another, the tasks are relational and constructive. They acknowledge the need for human interdependence in the world but also recognize the need continually to create the world. The growth tasks derive from the more fundamental conception that grounds the model, namely, its assumptions about human growth as a process of change.

The model rests on two interrelated premises about the nature of human change. It assumes that all living things have a life force or inherent "push for growth" that forms an inner dynamic for change. To be alive is to change. In this sense, growth is a naturally occurring process of change that is expressed in physical, emotional, intellectual, and spiritual dimensions. The catalyst for this naturally occurring process, however, is the interaction of the life force with physical and social environments (Weick, 1981). This view rests primarily on the assumption that human growth always occurs in a social context. To paraphrase John Donne, no one is an island. And equally important, no one is on an island with just family and loved ones. Although there is tremendous pressure to define the social environment as being composed of an individual and significant others, we must stretch the notion of environment to include social and physical forces being played out within and external to an individual. To state this understanding at the level of principle, we would say the following:

(1) All human beings grow and develop within the context of community.
(2) The idea of community embraces interlocking circles of connection among all human beings and, ultimately, all forms of life and matter.

The importance of these principles is worth clarifying. By establishing a rich and complex view of community, the notion of human growth is less likely to fall into a narcissistic interpretation. One of the current traps in our national preoccupation with human growth and fulfillment is that it is focused on narrow, egocentric concerns. Feeling better and looking better become goals in themselves, with little thought given to the matrix of relationships within which we live our lives. The more complex view of people in community expands the notion of person-in-environment. It reinforces the awareness of environmental forces and underscores an understanding of person as person-in-community. The notion of community is not meant to convey an idealized concept of a loving support system (although that is obviously desirable), but to reflect the social interconnectedness of people's lives and the social-institutional forces that shape them.

Having identified an inherent energy force and the contextual nature of its expression, we want to explore in more detail the processes by which growth tasks shape a developmental agenda. The five core tasks of intimacy, nurturance, productivity, creativity, and transcendence can be seen as channels through which each person's growth potential is challenged and exercised. The Growth Task Model assumes that these tasks coexist in every individual's life and that each presents a stage upon which growth issues are played out. The tasks center on the two most common elements of life: love and work. Intimacy and nurturance address the issue of love; productivity and creativity relate to the area of work. The fifth task, transcendence, speaks to the human capacity to develop beyond the intellectual, physical, and social limits accepted by culture. It is best described as the spiritual dimension because it calls people to explore beyond known and familiar realms of being.

Growth as Power

One way to conceptualize the energy that impels growth is as power. This connection of power with energy is not unfamiliar, but it challenges two more commonly held notions. When we associate energy with power, we may think of mechanical expressions of power, such as gasoline, electric, or nuclear power. Conversely, when we think of human power, we may equate energy with force, such as muscle power or political power, because contemporary models of power treat it as an agent to act upon someone or something. The third notion of energy as power, the one that is closest to the meaning intended here, is the vibrant energy experienced when one is feeling particularly healthy and content. It is the form of energy that we can identify as personal power because it resides within us. Its purpose is to fuel personal growth processes.

In applying the notion of power as a way of conceptualizing the energy force that impels growth, we see that each growth task is associated with a certain expression of this power. In the task of intimacy, individuals try to learn how to open themselves more fully to others. At the heart of this task is the willingness to be vulnerable to another without giving over one's own power. The language of dependence-independence is often used in this respect but it does not fully convey the notion of vulnerability that is related to power. If we think of personal power as one's own special, unique power, then the element of vulnerability means that we allow others to share in that aspect of ourselves without becoming confused about where the power resides. Learning to be comfortable with our own power to grow and not mistakenly attributing it to others is part of a lifelong task related to intimacy. Being open to the power of another while maintaining our own sense of value is a key to closeness with others.

Nurturance is a close companion to intimacy. It calls us to reach out to others to offer love and intimacy without letting our desire for control become dominant. The caring and compassion that develops through nurturing comes from our capacity to stimulate the power of others. When we nurture, we awaken and add to others' ability to grow. The crucial element is being able to give without taking charge, without overriding the other's power to grow according to his or her own light.

The tasks of love are closely joined to the tasks of work. In order to understand the element of power in this dimension, we must remove the idea of work from its cultural limitations, that is, work as paid employment. The notion of productivity has a larger meaning. It acknowledges the human need to engage in daily activities that contribute to the well-being of the community. This contribution may be in the form of paid work, but it may just as likely be associated with any of the myriad activities necessary to keep a society functioning and growing. It expresses the power to act in the world.

The task of creativity taps a slightly different dimension than productivity. While creative efforts may also be productive, creativity expresses power to add to or change one's world. The opportunity to discover and extend one's talents and abilities in artistic ways forms a bridge to the fifth task, transcendence.

In the task of transcendence, personal power is joined with the power of others to express a common goal or ideal. It may be expressed in service to the community, in religious commitment, or spiritual practices. It comes from the power of imagination about a better world or, for some, a world beyond known limits. Transcendence is more than altruism, although it may have this component. It is primarily an expression of a broader definition of power—one that attempts to lift humankind to a higher plane of awareness.

Needless to say, these various faces of human power are meant to be evocative, rather than descriptive. Attempting to draw lines of demarcation too starkly does not serve the metaphoric quality of these distinctions. What is important is recognizing that there are processes by which each individual's power is developed throughout a lifetime. The real challenge of this development is learning to recognize and express one's power without dominating or ignoring others.

The Role of Environment in Growth Processes

Environmental factors act as a catalyst in forming the expression of human growth. The base of all growth processes is dynamically interactive. The environment is always a crucial variable in eliciting or dampening human response. Something as simple and as vital as the exchange of oxygen in our lungs shows this fundamental linkage. Our survival depends on this process. The environment, both in physical and in social terms, provides the context within which a naturally occurring growth process occurs.

Because every environment is socially structured, it is difficult to appreciate the extent to which these patterns constrain or promote growth opportunities. The power of social structures lies in their ability to create the belief that accepted patterns are not only *a* way but the *only* way to organize human activities. Creating normative patterns for basic human activities, such as childbearing and child rearing, places limits on the ways these functions will be carried out. Tying human development too closely to these socially constructed forms limits the ways in which growth can be understood.

One of the points raised earlier in relation to current approaches to adult development was their unfortunate tendency to connect development to the framework of social roles. Although the concept of social roles is useful in considering how a society organizes its basic functions, it is not the best framework for understanding human development. When social roles are used as the organizing concept, all that one learns is how a society has created a normative structure for maintaining itself. The fact that many people live their lives within the constricting outlines of those rules and customs says more about the power of institutionalized patterns than it does about human development. In Western societies, the fact that many young adults marry in their early twenties is an artifact of their culture. One could cite other societies where the age of marriage and childbearing is much younger, or one could look to earlier periods of our own society for similar patterns. If one attributes developmental importance to the role itself or to the period of life when that role is lived out, then growth also becomes an artifact of human culture.

This leads us to reconsider the role of environment in the shaping of growth opportunities. In a Growth Task Model, the environment, in both its social and its physical dimensions, is of critical importance; however, it is considered precisely for the ways in which it has been shaped by human design. In other words, rather than taking institutional patterns as a given, they are approached with a critical view. Those patterns are central to an analysis that attempts to determine how a society, through its political, economic, and social institutions, both provides and constrains the opportunities for individuals to use their own personal power. Unless social patterns are open to critique, human growth can too easily be judged according to how well individuals carry out social roles, not on how well they develop their own capacities.

Let us take one example of this, the task of nurturing. Every culture that survives has a commitment to the nurturing of its young. The institution of marriage is an expression of this commitment in Western cultures because it establishes rules governing procreation and protection of the young. It seems logical, therefore, to consider the opportunity for nurturing within the context of marriage and family. Clearly, the opportunity for caring for a helpless infant and guiding a child to adulthood is a challenge to one's nurturing ability. At the same time, it is important to see what we lose by tying this task to the role of parenting. For one thing, we severely limit the context of nurturing. To see that task only in its most obvious expression dulls our sensitivity to the universal, ever-present need to care for others. We limit the power of nurturing if we imagine that it is mostly expressed in rearing children. Instead, the task of using our power to reach out to others is never absent. Whether it is with immediate loved ones or with strangers in our community, we are constantly called to be available to nurture. And the issue underlying that task is constantly with us: to be able to awaken and add to the power of another without controlling or weakening that person's own power.

Seen in this larger view, the environmental context is greatly expanded. Nurturing is not a private, family-oriented activity but a communal activity. The opportunities for nurturing are infinite because the communal needs for nurturing are infinite. Whether it is reaching out to a lonely neighbor or coworker, volunteering for community projects, or responding to the multitude of other needs in the local and world community, the challenge is to more finely hone our caring capacities. These challenges have less to do with social roles than with the constant needs that come from living in community. They also provide ways to be generative or socially responsible at midlife (see Maas, Chapter 12 of this volume).

Let us consider another important way in which the environment shapes growth opportunities. Earlier, we identified productivity as an essential growth task in human development. In identifying that area, we emphasized that productivity was not to be equated with paid employment, even though we live in a society whose economic structure has produced this connection. In a capitalist society, it is essential that human beings be viewed as laborers who are hired for the productive value they have to the employer. The return of wages is a symbol of their economic value. In other words, the institutionalization of a particular economic structure has created a certain definition of productivity and of those who produce. As with any such institutionalized pattern, there is a complex array of values, beliefs, and rules attached to it. To focus on the role of worker in American society is necessarily to concern oneself with the ways in which the economic institution has created an ideology surrounding the place of work in our society.

Given the profound shaping that has occurred in this area of our lives, it is obvious that the environment has produced a narrow definition of what it means to be productive. To be a productive person means that one must be employed, preferably with high pay, and must devote most of the hours of one's adult life to something called a job. It does not come as any surprise that most adults are thus concerned with the place of work in their lives: getting a job, keeping it, and worrying about how to survive. But we see once again that the issues related to employment are culturally produced. Worrying about finding and keeping a job only occurs because our society does not guarantee that our basic needs can be met in other ways. Nor, with its definition of work as paid employment, does it value activities that do not meet that criterion.

The growth task related to productivity cannot be properly understood by these cultural standards. The task of productivity concerns the power to act in the world and in some way shape and influence one's environment. The precise form that it takes is less important than the opportunity to contribute to the well-being of the larger community. To be productive means to express one's talents in ways that contribute to and sustain community life. Finding ways to do that throughout one's lifetime is the challenge of productivity.

As with nurturing, we see that the ability to be productive is much richer than the limited cultural version of paid work. In fact, the two notions are not necessarily related. One could argue that it is the separation of productivity and work that has given rise to the boredom and dissatisfaction many workers feel. Our cultural conception of work does nothing to ensure that people will be able to experience their power by making useful contributions through their work efforts. The ironic twist is that many people who make significant contributions to community life—the volunteers, the artisans, those who care for the children—are summarily dismissed as unemployed and, therefore, useless. Because many of those activities are typically considered part of the women's sphere, it is not surprising that so many women recognize that their productive powers are being ignored. If the need to be productive is a central growth task throughout human life, then the cultural thwarting of this natural expression for both women and men is a tragic and costly matter.

Growth Tasks in Midlife and the
Problems of Social Scripts

Given the inevitable restrictions that society places on the expression of human growth, let us turn our attention to an exploration of growth tasks in midlife. As will be clear from the outset, the Growth Task Model does not assume that the tasks are particularly related to any life stage. Implicit in the conceptualization of the Growth Task Model is its adherence to a transstage and transcultural view of development. Exploration of the notion of personal power as expressed in the growth tasks, however, might be helpful to people in their middle years.

By the time most people reach midlife, they are beginning to make an important discovery: life has not been what they were led to expect. The scripts society has written have become blurred because the things that were expected to happen did not and many things that did occur were not expected. In the marriage and family script, life events intervened, rewriting the lines about what marriage was to be. Finding a partner may have taken longer than one hoped or may not have happened at all. If found, the scenario of long-lasting love with a mate and 2.5 children has met with the real-life challenges of an imperfect world. Love may have faded and died, perhaps to be reborn again in a new relationship. Children may have arrived at the wrong time or not at all. Even when children arrived who were healthy and wanted, they may not have provided the emotional cement to keep a failing relationship together. Or perhaps, while marital love lived on, a child became a source of heartache and worry. The original script did not prepare adults for these real-life improvisations they were called on to cope with.

The problem with social scripts is exacerbated by similar scenarios in the workplace. Men who were raised to find good jobs and support their families in an adequate style may find by midlife that the work world does not cooperate with the dream they constructed (Levinson, Darrow, Klein, Levinson, & McKee, 1978). The hope for a good job has become obscured as a less than adequate job was taken. Or a good job was found but with sacrificial costs: stressful working conditions, fears about job security and advancement, the need to ingratiate oneself to demanding employers. And with good job or bad comes the specter of unemployment that could wipe out all the years of conscientious effort.

The arrival of women on the work scene in ever growing numbers has produced its own challenge to the work-role script. Many women carry into the workplace traditional role expectations that center on family responsibility. Bardwick (1980) identified the woman's dream as a relational one, where romantic attachment plays a central role. Because of the dream, work often takes second place to the intimate relationships in women's lives.

When women do enter the work force, some for the first time during midlife, they still find a gender-segregated world where they are excluded from certain jobs and from certain positions (Abramovitz, 1986). The secondary labor force is available but at wages that cannot support a family. Trying to continue as caretaker of children and overseer of domestic life has produced agonizing dilemmas of choice, regardless of the position held. How to mesh these real-life issues has forced the marriage and job scripts into a tangled and messy scrawl. Even if one's children are grown, these are dilemmas for women. Droege (1982) found that although midlife women may attempt to emphasize career over marriage, they have a split dream that diffuses the focus of their lives.

What we see in this abbreviated array of real-life possibilities is that the social scripts, developed around social roles, exist only in the mythical mind of society, not in our daily living. It is comforting to imagine that humans develop by responding to prescribed and expected role change, but that comfort only comes from a desire to make life appear tidy and well planned. The cost of abiding by these scripts, as with any such subterfuge, is to spend energy propping up a myth at the expense of our own lived experience. The cost is our own disempowering.

This disempowerment has two equally sharp edges. On one side is the cost of following the script and submerging one's own unique talents and capabilities under the expectations of social roles. Following this path takes away the power to define one's own life. But the other side presents an equally difficult dilemma. If one fails to follow prescribed scripts, either through choice or circumstance, the burden of social judgments leads to increased self-blame and doubt.

This loss of power shows itself in the demoralization that occurs when adults recognize that this experience does not meet external expectations about outcome. Because the script tells adults that it is both possible and desirable to find a good job and have an enduring relationship, there is no excuse for not doing so. The fault can only lie in the individual who has not shown the ability to accomplish these expected goals. Sennett and Cobb (1972) described this cost as one of "injured dignity" because there is no redress against our own deficits. If ability is rewarded and we do not win the reward, then it is our ability that must be questioned. Central to this demoralization, then, is a deep disbelief in our own worth and value. Our power to be and to do is deeply injured and it is socially held beliefs that have caused the injury.

Examples of injured dignity are poignantly represented in both women's and men's lives. The widespread occurrence of clinical depression in women can, in part, be attributed to society's devaluation of caregiving tasks. As the classic Broverman, Broverman, Clarkson, Rosencrantz, and Vogel (1970) study demonstrated, women are expected to express such traditional female characteristics as sensitivity, nurturance, and emotionality, but in doing so they are viewed as less mentally healthy than men. At the same time, the caregiving tasks that require such attributes are those least valued by society (De Lange, 1981; Kravetz, 1986). In light of these double-bind messages, depression can be seen as one way of trying to cope with untenable options.

Men too may experience crises of self-worth when their socially acceptable role of wage earner is called into question. Being laid off because of economic factors, or having one's skills become obsolete, present major challenges to the worker who was socialized to believe that work equals personal worth. To lose a job is not only a financial crisis but it also produces intense self-doubt and self-recrimination, factors that reverberate through the emotional life of the family and community. For both men and women, the social causes of these circumstances are often hidden under the personal, emotional responses they evoke.

We cannot underestimate the serious consequences of this pervasive form of oppression. To hold people responsible for living a life that is based on myth creates a permanent division within them. They believe that an ideal life is one in which everything works out "right"; that is, it meets all the socially constructed expectations about love and work. At the same time, they see how far short their own life falls and the resulting blame and self-doubt prevent them from learning the real meaning of their own life experience.

The topic of oppression is much larger than this discussion suggests. For our purposes, it is sufficient to recognize how institutionalized social patterns act as definitional boundaries for human behavior. When those boundaries are uncritically accepted, rather than critically examined, they "leak" into the professional-academic spheres, resulting in conceptions of human development that burden rather than enable people to discover their own definitions and meanings.

Regaining a Sense of Power

If disempowerment is to be reversed, a different developmental focus must emerge; one that, as in the Growth Task Model, centers itself not on what society expects of people but what people can learn about themselves. The power does not come from the outside. It is not given or granted by external authority or structures. It comes as a birthright for every individual and is, in its deepest sense, a personal gift. Power throughout a person's lifetime is a unique expression of the talents and abilities that each of us comes to discover in the process of growth. Let us see how the growth tasks can become the bridge to this deeper sense of power by exploring more fully the task of intimacy.

In the task of intimacy, there are many lessons to learn about the process of being close to others. This ongoing process challenges adults to explore the self in all its uniqueness. In Sherman's (1987, p. 217) study of midlife transitions, he emphasized "the unique personal meaning of the transitional events and experiences for the individuals undergoing them." Creating "structures of meaning" (p. 3) is one significant aspect of each person's own response to events and circumstances as they unfold throughout life. In midlife, one of the elements of intimacy may be the turning inward to discover who one is beyond a self defined by social roles.

In the task of intimacy, the discovery of a self not created by others is key. Finding out who one is apart from the expectations of others begins with the first glimmering sense that one is capable of and, more important, has the right to name one's own experience. In important ways, this recognition is a radical act because it springs from one's own power to act and to be. We see it in the woman or man who begins to challenge, even if in the privacy of their own heads, the constricted ways that they were taught and expected to act. Both on individual and collective levels, this process of redefinition is an affirmation of an interior power to grow in ways that more fully express individual talents.

A powerful contemporary example of collective and individual redefinition is that undertaken by women who no longer accept stereotyped expectations about women's behavior. Largely due to the political and social awakening engendered by the women's movement, many women have begun to explore who they might be underneath the paint of limited social roles. In the short run, some women respond to their new knowledge by pulling back from people with whom they have been close, that is, they desire to be less intimate. But if the process of self-discovery is supported, this new awareness can become the foundation for more authentic intimacy in both friendship and love relationships. By interacting with others, we are constantly provided with feedback about ourselves that can be reflected on and used in our own process of growth. Both interaction and reflection are key processes in the development of intimacy.

It is not surprising that sexual intimacy often stands as the penultimate expression of intimacy because it has the potential to bring together every aspect of a person's being. At the same time, in a culture such as ours where the human body is often seen as an embarrassing appendage to a rational mind, the use of the body as a medium of expression is likely to be fraught with great ambivalence. The development of intimacy in the sexual arena thus has its own lifelong challenges because individuals continually have to grapple with their ability to open themselves emotionally, physically, and intellectually to others in the midst of a culture that still treats sex as a guilty secret. Because we are not encouraged to develop a more genuine sense of ourselves through intimate relations, sex becomes merely a physical act. Without the full presence of self, there is no relationship (see Weg, Chapter 1 of this volume).

The other growth task areas can be understood in a similar way. In each case, there are social factors that make it difficult for us to recognize our own power. The nurturing task is given a socially limited definition and within those limits is undervalued. Women's contribution in child care goes unrecognized and men are largely cut off from their nurturing capacities. The social definitions surrounding productivity go in the opposite direction. Men bear the burden of maintaining paid employment, while many women who want and need to work are relegated to the low-wage labor force. The tasks of creativity and transcendence do not find a comfortable place within our dominant social beliefs unless one equates transcendence with the presence of organized religion. Instead, the social emphasis on work and material gain stunt the possibility of creativity and transcendence in the marketplace. For creativity and transcendence to reemerge, they need to be seen as expressions of power that can lead people to venture beyond the confines of social definitions. Creativity calls upon us to put into a sharable form the special insights we have about the world, and transcendence is the process of synthesizing the special insights of self and others. Transcendence thus engages us in the expansion of our view of the world into the spiritual realm.

Links with Practice

The Growth Task Model, with its emphasis on process and power, can create an orienting perspective for professional practice. Its conception of human development places attention on processes of change, and in so doing calls into question some prevailing beliefs about the role of the professional practitioner in the helping process. The underlying process of growth, as envisioned in this model, is far more elusive than many adult developmental theories would lead us to believe. It is this "aleatory" or "chance dependent" aspect of human development that Gergen (1982, p. 153) emphasized in his account of the evolution of developmental theory. Once growth is detached from its stage-age-role-related aspects, the process of change becomes far less predictable and the role of the practitioner far less determinate than we have chosen to believe.

The elusive quality of human development has important consequences for our view of practice. Based on a growth task perspective, we would need to relinquish our preoccupation with techniques. We often speak of what we do as "intervention" and think of ourselves as "change agents." The techniques we learn often become instruments of power to direct what we think to be the desired course of change. Professional values to the contrary, we often find it difficult to grant to individuals the power to direct their own lives. Our reliance on techniques makes us forget that showing our power and ability is not the purpose of helping. Rather, everything we do should serve the purpose of helping people discover and develop their own power to grow and to change.

Feminist therapy is one important development in this approach. To counter sexist assumptions prevalent in practice, practitioners help both women and men develop the full range of their potential (Rosewater & Walter, 1985). The content for this is a new power relationship, in which both the worker and the client are seen as powerholders and where the capacity of the client to know and to act is maximized (Miller, 1976).

A belief in the human capacity to develop all the dimensions of human growth is a way of adding to, rather than decreasing, an individual's own power. The practitioner enhances power by not preempting the individual's story by assigning diagnostic categories or by offering intrusive interpretations. The professional will undoubtedly have judgments about the growth needs implicit in the story but, at the same time, will find many ways in which the person has shown a desire and ability to respond to the tasks life has set out. In other words, the person will have shown strength in meeting life's challenges, even though there are many additional ways in which growth is possible.

An emphasis on strengths recognizes that individuals have and can come to appreciate more fully their own power to develop in ways that best express their strivings and capacities. The professional helper uses a broad perspective of the human growth process to help people sit up and take notice of their lives. It is akin to the role Watson (1977, p. 136) ascribed to healers who help stimulate the regenerative capacity within individuals by "prodding them into the natural business of healing themselves." This growth-oriented approach is further reinforced by the conscious awareness on the part of the helper that, except in the most extreme circumstances, the helper does not really know how best to proceed. This acknowledges the uncertainty underlying most of human life. We will have judgments and guesses but, for the most part, we do not know with any certainty what direction a person should take. Guggenbühl-Craig (1978, p. 2) recognized the stakes in this when he said, "Acting against the will of the client demands conviction. One must be certain that one's ideas are right." Short of such certitude, how much better it is to see ourselves as ones who enlist the energy of clients to grow in their own light. To borrow the words of Belenky and her colleagues (1986, p. 19), the goal is "to put the knower back into the known and [help them] claim the power of their own minds and voices."

As we consider the five growth task areas of intimacy, nurturance, productivity, creativity, and transformation, we see that they can serve as a framework for working with clients to help them assess their own growth. Because the tasks are separated from social roles, people have an opportunity to reflect on how they are meeting their personal growth needs. For example, in the area of nurturance, as indicated before, they may consider what broadened opportunities they have for caring for others.

One useful consequence of the larger view of growth tasks is that it reframes in a positive way circumstances that might be considered pathological from a traditional view. For example, adults who are not married may be judged as being fearful of intimacy or couples who do not have children may be seen as immature or unwilling to make a commitment. If social roles are used as norms of behavior, then many behaviors can be considered abnormal. If growth tasks are used as the framework for assessment, however, individuals have much more latitude for seeing ways in which they express or can learn to express the powers the tasks represent. The woman who feels depressed because her children have left home can be helped to see that her need for nurturing is still vital. Helping her discover new ways to express this need can be an important aspect of the helping process.

The framework provided by a growth task perspective necessarily requires a clear focus on the individual in community. Both clients and community are viewed as rich resources for mutual well-being. The expanded perspective of human development joins with an expanded view of human community, making the professional person an important resource coordinator. For example, in helping the woman mentioned above find new expressions for her caring, she and the worker team together to assess opportunities that exist in her community. Youth programs, hospice care, senior citizens' clubs, Brownie or Scout troops are only a few obvious possibilities. The worker helps her see herself as a valuable resource whose caring capacity is deeply needed in her community.

An assessment that embraces a growth task perspective is not intended to become rigid or formalized. It is recognized that at any one point in time, most individuals are not able to focus with equal interest and intensity on all growth areas. A conscious assessment of these areas may lead an individual to choose one for more focused attention. It is equally likely that the area selected may not be the one that seems most obvious. A women who is dealing with a sense of loss as children leave home may decide that other task areas such as productivity or creativity have been too long neglected. This awareness may lead to new growth ventures in these arenas. By incorporating a growth task perspective into professional practice, the worker can provide a context within which clients may see their own life in a more positive light and may identify a wider range of options for expressing their personal power.

Conclusion

The view of human behavior engendered by the Growth Task Model offers a useful alternative to more traditional formulations. It acknowledges that the processes of human growth are elusive and dynamic, rather than orderly and predictable. The tasks of growth, while identifiable, do not proceed in a linear fashion from birth to death. Because the personal power inherent in each individual is expressed through her or his unique blend of talents and abilities, the actual expression of this power in time and over time is, in some essential way, unpredictable. Certainly, we can recognize broad patterns of development, particularly as they have been shaped by cultural or physical forces. But those broad patterns do not predict, in any individual life, what course will actually develop. There is room for enormous variation as each person attempts to develop the raw materials available. This development is dynamic and ever changing as the life energy seeks to be expressed in its many forms.

References

Abramovitz, M. (1986). Social policy and the female pauper: The family ethic and the U.S. welfare state. In N. Van Den Bergh & L. Cooper (Eds.), *Feminist visions for social work* (pp. 211-228). Silver Spring, MD: National Association of Social Workers.

Bardwick, J. (1980). The seasons of a woman's life. In D. McGuigan (Ed.), *Women's lives: New theory, research and policy* (pp. 35-57). Ann Arbor: University of Michigan, Center for Continuing Education.

Becker, E. (1973). *The denial of death*. New York: Free Press.

Belenky, M., Clinchy, B., Goldberger, N., & Tarule, J. (1986). *Women's ways of knowing*. New York: Basic Books.

Broverman, I. K., Broverman, D. M., Clarkson, F. E., Rosencrantz, P. S., & Vogel, S. R. (1970). Sex-role stereotypes and clinical judgments of mental health. *Journal of Consulting and Clinical Psychology, 34*, 1-7.

Colarusso, C. A., & Nemiroff, R. A. (1981). *Adult development: A new dimension in psychodynamic theory and practice*. New York: Plenum.

Dannefer, D. (1984). Adult development and social theory: A paradigmatic reappraisal. *American Sociological Review, 40*, 100-116.

De Lange, J. (1981). Depression in women: Explanations and prevention. In A. Weick & S. Vandiver (Eds.), *Women, power and change* (pp. 17-26). Washington, DC: National Association of Social Workers.

Droege. R. (1982). *A psychosocial study of the formation of the middle adult life structure in women*. Unpublished doctoral dissertation, California School of Professional Psychology, Berkeley, CA.

Erikson. E. H. (1963). *Childhood and society* (2nd ed.). New York: Norton.

Gergen, K. J. (1982). *Toward transformation in social knowledge*. New York: Springer-Verlag.

Guggenbühl-Craig, A. (1978). *Power in the helping professions*. Zurich, Switzerland: Spring.

Kravetz, D. (1986). Women and mental health. In N. Van Den Bergh & L. Cooper (Eds.), *Feminist visions for social work* (pp. 101-127). Silver Spring, MD: National Association of Social Workers.

Levinson. D., Darrow, C., Klein, E., Levinson, M., & McKee, B. (1978). *The seasons of a man's life*. New York: Ballantine.

Miller, J. B. (1976). *Toward a new psychology of women*. Boston: Beacon.

Neugarten, B. L. (Ed.). (1968). *Middle age and aging: A reader in social psychology*. Chicago: University of Chicago Press.

Rosewater, L. B., & Walter, L. E. (Eds.). (1985). *Handbook of feminist therapy*. New York: Springer.

Sennett, R., & Cobb, J. (1972). *The hidden injuries of class*. New York: Knopf.

Sherman, E. (1987). *Meaning in midlife transitions*. Albany: State University of New York Press.

Watson, L. (1977). *Gifts of unknown things*. New York: Simon & Schuster.

Weick, A. (1981). Reframing the perspective of person in environment. *Social Work, 26* (2), 140-143.

Weick. A. (1983). A growth-task model of human development as a basis for practice. *Social Casework, 64* (3), 131-137.

12

Social Responsibility in Middle Age: Prospects and Preconditions

Henry S. Maas

According to popular belief, in middle age the life course narrows and begins a downhill stretch through the wastelands of old age, terminating in death. As in many such widespread public assumptions, specific referents are hazy, boundaries are not stipulated, and when evidence is presented it is selective and anecdotal. A flourishing literature on midlife continues, bearing titles that spotlight presumably universal ("normative") crises and other survival pains or decremental changes. It seems to be assumed, moreover, that any change is stressful. These and other untested (untestable?) propositions are sometimes documented from clinical case records, with shades of Freudian overgeneralization extended to include people who never use the couch or variants thereof.

The thesis of this chapter is that the life course in Western societies today broadens and branches out in middle age. This allows for, among other choices, an expansion of involvements especially in community-based, socially responsible activities. These may enrich the lives of both participants and beneficiaries. Ideally, in a democratic society the beneficiaries become, in time, if not to start with, participants on their own behalf.

Some middle-aged men and women extend their horizons by developing new socially responsible involvements as changes occur in their families and at work. Midlife contextual changes in occupational and parenting or other familial situations vary greatly for women and for men. Such changes vary also for both genders within individual lives that may or may not, for example, be childless or include marriage. Still, studies of midlife changes, as specified in the next section of this chapter, indicate a probability of release from young adult constraints, regardless of gender. Such release enables the middle-aged to participate more actively in community life and with broader concerns than those of young adulthood, which focus primarily on problems of jobs, intimate relationships, or young children.

The pursuit of socially responsible interests in middle age depends on both concurrent and earlier environments or contexts. Among these are the options for democratic social participation and decision making a society provides, as well as the many contexts that foster personal development. The abilities to make socially responsible commitments, and having the capacities in middle age to pursue them, depend on a person's prior social development. The relevant developmental tributaries and their contextual shores are mapped in this chapter and discussed at book length elsewhere (Maas, 1984).

Midlife Changes in Work and Family Contexts

The contexts that provide or limit people's accessible options change over the life course and in roughly patternable ways at midlife in Western societies today. "Life course" refers here to the range and approximate sequence of contexts through which people travel over their lives. "Contexts" define environments as both physical-social realities *and* people's perceptions of them (Maas, 1984, pp. 10-14). We are thus dealing with changing physical-social settings, like families and workplaces, about which almost all observers might share some consensus and, moreover, experience some individual variant interpretations. Most important to remember, however, is that accessible contexts along the life course foster or inhibit people's development at all times of life.

This chapter began by proposing that, contrary to popular belief, the life course of middle-aged women and men in today's Western world spreads out. The width of the life course and new side roads radiating from it increase. Less metaphorically, this means that new options for living arise as changes in contexts occur at midlife. This proposition is based on evidence of the subsiding, in middle adulthood, of the kinds of pressures in nuclear family life and workplaces that many young adults experience. Several empirical studies will be examined so that readers not only obtain firsthand contact with study findings but also see how related conclusions appear in different investigations. When researchers in California, Michigan, and Massachusetts discover similar findings, one may be getting close to a regionally diverse American truth.

As life course (contextual) changes occur, psychological developments are simultaneously in process. How these developments can be expressed hinges in part on the available options of relevant contexts. One development, for example, in middle age is a new kind of idealistic concern about young people called "generativity" by Erikson (1959), "mentorhood" by Levinson (1978), or "interest newly taken in guiding the young" (Tamir, 1982). Settings in the life course must foster, or at least not impede, the pursuit of such new interests. Therefore, we turn first to midlife contexts for men and women before considering the expression of social responsibility in middle age.

Middle-Aged Men in the Workplace and Beyond

Reviewing the Berkeley longitudinal study findings on changes between age 38 and 49 in men's investment on their jobs, Clausen (1981, p. 337) reported that by about age 50, "those who had achieved or exceeded their aspirations were satisfied with their current situations. . . . Men who had to lower their sights were somewhat less satisfied, but most of them expressed generally positive feelings about their jobs and were reconciled to having reached their ceilings." Moreover, "for men in lower middle-class occupations and those who have not been upwardly mobile," there is "a marked decline in job and career satisfaction from the early to the late forties" (p. 329). Thus all of these California men seemed to have come to terms with or undergone a reduced involvement in their work. Jobs ceased to be the center of concern they had been earlier in life. These men, like those in other studies cited below, had reached an occupational plateau by middle age. Thus the psychosocial space appeared to be clear for these men to take on new involvements in the pursuit, for example, of their new generative or "mentorhood" interests.

Concluding her findings on men's work satisfaction, Tamir (1982, p. 121) stated: "It appears that the middle-aged man may disengage from the job he does, as a source of personal fulfillment. The process of disengagement from the work arena is most likely subtle" because it occurs at a time of satisfactions that "come not only from reaching the peak of one's work career, but also from the interpersonal side of exchanges of the job." She continued:

> Hence by middle age, work, a major value for men and source of social identity, recedes into the background, despite the fact that success may be high by middle age. The drive toward achievement and material success diminishes by this age. The less educated continue to be concerned with security needs, presumably due to realistic assessments of present and future finance. The more educated, however, appear to be more materially secure. . . . In either case, both

groups of men no longer rely on the act of work to offer self-fulfillment and to enhance their state of well being. (Tamir, 1982, pp. 122-123)

According to Tamir's (1982, p. 123) findings on men in their forties, "life after the middle-age transition proceeds along a new plane of adult development" in which face-to-face social relationships "can develop on a new level." Family relations "become less role constrained past middle age. Children are considered as competent adults . . . and wives no longer need to be viewed in the all-encompassing role of mother." Thus men's family roles also become less constraining.

Levinson concluded his study of men in four occupational categories with a discussion of the "developmental work of early and middle adulthood," seeing early adulthood (the twenties and thirties) as "perhaps the most abundant and stressful decades in the life cycle" urgently needing the kind of "mentoring relationships"—which combine fathering and friendship— that the middle-aged can provide. "Many middle-aged men never experience the satisfactions and tribulations of mentorhood. This is a waste of talent, a loss to the individuals involved, and an impediment to constructive social change." Thus Levinson (1978, pp. 334, 337) touched on one kind of socially responsible behavior in middle adulthood. He continued:

> We need more people who can contribute as leaders, managers, mentors, sources of traditional wisdom as well as vision and imagination. Modern society *requires* a vital, developing contingent in middle age. The required work of middle adulthood is different from that of youth. It involves greater responsibility, perspective and judgment. A person in this era must be able to care for younger and older adults, to exercise authority creatively, to transcend the youthful extremes of shallow conformity and impulsive rebelliousness. The moderate mid-life decrease in biological capacity must be counterbalanced by an increased psychosocial capacity. In countless intellectual, emotional, moral, esthetic, managerial and reparative ways, the middle-aged must help in maintaining and developing the culture. (p. 329)

The potentials and mandates for socially responsible contributions in middle age are thus clearly stated for men.

In summary, then, according to both Clausen and Tamir, young men's involvements with their jobs typically diminish by midlife. This holds for both more and less educated workers, and for men who have either attained their occupational goals or have not, by middle age. In addition, familial roles become less pressured as children become independent. When what Levinson called "the most abundant and stressful decades in the life cycle" for men—the twenties and thirties—are over, middle-aged males are free to devote some of their energy and "increased psychosocial capacity" to community issues and causes of broad social concern. Evidence suggests that contextually there is the "space" for them to do so.

Middle-Aged Women's Extrafamilial Lives

In a 1984 collection of studies called *Women in Midlife* (Baruch & Brooks-Gunn, 1984), written by more than two dozen women, a repeated theme was well stated, as follows:

> Although a woman may have enacted only her family roles to the exclusion of all others in early adulthood, at midlife as family demands slack off, she is capable of launching a delayed career in spheres other than the family. At this point in her life-course, a woman may complete an education or begin one, train for a new job or seek a promotion, join a volunteer association or found one. A midlife woman is much more than her familial roles, more than "just a wife" or "just a mother." (Long & Porter, 1984, pp. 140-141)

Other analyses of women's work and familial roles present equally relevant messages. Giele (1982, p. 142) discussed what she called a "cross-over model" for women's life course with the implication that "a positive value is attached to the number and variety of life experiences, continued learning, and flexible adaptations in the face of new challenges." Stroud's (1981, p. 389) report on Berkeley's longitudinal studies of middle-aged women stated: "Serious involvement with work is found in this sample mainly among well-educated women who are single in mid-life. . . . At 40, work-committed women are functioning better than ever before. Their psychological resources seem to have been liberated by the ending of unhappy marriages." These findings echo an earlier report on some of the mothers of these same Berkeley women when, at about age 70, they scored high on Life Satisfaction Ratings. In middle age, through either widowhood or divorce, they were freed from familial situations that they had found stressful. In midlife they entered the world of work and became happily engaged as "work-centered mothers" in full-time employment (Maas & Kuypers, 1974, pp. 62-66, 118-120).

The work-centered mothers belonged to a generation born about 1900. When they were liberated from depressing daily schedules in their homes, they extended their friendship networks but rarely got involved in political volunteer work or any formal organizations. By contrast, in an empirical study of "relatively traditional" women of a later generation in Chicago, Lopata and Barnewolt (1984, pp. 105-106)) reported that "societal roles" fared best among the unmarried working women, although women of all ages expected "roles outside the home, such as those of friend, member of religious group, citizen or neighbor . . . to increase in importance in their future." Still, the actual "societal" involvement rates of respondents in their early fifties were not high.

But midlife for still younger generations of women promises to be quite different from their mothers' and grandmothers' middle age. The 1980 United States census data indicated generally later marriages, more divorces, fewer and later-born children, and greater independence in living arrangements for women. The rise in the proportion of living units headed by women was indicative of their more independent ways of life (Bianchi & Spain, 1986). With greater independence in young adulthood, women may find opportunities for socially responsible involvements in middle age more "on course" and compatible with their increased freedom of choice.

Young women's increasing independence still involves obligations both at home and at work. According to the 1980 United States census, motherhood was combined with simultaneous paid employment for about half of American women with preschool children and three-fifths of those with school-aged children (Bianchi & Spain, 1986). Thus, by the time children become independent and some begin to live on their own, middle-aged women who have successfully managed to balance their work both at home and in the labor market may be ready for more expansive kinds of activity.

Beyond the boundaries of family and job, for women who are curious, concerned, and adventuresome, there are groups and organizations whose members address human problems at neighborhood, national, and international levels. The doors are always open to new volunteers. In the course of cooperative efforts on behalf of physically or mentally handicapped people, or newcomers to a given region, participants enlarge their understandings and social networks and thus further their personal development. Women's increasing independence at midlife may have multiple payoffs for both others and themselves.

Psychology and Midlife
Social Responsibility

In the previous section, research findings were presented on contextual changes for women and men in middle age, starting with a sociologist's analysis of men's occupational careers (Clausen, 1981) and ending with demographers' interpretations of census data on women's increasingly independent life-styles (Bianchi & Spain, 1986). Psychologists have also contributed to our understanding of commitments and capacities involved in socially responsible involvements at middle age. Review of the relevant psychological literature, however, resulted in only a slim yield. The problem falls simultaneously into areas of developmental psychology (middle age) and personality theory (commitments and capacities). Only studies peripheral to or merely superficially touching on the problem could be located. Perhaps psychology's primarily autonomy-focused (e.g., individuation) and essentially amoral (in the guise of being more scientific) perspectives on person and self account for the relative lack of attention to socially responsible behavior. Sampson (1977) proposed that psychology's neglect of studies of interdependence and collaboration reflect the values of an individualistic, competitive society. The relevant literature found was written, for the most part, by clinical or social psychologists with an action orientation and concern about personal if not social change.

In the 1950s Havighurst (1952) proposed, as a primary developmental task of middle age, achieving adult civic and social responsibility, but he provided little illumination about the psychological bases for this "task." In the eighth and last stage of Erikson's (1959) "eight stages," "ego integrity" arises as the antithesis of "despair and disgust," under the dark clouds of which people are unlikely to become committed to and act upon social causes. Erikson (1959, pp. 97-99) specified: "Ego integrity . . . implies an emotional integration which permits participation by followership as well as acceptance of the responsibility of leadership: both must be learned and practiced in religion and in politics, in the economic order and in technology." In Erikson's schema, ego integrity follows upon "generativity," which concerns "interest in establishing and guiding the next generation" and includes "forms of altruistic concern and creativity." Erikson's observations, based primarily on clinical work, ring true but are not systematically grounded nor do they attend to the why of commitments in socially responsible behavior.

Maslow (1962, pp. 106-107) proposed that following "peak-experiences" "a common consequence is a feeling of gratitude," which "is expressed as or leads to an all-embracing love for everybody and everything . . . often to an impulse to do something good for the world, an eagerness to repay, even a sense of obligation." His observation is quoted because it grows out of a developmental and not a deficit concept of human motivation for doing social good—that is, not out of personal deprivation or as substitutive behavior for a lack in personal intimacy. A deficit approach was used, for example, by psychoanalytically oriented psychohistorians to explain Mahatma Gandhi's commitments and capacities as a leader in social reform in terms of his difficult relationship with his father (Muslin & Desai, 1985). With greater parsimony in his theory, Maslow suggested that a sense of social obligation may arise from thankfulness for prior enriching experience. This is the situation reached by "successful" or fulfilled and satisfied middle-aged men and women, who might then turn their attention and accumulated capacities to societal issues, with a sense of gratitude and a desire to repay.

Findings from longitudinal research on personality reveal that, by comparison with measures made earlier in their lives, middle-aged women and men become "more cognitively invested, nurturant, and intraceptive [attuned to inner messages]. . . . Our middle aged had also become considerably more giving and self-extending . . . as well as interpersonally predictable and accountable to others—or generative, to use Erikson's term" (Haan, 1981, pp. 149, 151). Here, then, in the Berkeley data, are both systematically based confirmation of Erikson's clinical inferences and evidence of psychological substrata for midlife socially responsible investments—being nurturant, self-confident, giving, self-extending, and accountable to others.

Contributions to an understanding of socially responsible behavior derive also from theory in social psychology on such matters as socialization in a democratic society and satisfactions deriving from cooperation and teamwork when, as Gordon Allport (1960, p. 189) put it, "ego-boundaries are enlarged" and members' "identity of interest are clearly understood." In a later section of this chapter on reciprocity and collaboration, these issues are pursued.

The central issues of this section on midlife social responsibility can be summarized as follows:

> The essence of social responsibility . . . is twofold. First, it involves a person's sense of obligation. The obligation is to work on behalf of or otherwise contribute to the general welfare beyond self-interest. The obligation is based on a keen awareness of one's group memberships—ultimately, the human race—and of human interdependence in society. Having obtained by the middle adult years some of the advantages of such interdependence, a middle-aged person should be ready to make some repayments. Thus, the sense of obligation. One cannot be responsible, however, for somebody or something about or for which one cannot do anything. Thus, the second component of social responsibility involves, as the dictionary says, "capabilities of fulfilling an obligation or trust." Again, the idea of competence arises. At this time of life, the middle-aged become especially crucial links in responsive environments, in supportive networks needed for attachments or collaborative communities important not only in helping but also in modeling and developing reciprocity in others. Together with the competence is its contextual base in

positions of power which the middle-aged have access to. Thus, social responsibility has a value or "should" component, experienced as obligation, and a capability or power component. (Maas, 1984, pp. 240-242)

Development and Contexts as Preconditions for Midlife Social Responsibility

Given the previously documented psychosocial space of middle-aged women and men in Western societies, it is of concern that relatively few people are involved in socially responsible activities (Lopata & Barnewolt, 1984; Meister, 1984). Such concern arises not only from principles of social justice and a good and proper life, but also from assumptions about how democracies and their freedoms are supported and extended as the locus of power in society changes.

There are widespread needs and opportunities for social participation in local community life, voluntary associations, health and educational facilities, and social change organizations. These groups and organizations address such problems as the maldistribution of resources, international relations and militarism, and environmental conservation. People in middle age are unlikely to participate in such endeavors if their previous lives have not prepared them to do so.

The chart on social development (see Table 12.1) outlines capacities and conducive contexts that are theoretically relevant to midlife social responsibility. As the discussion of this framework indicates, socially responsible commitments and capacities in middle age may be considered an ultimate outcome of an antecedent developmental sequence. Schemata of this sort suggest a far simpler and much tidier view of the life course and human development than reality's complexities so clearly reveal. Without such schemata, however, we have only a blur of confusion to orient practical work.

This schema is called the CDI approach: "C" for contexts without which development may be warped or aborted, "D" for the developing capacities themselves, and "I" for the interaction between incipient-and-emerging development and the conducive contexts that are growth-fostering. The framework is presented on the assumption that professional workers and others concerned about the future of humankind (in a socially responsible way) will find it useful (Maas, 1985). Among other uses, the CDI schema orients people to those contexts that facilitate social development and ultimately the emergence of a sense of social responsibility. By helping to

TABLE 12.1.

Development Relevant to Midlife Social Responsibility

Capacities for	Conducive Contexts	Relevance (feelings, attitudes)
attachment	supportive social networks	interpersonal security
exploration of novelty	accessible, varied, explorable arenas	curiosity fostered, to understand how, why
coping with new situations	environments responsive to coping effort	efficacy (feeling "I *can* do")
reciprocity, mutuality, collaboration	caring & sharing groups, cultures, communities	team-play spirit, group belonging, in games, with peers
intimacy, love	groups supportive of twosome caring	pleasure in caring, sharing
cooperative work	workplace fostering cooperation	pleasure in teamwork
cohabiting, coparenting	familial social supports	partnership commitments, future commitments
social responsibility in midlife	neighborhood and societal options	readiness for social participation

shape these environments, all along the life course, users of the CDI framework may be promoting, together with other desirable personal capacities, the development of socially responsible involvements in middle age. Practical implications of this schema have been presented for child welfare (Maas, 1983) and for social work as a profession, a central purpose of which should be fostering social development in both its micro and its macro meanings (Maas, 1986). In the following sections, some general practical proposals deriving from the CDI framework are discussed.

Attachment and Supportive Networks

A sense of social responsibility begins with the capacity to put oneself in the shoes of others and, more specifically, to feel empathically and sympathetically with them. To be able to do so, one must first of all be able to relate trustingly, not warily but with a sense that one can count on the other person in a dyadic relationship. Without such an ability, the messages one gets from another person are likely to be distorted by self-defensive maneuvers or efforts to test that person's trustability before one can interact more openly with or on behalf of the other person.

The ability to form trusting relationships begins normally (but not always) in the first year of life. Then, the fortunate infant repeatedly experiences appropriate responsiveness from a person who typically is a parent or caretaker. None of this is likely to be new to readers of this chapter. It is widely known that the young need not only sympathetic but also properly paced and reliably available kinds of interactions with another person who nourishes the child's early capacity for attachment.

Less widely appreciated are the propositions that (a) parent-child attachments are normally two-way or reciprocal attachments, the parent to the child as well as the child to the parent; (b) the parent him- or herself should be embedded in a personally supportive social network of friends, kin, and/or neighbors whose help enables the parent to relate to a child's needs without serious neglect (underattachment) and whose balancing relationships with the parent can prevent parental smothering care (overattachment); (c) the parent's social network can also provide opportunities for the child to develop attachments to persons in addition to the child's primary caretaker; and (d) the child's capacity for multiple attachments develops in a context in which families (parent and child) are not socially isolated but rather engaged in neighborhood and/or kinship and/or more broadly based supportive networks.

With the fostering of capacities for social responsibility as a long-range developmental goal, professional workers and others try to ensure the availability and use of social network supports, especially wherever there are young families with a new firstborn. Kin, friends, and neighbors provide informal supports, but young and particularly single parents have many needs that require formal supports. Incidentally, such programs not only are a response to immediate and normal needs, but also demonstrate and model social responsibility by people who are professional or volunteer service providers. One focus of such provisions could be the furthering of normal capacities for attachment in both parents and children, together with the generation of feelings of faith in and concern about other people, so fundamental to socially responsible involvements.

Exploration, Competence, and Responsive Contexts

Social responsibility focused on public concerns brings one into arenas beyond one's immediate family and work settings. The capacity to move out into the larger world with feelings that one can effectively modify environments has its origins and paradigms in early life.

With the sense of security or trust about one's immediate world that early attachments provide, children (and their elders) are enabled to reach out and explore new situations. The personal dynamic of curiosity, about which so little is understood, propels the young to investigate what is available in their surroundings. The more varied the accessible options, the wider are their investigations and the richer their subsequent understandings. And the more diverse the settings they can explore, the less the likelihood that new situations will seem frighteningly strange, overwhelming, and, therefore, stressful. If early inquiries are met frequently with appropriate responsiveness rather than deterrents, capacities for exploratory behavior are likely to expand and curiosity is fostered. Midlife social responsibility often begins with questions and inquiries about conditions and causes of concern, a kind of behavior for which ideally earlier experience had brought rewards and increased capacities.

In the process of exploration, the young develop other competencies, using and furthering abilities to manipulate and understand the workings of their environments. A sense of one's own competence or feelings of efficacy (White, 1960) grow when one's efforts to influence one's contexts are seen to bring about desired effects. By contrast, repeated experiences of environmental nonresponsiveness generate feelings of incompetence. Such feelings reduce efforts to change or otherwise affect one's environs. People who engage in socially responsible activities are likely to be people who have found that their efforts to modify their surroundings have been productive. They can do. There is no point in trying if the end result expected is failure.

Reciprocity and Collaboration in
Caring, Sharing Groups

The expression of social responsibility calls not only for commitments to people regarding social concerns but also for the competence to do something about the problems. The kinds of competence preschool children develop normally involve them as individuals in transactions with their immediate environments and primarily for personal gain. As children move into preadolescence during the years prior to puberty, they normally become cognitively able to take the roles of other people or develop what psychologists call the capacity for reciprocity (Maas, 1984, pp. 111-117). Reciprocity enables one to play team games (anticipating what other team members will do in a game) and experience a sense of belonging to a group of peers. One begins to be able to collaborate with peers toward commonly accepted goals.

The development of reciprocity and collaboration is fostered by familial, peer group, and other contextual supports. In groups, communities, and subcultures that encourage a caring and sharing approach to members, reciprocity is both demonstrated and rewarded. Such contexts seem essential for the growth of the ability to take the role of the other, to respond sympathetically, and to collaborate—all capacities needed by socially responsible people. For example, research on student activists of the 1960s reported on "the importance of permissive, democratic child-rearing practice in the development of the young activist," practices in which "the child is encouraged to see the relationship between his own actions and their subsequent effects on other people." In this way there was an early promotion of "the development of empathy and concern for others" (Block, Haan, & Smith, 1974, p. 93).

Children who are able to interact with peers in ways that show an awareness of their agemates' feelings have made a great step forward in their social development. Earlier, they may have used others simply as objects in the attainment of their own satisfactions, a form of behavior sometimes seen in adults too. When this appears as a person's characteristic pattern of social interaction, it probably reveals deficient capacities for reciprocity, collaboration, and any kind of socially responsible involvement (Mussen & Eisenberg-Berg, 1977; Rushton & Sorrentino, 1981).

Intimacy and Love in
Peer Relations

The experience of love normally encompasses pleasures in caring for and sharing with another person in ways that rarely occur in nonintimate relationships. This goes beyond sexual behavior to include the concerned helpfulness and ministrations in which lovers are likely to engage. Some elements of such behavior may reappear in neighborhood work with old people, battered partners, or abused children, or in other socially responsible activities on a face-to-face level with troubled people or people in trouble. With no good evidence to draw upon and thus with considerable tentativeness, it is proposed that social responsibility is likely to be exercised most effectively by adults who have (or have had) a gratifying intimate relationship. Negative instances like the lonely Secretary General of the United Nations,

Dag Hammarskjold (Auden, 1964; Urquhart, 1987) could be counterbalanced by countless others who were simultaneously and actively committed to important social causes and to a loving partner. With both commitments, one does not seek in one setting—for example, loving responses for service—what is appropriately found in the other.

Following the development of capacities for team play and collaboration toward shared goals based in reciprocity, one seems better prepared to sustain a loving relationship. Sullivan (1947) distinguished between what he called lust and love, the latter dynamic transforming concern about the welfare of the other person into an equivalent of one's concern for one's own welfare. In a loving relationship, caring and "consensual validation" and other kinds of sharing deepen a person's capacities for reciprocity and collaboration—that is, for doing on behalf of and together with another—in a dyadic relationship.

Cooperation in Workplaces

Socially responsible activity in midlife, though it may be done as a volunteer in one's leisure time and without compensation, nevertheless calls upon competencies in worklike behavior and/or work settings. Working on behalf of neighborhood youth or helping new immigrants is usually a collaborative enterprise, sometimes under formal organizational auspices. People who have learned on jobs to work conjointly with coworkers are well prepared for those aspects of volunteer efforts that require cooperation.

Any discussion of the life course leading to midlife social responsibility that fails to allude to youth's exclusion from the world of work would be seriously deficient. Youth who begin their working life with an unsuccessful search for jobs have, as one intensive interview study concluded, "few avenues or opportunities for developing a sense of responsibility and purpose" and find themselves on a course that "leads into more destructive behavior" (Reilly et al., 1982, p. 72). Work is not only a necessary means of economic support but a major integrative force for youth and adults in their relationships with their society. Democratic governments require the social participation of their citizens to survive, and fundamental to such participation are people's sense of belonging and integrative sentiments. A society that cannot provide its able members, and particularly its youth, with productive employment fosters a sense of alienation and in no way induces the feelings of indebtedness and obligation that may underlie, as suggested earlier, some people's socially responsible involvements in midlife.

Cohabiting, Coparenting, and Familial Support

Most, although not all, young adults at some time share in a familial household with a sexual partner, and most of these become parents together. On the route to a socially responsible middle age, young adults who parent a child together, increasingly with the androgynous ideals of the contemporary Western world (at least its middle classes), learn to coparent. They learn to share the responsibilities and activities, the pains and pleasures, of taking care of a young child. Although the balance of pressures still weighs more heavily on women, coparenting (or even childless cohabitation) calls upon both women and men to exercise all the capacities cited earlier: capacities for attachment, exploration of novelty, coping as an individual with new situations, reciprocity and collaboration, intimacy and love, and cooperative work. Relevant also are the feelings and attitudes of interpersonal security, interest in understanding how and why, feelings of competence, a spirit of team play, a sense of group (family, household) belonging, the pleasures of caring and sharing as a twosome (or threesome) and in teamwork.

Out of such experience—provided that extrafamilial supports are available to buttress the partners as needed—should emerge a capacity for working in twosomes useful in settings beyond the home. This entails a commitment not only to one's partner, but also a commitment to the future (as well as the present) growing out of a normal concern, for example, for what may happen to a couple's child in the years ahead and especially in the event of major catastrophes. The new future orientation of young parents feeds directly into socially responsible activities, which require more than a now-focused sense of urgency. Tomorrow's ecological conditions must be anticipated by planning and prevention today so that forests are not totally denuded, waterways irretrievably polluted, and cities made completely uninhabitable. At stake are the lives of one's children and their children, and generations beyond them. These are among the issues that the middle-aged have the psychosocial space, the capacities, and ideally the commitments to address.

Midlife Contexts for Social Responsibility

Whether and how the middle-aged use their capacities in the pursuit of social commitments depends on macro-societal and local community options. In neighborhoods where local area problems might involve the middle-aged, programs that combine the efforts of residents and professional workers may be available—or generated by concerned people (in midlife?) when such programs are not on the scene. All communities should have neutral meeting places for public discussions of existing or incipient problems, or for planning developmental or preventive programs. Schools, churches, and recreation centers provide small rooms or assembly halls for public gatherings on emergency issues. Ideally, however, clusters of neighborhood buildings like the Britannia Community Services Centre in Vancouver, Canada—housing child care, library, arts and crafts, family activity, community information, and other programs—provide local forum space (Clague, 1979). In such multiservice facilities, interested citizens and, for example, municipal bureaucrats, might meet on neutral ground and, with professional workers as resource people, work on plans and follow through on changes for improving aspects of neighborhood life.

In some situations specific populations, such as persons who have mental health problems, become both the focus and coparticipants in planning (Heginbotham, 1987). An advantage in having and using a multipurpose services center is that several such groups may simultaneously use the facilities and, in the process, through staff involvement, discover how their concerns are interrelated. Moreover, with many such planning groups in process, residents in an exploratory stage of social participation may consider several options.

There are many definitions and examples of citizen participation at a local level, from board memberships to volunteer direct services to work aimed at "a redistribution of decision making power and resources" (Hooyman, 1981, p. 114). An organizational model that makes sense at a local level calls for partnerships between nonprofessionals and professional workers, bureaucrats in the power systems of government, and local people who are most directly affected by whatever problem is being addressed (Clague, 1979; Hooyman, 1981; Meister, 1984). In this process, the collaborative capacities (in the CDI framework) of all participants are likely to be put to the test.

The options for socially responsible midlife involvements at the local level, however, are likely to reflect macro-societal values and sanctions, both codified and unwritten. There is a wide range of options in liberal democracies of the Western world, especially bearing on citizens' social participation and supportable purposes therefor. Fundamental to such values and sanctions are assumptions about freedoms that individuals in a democracy may enjoy, as well as the central purposes and, consequently, the desirable options of a democratic society. The kind of question about democracies that must be considered by socially responsible people in our times is posed by one astute political theorist, as follows:

> We should be considering whether we have been asking the wrong question all this time, in asking, as we have done, how to hold on to the liberty we have got—the liberty of possessive individualists—while moving a little towards more equality. Perhaps we should be asking, instead, whether meaningful liberty can much longer be had without a much greater measure of equality than we have hitherto thought liberty required. (Macpherson, 1973, p. 184)

As examples, increasing equality for women reduces liberties for men, just as land reform in developing nations aimed at raising the living standards of impoverished landless peasants reduces liberties for powerful landowners. Socially responsible commitments derive from principles of social justice and fundamental beliefs about the interdependence of all humankind.

In light of the CDI focus on people's developing capacities and conducive contexts for such development, additional remarks by Macpherson are relevant:

> A democratic theory must assert an equal right of individuals to develop their capacities to the fullest: an equal right merely to use the capacities each has at a given time is not equality as between those whose capacities had been stunted by external impediments and those whose capacities had not been so stunted.

> Finally we should notice that this view of capacities and their development, while it does assume that all . . . [people] are at least potentially exerters and developers of their essentially human capacities, and does therefore treat the development of capacities as a process which would go on if society placed no impediments in anyone's way, does not imply that society is only an impeding agent. It does not deny that society is also a positive agent in the development of capacities. It does not deny that every individual's human capacities are socially derived, and that their development must also be social. Human society is the medium through which human capacities are developed. A society of *some* kind is a necessary condition of the development of individual capacities. A *given* society, with all its enabling and coercive institutions, may be judged more of a help than a hindrance, or more of a hindrance than a help, at any given time. Societies have usually been both, in varying proportions. (Macpherson, 1973, p. 57)

Illustrations of Macpherson's "enabling and coercive" environments are presented as "conducive contexts" in the chart (Table 12.1) and CDI framework. These ideas could feed into deliberations and policy about the initiation and support of environments that foster the development of human capacities. Herein lies a huge arena of issues for the socially responsible to consider and act upon.

The public media sometimes provide an impetus to such service. On the cover of the May 25, 1987, issue of *Time*, the editors asked, "What Ever Happened to Ethics?" and inside (pp. 16-41) published a spread of photographs of more than fifty primarily middle-aged men and women whose morality is in doubt—former government officials, Wall Street traders, televangelists, members of the military, industrialists, bankers, and others. Following some details on the essentially self-seeking lives of these people, the editors commented on the "diminished sense of commitment" and called for "a redefinition of wants so that they serve society as well as the self" and "a new morality in which freedoms we struggled for will be counterbalanced with a sense of responsibility."

Who are in a better position than middle-aged men and women to respond to such a call? But can they do so without the prior development and contextual supports that this chapter proposed?

References

Allport, G. W. (1960). *Personality and social encounter*. Boston: Beacon.

Auden, W. H. (1964). Foreword. In D. Hammarskjold, *Markings* (pp. 9-26). London: Faber and Faber.

Baruch, G., & Brooks-Gunn, J. (1984). *Women in midlife*. New York: Plenum.

Bianchi, S. M., & Spain, D. (1986). *American women in transition*. New York: Russell Sage.

Block, J. H., Haan, N., & Smith, M. B. (1974). Activism and apathy in contemporary adolescents. In M. B. Smith (Ed.), *Humanizing social psychology* (pp. 57-94). San Francisco: Jossey-Bass.

Clague, M. (1979). The Britannia community services centre. In B. Wharf (Eds.), *Community work in Canada* (pp. 51-86). Toronto: McClelland and Stewart.

Clausen, J. A. (1981). Men's occupational careers in the middle years. In D. H. Eichorn, J. A. Clausen, N. Haan, M. P. Honzik, & P. H. Mussen (Eds.), *Present and past in middle life* (pp. 321-351). New York: Academic Press.

Erikson, E. (1959). *Identity and the life cycle*. New York: International University Press.

Giele, J. Z. (1982). Woman's work and family roles. In J. Z. Giele (Ed.), *Women in the middle years: Current knowledge and directions for research and policy* (pp. 115-150). New York: John Wiley.

Haan, N. (1981). Common dimensions of personality development: Early adolescence to middle life. In D. H. Eichorn, J. A. Clausen, N. Haan, M. P. Honzik, & P. H. Mussen (Eds.), *Present and past in middle life* (pp. 117-151). New York: Academic Press.

Havighurst, R. J. (1952). *Developmental tasks and education*. New York: McKay.

Heginbotham, C. (1987). Consumers in mental health planning: The Camden consortium. In D. Clode, C. Parker, & S. Etherington (Eds.), *Towards the sensitive bureaucracy: Consumers, welfare and the new pluralism* (pp. 105-115). Aldershot, Hants, England: Gower.

Hooyman, N. R. (1981). Strategies for citizen participation. In J. F. Jones & R. S. Pandey (Eds.), *Social development: Conceptual, methodological and policy issues* (pp. 108-138). New York: St. Martin's.

Levinson, D. J. (1978). *The seasons of a man's life*. New York: Knopf.

Long, J., & Porter, K. L. (1984). Multiple roles of midlife women: A case for new directions in theory, research and policy. In G. Baruch & J. Brooks-Gunn (Eds.), *Women in midlife* (pp. 109-159). New York: Plenum.

Lopata, H. Z., & Barnewolt, D. (1984). The middle years: Changes and variations in social role commitments. In G. Baruch & J. Brooks-Gunn (Eds.), *Women in midlife* (pp. 83-108). New York: Plenum.

Maas, H. S. (1983). *Social development, its contexts, and child welfare* (Social Work Papers, 17, pp. 1-9). Los Angeles: University of Southern California, School of Social Work.

Maas, H. S. (1984). *People and contexts: Social development from birth to old age*. Englewood Cliffs, NJ: Prentice-Hall.

Maas, H. S. (1985) The development of adult development: Recollection and reflections. In J. M. A. Munnichs et al. (Eds.), *Life-span and change in a gerontological perspective* (pp. 161-175). New York: Academic Press.

Maas, H. S. (1986). *From crib to crypt: Social development and responsive environments as professional focus* (2nd Werner and Bernice Boehm Distinguished Lectureship in Social Work). New Brunswick, NJ: Rutgers University, School of Social Work.

Maas, H. S., & Kuypers, J. A. (1974). *From thirty to seventy: A forty-year longitudinal study of life styles and personality*. San Francisco: Jossey-Bass.

Macpherson, C. B. (1973). *Democratic theory: Essays in retrieval*. Oxford: Clarendon Press.

Maslow, A. H. (1962). *Toward a psychology of being*. Princeton, NJ: Van Nostrand.

Meister, A. (1984). *Participation, associations, development, and change*. New Brunswick, NJ: Transaction.

Muslin, H., & Desai, P. (1985). The transformation in the self of Mahatma Gandi. In C. B. Strozier & D. Offer (Eds.), *The Leader: Psychohistorical essays* (pp. 111-132). New York: Plenum.

Mussen, P. H., & Eisenberg-Berg, N. (1977). *Roots of caring, sharing, and helping: The development of prosocial behavior in children*. San Francisco: Freeman.

Reilly, L. et al. (1982). *Pinball parlours in Brisbane: A study of the parlours and the young people who use them*. Unpublished manuscript.

Rushton, J. P., & Sorrentino, R. M. (Eds.). (1981). *Altruism and helping behavior: Social, personality, and developmental perspectives*. Hillsdale, NJ: Lawrence Erlbaum.

Sampson, E. E. (1977). Psychology and the American ideals. *Journal of Personality and Social Psychology, 35*, 767-782.

Stroud, J. G. (1981). Women's careers: Work, family, and personality. In D. H. Eichorn, J. A. Clausen, N. Haan, M. P. Honzik, & P. H. Mussen (Eds.), *Present and past in middle life* (pp. 353-390). New York: Academic Press.

Sullivan, H. S. (1947). *Conceptions of modern psychiatry: The first William Alanson White memorial lectures*. Washington, DC: William Alanson White Psychiatric Foundation.

Tamir, L. M. (1982). *Men in their forties: The transition to middle age*. New York: Springer.

Urquhart, B. (1987, October 1). United Nations: Hammarskjold, Thant, Waldheim. *International Herald Tribune*, p. 8.

White, R. W. (1960). Competence and the psychosexual stages of development. In M. E. Jones (Ed.), *Nebraska Symposium on Motivation 1960* (pp. 97-141). Lincoln: University of Nebraska Press.

Conclusion: Toward Applying Research Knowledge About Midlife in the Helping Professions

Martin Sundel
Ski Hunter

This chapter begins with an overview of recent attempts to integrate research findings on midlife with practice. The major questions and key findings of the volume are then examined, including their implications for practice. Crosscutting issues are also identified in regard to the generalizability of findings and gender differences. A concluding section offers suggestions for a demythologized orientation to practice with middle-aged persons.

The major gap in practitioner knowledge about middle age has been related to the lack of research; for many years there have been few studies to consult. Mental health professionals have typically relied on Freudian (Freud, 1923/1953) developmental theory to guide them in their therapeutic work. Beyond that, the primary reference to adult development has been Erikson (1950), who presented a scheme of stage-related developmental tasks to be achieved over eight life periods, including adulthood. Behavior therapists have tended to eschew stage-dependent theories of development and do not use a particular model of adult development (e.g., Gambrill, 1977; O'Leary & Wilson, 1987; Sundel & Sundel, 1982; Wolpe, 1982).

The availability of a body of empirically validated knowledge in key areas of midlife could be valuable to helping professionals concerned with assessment, treatment, and prevention of social and mental health problems of adults at midlife. Such integration has been slow to develop, however, and counseling, therapy, and direct practice texts typically include little or no content specifically dealing with middle age (e.g., Brown & Srebalus, 1988; Gambrill, 1983; Garvin & Seabury, 1984; Germain & Gitterman, 1980; Hepworth & Larsen, 1986; Ivey, Ivey, & Simek-Downing, 1987; Shulman, 1984). There is often a schism between clinical practice and human behavior courses, so that students are left to integrate practice and human development content themselves.

Mahoney and Gabriel (1987) recently noted that there is increased interest in incorporating developmental approaches in clinical practice that emphasize psychological growth and processes of change. The applicability of such knowledge would have to be tested in terms of its utility when combined with a particular psychotherapeutic or helping methodology. There are models for research-based practice in various areas, such as the University of Michigan Group Work Model (e.g., Sundel, Glasser, Sarri, & Vinter, 1985) that applies research findings from small group theory, the social psychology of interpersonal influence, and personality theory.

Helping professionals have only recently begun to explore the gap between adult development theory and practice. Various formulations of adult developmental therapy have been proposed (e.g., Carlsen, 1988; Ivey, 1986). A number of texts, edited books, and readers have been written on adult development with selected practice applications to midlife (e.g., Baruch & Brooks-Gunn, 1983; Berardo, 1982; Colarusso & Nemiroff, 1981; Howells, 1981; Nemiroff & Colarusso, 1985; Norman & Scaramella, 1980; Schlossberg, 1984; Schlossberg & Entine, 1977; Schlossberg, Troll, & Leibowitz, 1978). Recent journal articles (e.g., Simmermon & Schwartz, 1986) and the *Encyclopedia of Social Work* (Sze & Ivker, 1987) have also included midlife content in their presentations of adult development.

Practice books on midlife are rare and only a recent phenomenon. For example, Golan (1986) and Sherman (1987) have attempted to apply midlife knowledge to counseling, therapy, and social casework. Recent journal articles relevant for practice with middle-aged persons can also be found (e.g., Coche & Coche, 1986; Sands & Richardson, 1986). The dual perspective of "midlife development" and helping methodology suggests an evolutionary process in which midlife knowledge becomes increasingly applied and tested in the various practice situations encountered by helping professionals. When findings become firmly established, helping professionals can consider them with greater confidence as appropriate for their clientele.

The contributors to this volume have presented research findings or conceptual perspectives that challenge the myths surrounding their topics. The range and kinds of implications presented by the contributors vary because implications can be drawn more readily in some places than others. Also, researchers are often cautious in making recommendations for practice based on the results of their studies, especially when a field is young and lacks corroborative findings. Progress in a new field usually requires extensive generation and testing of research knowledge before new conceptual frameworks are accepted in the mainstream of practice. This volume might be considered as an evolutionary step toward making research findings on midlife available for testing in the helping professions.

Major Questions Addressed by the Volume and Key Findings

A number of midlife myths have been identified and evaluated by the contributors to this volume. We have formulated a set of 10 major questions that are addressed by the key findings. Considered together, the answers to these questions provide an alternative perspective to prevalent beliefs depicting midlife as a tumultuous pessimistic period of crisis and emotional upset, physical and intellectual decline, dissatisfaction with marriage and career, and detachment and isolation between children and their parents.

The 10 questions will be presented first and then answered individually. Chapters pertaining to the individual questions and answers will be noted in parentheses at the end of each answer.

Questions

(1) Can sexual pleasure be maintained by men and women during midlife?
(2) Does menopause cause emotional disturbance in women?
(3) Are individuals at midlife less mature in the way they think?
(4) Does intelligence decline during midlife?
(5) Does the individual at midlife experience a crisis?
(6) Does an individual's personality become dull and inflexible during midlife?
(7) Does marital satisfaction decline and divorce peak at midlife?
(8) Do the stresses of a dual-career marriage outweigh the benefits during midlife?
(9) Are middle-aged individuals isolated and alienated from their families?
(10) Is there personal development beyond self-absorption at midlife?

Question 1. Can sexual pleasure be maintained by men and women at midlife? Middle-aged men and women can continue to experience pleasurable sexual and sensual activities. Physiological changes have minimal consequences for sexual pleasure. In fact, pleasure can be enhanced by increased emphasis on sensuality, which includes intimate behaviors other than genital intercourse—for example, touching and holding. Practitioners can inform their clients about expected physiological changes but emphasize the minimal consequences of those changes for sexual competence and enjoyment. Continued sexual activity is a way of preventing decline in sexual capacity and desire. Professional helpers can also stress the importance of sensuality and its association with sexual pleasure. (See Weg, Chapter 1, and Dan and Bernhard, Chapter 2.)

Question 2. Does menopause cause emotional disturbance in women? Menopause presents few problems for most women; the "hot flash" is the only universal symptom. Vaginal changes that could interfere with sexual pleasure are uncommon, especially for women who remain sexually active. After experiencing menopause, women tend to feel more positively about both this bodily change and their overall lives. Fortunately, most women do not believe health care personnel who view menopause as creating a major emotional disturbance for women. Accurate information about menopause can be provided that portrays it as a positive experience and not disruptive to mental health. (See Dan and Bernhard, Chapter 2.)

Question 3. Are individuals at midlife less mature in the way they think? Adult thought can grow and progress beyond the formalistic, abstract, objective, youth-centered mode valued as the highest form of thought in Western society. A different mode of thought that is pragmatic, concrete, and subjective emerges in adulthood. The pragmatic mode has been considered to be a sign of regression from the more valued youth-centered mode, and has been feared as a harbinger of decline and deficit in intellectual functioning. Research has shown, however, that the pragmatic mode is a qualitative, adaptive, and mature progression—not regression—in adult thought. In other words, the emergence of the pragmatic mode can be viewed as a positive rather than negative development.

The formalistic mode is an emotionally controlled, external, and impersonal way of knowing. The pragmatic mode is a more emotional, inner, and personal way of knowing. Optimal progression in adult thought involves an integration of the two modes, a development that appears to emerge at midlife. Other progressive changes in emotional functioning are linked to this change in cognitive reorganization. The changes include greater flexibility in interpreting one's experiences; for example, an event previously assessed as negative can be reassessed in a more positive way. In addition, emotions are not "backed up" or overly controlled. Emotional experience is more fully acknowledged and examined, and more spontaneously expressed. There is less reliance on immature coping strategies such as projection, escape, avoidance, distancing, repression of emotional tension, and blaming others for one's negative emotions.

Before concluding that a pragmatic, middle-aged person has experienced decline in cognitive or emotional functioning, the professional helper can determine, instead, if the client's mode of thought is adaptive to the client's circumstances. A client who achieves integration of both the formalistic and the pragmatic modes is more likely than ever to be functioning at a maturity level for achieving positive effects from counseling, casework, or psychotherapy. Individuals who appear to have achieved such integration might also function well in leadership roles in therapy groups and self-help organizations, or assume key volunteer roles in the community or larger society. (See Labouvie-Vief and Hakim-Larson, Chapter 3.)

Question 4. Does intelligence decline during midlife? Intellectual ability continues to develop throughout the adult years. Longitudinal studies of intelligence have dramatically refuted the pessimistic findings of cross-sectional studies showing age-related decline in overall intellectual performance. The findings revealed that different intellectual abilities follow different patterns of change, with some abilities declining sooner than others.

Although age-related changes occur, they usually do not take place until the early sixties. Intellectual functioning at midlife is basically stable. In fact, some abilities (for example, verbal ability) do not even reach peak levels until late middle age. These are normative or average patterns. Individual differences can show wide variations in performance at all ages. Some individuals show significant decline in intelligence during middle age, whereas a few exceptional individuals remain stable into the eighties.

What are the conditions that accelerate premature decline and those that hold it off? Lack of mental stimulation and challenge, or inflexible attitudes, can lower intellectual performance. On the other hand, active, stimulating, and challenging engagement in life and mental flexibility hold off decline. Work is an important source of mental stimulation and challenge if it is complex and calls upon initiative and independent decision making.

Adults can benefit from stimulating environments that contribute to the maintenance and possible increase of their intellectual performance. Professional helpers can encourage adults to pursue mentally challenging learning opportunities and update the knowledge base and skills related to their employment and other areas of their lives. Educational and vocational counselors can inform middle-aged adults that they are capable of maintaining and even enhancing their intellectual abilities to pursue new learning opportunities or train for new careers. Organizational consultants can advise employers to provide job enrichment opportunities such as employee seminars, discussions, brainstorming, and other educational courses and training that provide mental stimulation, as well as encourage continued learning and mental flexibility. (See Willis, Chapter 4.)

Question 5. Does the individual at midlife experience a crisis? Mental health problems such as depression are not more common during midlife. In addition, many research studies have failed to substantiate a universal midlife crisis. Although there may be questioning of one's life and personal goals, this typically does not result in a crisis.

The notion of a midlife crisis is more associated with men than with women. The studies of men, however, indicate that their responses at midlife vary considerably on issues such as personal awareness of mortality, attaining one's career peak, and determining how to leave a legacy. All things considered, men are more highly satisfied with their jobs than ever before, most having adjusted to their achieved level rather than being bitter or disillusioned about not going further in their careers. What remains strong, however, is the desire for work that is challenging.

For men at midlife, especially those who are well educated and middle class, marital satisfaction is the primary correlate to well-being—rated higher than occupational achievement. Conventional wisdom emphasizes "climbing the career ladder" as the primary concern of men at midlife. "Midlife crisis" symptoms of depression and disillusionment might be more related to marital dissatisfaction than to unrealized career aspirations. Perhaps a more balanced look at both factors, marriage and job, could enable professional helpers to clarify the focus for their male clients.

Reevaluation of issues such as job and marriage appears to be an important task for middle-aged men. Reactions to this self-examination vary; for some men it could elicit a crisis, whereas for others there might be a lesser struggle or even a denial of the issues. For some individuals these issues might not be applicable, or if they were, they would be relatively unimportant. For example, some individuals might be content with their career achievements and feel no need for reassessment of their career status. (See Hunter & Sundel, Introduction; Chiriboga, Chapter 5; Haan, Chapter 6; and Tamir, Chapter 7.)

Question 6. Does an individual's personality become dull and inflexible during midlife? Longitudinal research studies have not supported the claim that an individual's personality is fixed in childhood and impermeable to change during middle age. Substantial change has been shown to occur at least up to the middle fifties, especially for women. Overall, an individual's personality has been found to be more fluid and adaptable than portrayed by psychoanalytic theory, which has exerted a major influence in the training of counselors, therapists, and educators in the mental heath and human service professions.

In contrast with the belief that personality change results from some inner push, personality has been found to change most markedly when life conditions are altered. The potential for personality change for individuals at midlife, therefore, depends primarily on their adaptations to changing situations. This finding also indicates that environmental change can have more immediate and clearer effects than psychodynamically oriented counseling and therapy. (See Haan, Chapter 6.)

Question 7. Does marital satisfaction decline and divorce peak at midlife? According to popular myth, marital satisfaction declines during middle age and leads to a peak in divorces during this life period. Only part of that belief has been validated by research studies: marital satisfaction declines at midlife, but divorces are less common than for couples in their teens or twenties. In fact, midlife couples are more likely to stay together than to divorce.

Marital satisfaction declines during the years of child rearing. The difficulties of handling multiple roles (for example, parent, marital partner, employee, and daughter-in-law) take away from the time couples can devote to each other. Particularly as a result of "roles overload" related to caring for children, marital quality can diminish as communication and companionship decline. These circumstances, however, suggest a key to avoiding the negative consequences of "roles overload": not letting communication and companionship drift to low levels.

Professional helpers can encourage couples to communicate and spend time with each other around issues of importance to each individual. Couples can also be informed that temporary gaps in communication and companionship are common, and that sacrifice and delayed gratification will be required from both partners. Those gaps, however great they might seem at the time, can be filled after the children leave home, thereby making it more likely that marital satisfaction will be restored. (See Rollins, Chapter 8.)

Question 8. Do the stresses of a dual-career marriage outweigh the benefits? Research studies have shown a number of benefits or rewards to individuals in dual-career marriages, such as shared economic responsibility for the family, intellectual contentment and companionship, and the challenge to be innovative and flexible in creating alternative models of marriage. The majority of women are working outside the home and their incomes are often necessary to maintain their households. Supportive organizational policies such as flex-time, parental leave, and on-site child care can help reduce the complexities of managing dual careers.

Counselors and therapists can help couples in dual-career marriages to examine not only the stresses they experience, but also resources that can help them cope with the stresses. The couple's personal and environmental resources can be identified, as well as the strengths in their relationship. The knowledge gained from this analysis can be used by the couples to formulate and choose among alternatives a strategy that best fits their situation. (See Gilbert and Davidson, Chapter 9.)

Question 9. Are middle-aged individuals isolated and alienated from their families? Research studies have refuted the myth that middle-aged individuals are isolated and alienated from their families. Most middle-aged men and women are involved with both their children and their parents. Families generally enjoy and are enriched by their intergenerational ties. The pleasure is greatest when individuals can also seek self-realization through the pursuit of independent goals.

The finding that parents and their adult children usually stay involved with each other throughout their adult lives might not always be viewed as positive. Some counselors and therapists, for example, might inappropriately label as pathology the desire of adults to remain close to their parents and grandparents. Just as middle-aged children are ready to help their parents when needed, their parents and grandparents similarly are available to help their children and grandchildren.

If both spouses are working to sustain the family, other support systems may be necessary to assist with ailing parents, such as relatives, friends, neighbors, and public or private social services. During certain career moves and other times of family instability related to child rearing or unemployment, families may need additional resources in managing crises involving older parents. Middle-aged women who work outside the home, in addition to providing care for elderly parents and in-laws, may have to enlist more active participation from men in caring for the elderly. Helping professionals can encourage middle-aged persons to be flexible and equitable in the performance of work and family roles, and to maintain a balance between the norms of self-realization and filial obligation. (See Troll, Chapter 10.)

Question 10. Is there personal development beyond self-absorption at midlife? According to popular belief, individuals at midlife are preoccupied with such things as their changing physical appearance, health status, accumulation of material wealth, and unrealized aspirations. This notion of self-absorption at midlife is countered by the alternative perspective that throughout the life course individuals encounter various challenges to perform and reperform certain tasks. The tasks involve cyclical themes (for example, nurturing and intimacy) that contribute to the evolution of an individual's personal growth and development beyond self-absorption. The cyclical theme of nurturing, for example, can resurface as a challenge at various times in one's life and assume different forms. In young adulthood nurturing might involve taking care of one's young children, whereas in middle age nurturance could involve serving as a volunteer in a hospital or a group home for individuals with mental retardation.

Individuals at midlife, particularly those who are less preoccupied with child rearing and job advancement, have time and energy to expand their interests beyond their families to community activities and social issues from local to international levels. Aside from the benefits to others, the efforts of middle-aged individuals are rewarded with enhanced personal development, which is generally defined in terms of Erik Erikson's concept of generativity.

The commitment and capability for socially responsible generativity is based on prior development of capacities such as caring, empathy, sharing, competence, and commitment to future generations. Development of those capacities requires various contextual supports, including individuals and groups who model and encourage social responsibility.

Helping professionals can encourage individuals at midlife to become involved in community activities and social issues that affect the well-being of present and future generations. In fostering such involvement, they can explain the reciprocal benefits for both the middle-aged adult and the community. Emphasis can be placed on assuming social responsibility as a means of broadening one's understanding of the community and participating to solve its problems. (See Weick, Chapter 11, and Maas, Chapter 12.)

Crosscutting Issues and Conclusions

This section will address two major crosscutting issues of the volume: concerns about the generalizability of findings and gender differences. We will conclude with suggestions for an orientation to practice with middle-aged persons.

Concerns About
Generalizability of Findings

The research studies reported in this volume involved groups of individuals; therefore, the findings might not be applicable to a specific person. Variations exist among individuals, their idiosyncratic situations, and the unique historical events that occur during their lives. Also, the predominant use of middle-class White men as subjects in the research studies raises questions about the applicability of the findings to women and different socioeconomic, racial, and ethnic groups. For example, recent research conducted on the mental health of Black persons by Rose Gibson at the University of Michigan suggested that midlife was the most tumultuous period for Blacks in terms of marital and family difficulties and emotional disturbance ("New Perspectives on Black America," 1987, p. 7).

Although the findings in this volume can be applied to the majority of middle-aged persons, exceptions can always be found. For example, sexual pleasure can decline with physical illness or psychological problems; a particular woman's experience of menopause may result in depression or other emotional disturbance; mature adult thought is not realized by every adult; intelligence can be adversely affected by factors such as educational level, malnutrition, or birth cohort; the mental health of some individuals may deteriorate; some traditional men and women might have difficulties adapting to changes in their work or parental roles; and some individuals might experience crises, get divorced, feel their life is over, and so on. Other factors have been identified that can affect variations among middle-aged persons, such as the number and intensity of social stressors or the cognitive interpretation of life events (for example, one individual might feel fortunate, another overwhelmed about the same event).

Gender Differences

Gender bias has been identified in various theories of personality. For example, classical psychoanalytic theory stereotyped the woman's personality as rigid and unchangeable, as compared with men who were considered more likely to change and develop through analysis. The legacy of such gender bias in certain theories and research studies is still evident (e.g., Gilligan, 1982). Men are still more frequently studied, and the "midlife crisis" is concerned almost entirely with middle-class, White males. Two consequences of the male bias are particularly relevant. First, the emphasis on crisis conveys an exaggerated, negative image of midlife in general. Second, because the research has often excluded women, the differences between men and women at midlife have been masked—particularly the more positive experiences of women.

The contributors to this volume pointed out gender differences at midlife that appear to favor women, such as that women experience more positive personality changes than men; women have shown greater variability in life patterns than men, who tend to be influenced more by socially defined age expectations (for example, in the development of their careers); women are more articulate and comfortable in expressing their feelings than men; and the career benefits for women in dual-career marriages seem to be greater for women than men.

Toward a Practice Orientation with
Middle-Aged Persons

The main thesis of this book is that midlife is a period of many more positives than negatives. Research findings reported in this book have shown, for example, that many middle-aged people are self-confident, assertive, outgoing, generous, nurturant, dependable, and warm. They are often more comfortable with their lives than during any previous period, and they deal with their worlds efficiently and productively. There is no significant decline for the majority of middle-aged persons in their physical, psychological, social, intellectual, or cognitive functioning. Most middle-aged people are neither stagnant nor stodgy, and they are not experiencing a "midlife crisis."

Research on midlife has been a relatively recent phenomenon emerging during the past two decades; it is now finding a niche in the developmental research spectrum including children, adolescents, young adults, and the elderly. As more research is conducted with middle-aged individuals, the studies will begin to fill in gaps in knowledge about this life period. The research findings will be interpreted by researchers, academicians, practitioners, the mass media, and the general public. Analysis and interpretation of the findings by helping professionals and others will lead to guides for applying them in assessment, prevention, and intervention.

The major conclusion of this book for helping professionals is that they endeavor to become knowledgeable about development at midlife to avoid negative stereotypes and biases about middle-aged people. Such knowledge can also help middle-aged practitioners become more aware of their own stereotyped views of themselves that could be detrimental if projected onto midlife clients.

Middle-aged persons, like all people, are diverse in culture, social class, race, and ethnicity. By growing older they have also become more different from others in their age group because of varying life events and experiences, as well as the interpretations given to them. Practitioners can avoid misperceptions and faulty judgments of middle-aged persons by viewing them less on the basis of their chronological age than on their particular circumstances and how they interpret them. Professional helpers can also encourage their clients to act in more flexible ways and to make choices among diverse alternatives.

College courses, continuing education workshops and seminars, and agency in-service training can be used to disseminate midlife knowledge to students, practitioners, and the general public. Midlife content can also be included in certification and licensing examinations for professional practice.

Although at present there is no journal that deals exclusively with middle age, a number of journals in the area of adult development periodically publish pertinent articles. These journals include the following: *Aging and Human Development, Developmental Psychology, The Gerontologist, Human Development, International Journal of Aging and Human Development, Journal of Applied Developmental Psychology,* and *Journal of Gerontology.* The professional journals in social work, psychology, nursing, education, medicine, and the various counseling professions (for example, pastoral counselors, marriage and family counselors) also include occasional content on middle age. Consulting these journals is a way of keeping abreast of new developments in the field until the emergence of a specialty journal on midlife.

Ultimately, the adoption of a demythologized orientation to practice will be achieved through the practitioner's integration of updated empirical knowledge with the personal experiences and perspectives of their clients. We hope this book contributes toward that end.

References

Baruch, G., & Brooks-Gunn, J. (Eds). (1983). *Women in midlife.* New York: Plenum.

Berardo, F. M. (Ed.). (1982). Middle and late life transitions. *The Annals of the American Academy of Political and Social Science, 464,* 47-56.

Brown, D., & Srebalus, D. J. (1988). *An introduction to the counseling professions.* Englewood Cliffs, NJ: Prentice-Hall.

Carlsen, M. B. (1988). *Meaning-making: Therapeutic processes in adult development.* New York: Norton.

Coche, J. M., & Coche, E. (1986). Leaving the institutional setting to enter private practice: A mid-life crisis resolution. *Psychotherapy in Private Practice, 4*(3), 43-50.

Colarusso, C. A., & Nemiroff, R. A. (1981). *Adult development.* New York: Plenum.

Erikson, E. H. (1950). *Childhood and society.* New York: Norton.

Freud, S. (1953). *The ego and the id. Standard edition of the complete psychological works of Sigmund Freud* (Vol. 19, pp. 3-66) (Trans. and Ed., James Strachey). London: Hogarth Press. (Original work published 1923)

Gambrill, E. (1977). *Behavior modification: Handbook of assessment, intervention, and evaluation.* San Francisco: Jossey-Bass.

Gambrill, E. (1983). *Casework: A competency-based approach.* Englewood Cliffs, NJ: Prentice-Hall.

Garvin, C. D., & Seabury, B. A. (1984). *Interpersonal practice in social work: Processes and procedures.* Englewood Cliffs, NJ: Prentice-Hall.

Germain, C. B., & Gitterman, A. (1980). *The life model of social work practice.* New York: Columbia University Press.

Gilligan, C. (1982). *In a different voice: Psychological theory and women's development.* Cambridge, MA: Harvard University Press.

Golan, N. (1986). *The perilous bridge: Helping clients through mid-life transitions.* New York: Free Press.

Hepworth, D. H., & Larsen, J. A. (1986). *Direct social work practice: Theory and skills.* Chicago, IL: Dorsey.

Howells, J. G. (Ed.). (1981). *Modern perspectives in the psychiatry of middle age.* New York: Brunner/Mazel.

Ivey, A. E. (1986). *Developmental therapy.* San Francisco: Jossey-Bass.

Ivey, A. E., Ivey, M. B., & Simek-Downing, L. (1987). *Counseling and psychotherapy: Integrating skills, theory, and practice* (2nd ed.). Englewood Cliffs, NJ: Prentice-Hall.

Mahoney, M. J., & Gabriel, T. J. (1987). Psychotherapy and the cognitive sciences: An evolving alliance. *Journal of Cognitive Psychotherapy, An International Quarterly, 1*(1), 39-59.

Nemiroff, R. A., & Colarusso, C. A. (1985). *The race against time: Psychotherapy and psychoanalysis in the second half of life.* New York: Plenum.

New perspectives on Black America. (1987, November-December). *Research News,* pp. 2-7.

Norman, W. H., & Scaramella, T. J. (Eds.). (1980). *Midlife: Developmental and clinical issues.* New York: Brunner/Mazel.

O'Leary, K. D., & Wilson, G. T. (1987). *Behavior therapy: Application and outcome.* Englewood Cliffs, NJ: Prentice-Hall.

Sands, R. G., & Richardson, V. (1986). Clinical practice with women in their middle years. *Social Work, 31*(1), 36-43.

Schlossberg, N. K. (1984). *Counseling adults in transition: Linking practice with theory.* New York: Springer.

Schlossberg, N. K., & Entine, A. D. (1977). *Counseling adults.* Monterey, CA: Brooks/Cole.

Schlossberg, N. K., Troll, L. E., & Leibowitz, Z. (1978). *Perspectives on counseling adults: Issues and skills.* Monterey, CA: Brooks/Cole.

Sherman, E. (1987). *Meanings in mid-life transitions.* Albany: State University of New York Press.

Shulman, L. (1984). *The skills of helping: Individuals and groups* (2nd ed.). Itasca, IL: F. E. Peacock.

Simmermon, R., & Schwartz, K. M. (1986). Adult development and psychotherapy: Bridging the gap between theory and practice. *Psychotherapy, 23*(3), 405-410.

Sundel, M., Glasser, P., Sarri, R., & Vinter, R. (Eds.). (1985). *Individual change through small groups* (2nd ed.). New York: Free Press.

Sundel, M., & Sundel, S. S. (1982). *Behavior modification in the human services: A systematic introduction to concepts and applications* (2nd ed.). Englewood Cliffs, NJ: Prentice-Hall.

Sze, W. C., & Ivker, B. (1987). Adulthood. In *Encyclopedia of social work* (18th ed., pp. 75-89). Silver Spring, MD: National Association of Social Workers.

Wolpe, J. (1982). *The practice of behavior therapy.* New York: Pergamon.

About the Contributors

Linda A. Bernhard is Assistant Professor in the College of Nursing and Center for Women's Studies at the Ohio State University. She earned her Ph.D. in Nursing Sciences, with an emphasis on Women's Health, from the University of Illinois at Chicago in 1986. Her major research interest is women's experience of hysterectomy, including conditions and symptoms leading to hysterectomy and outcomes related to hysterectomy.

David A. Chiriboga is Associate Professor and Director, Graduate Studies Program, School of Allied Health Sciences, University of Texas Medical Branch, Galveston, Texas. For over 17 years, he was on the faculty of the Department of Psychiatry, University of California, San Francisco, where with Marjorie Fiske and Majda Thurnher he conducted a series of longitudinal studies on the impact of normative and nonnormative transitions across the life course. His current research focuses on the stresses experienced by adult child caregivers of Alzheimer's victims.

Alice J. Dan is a psychologist and Associate Professor in the College of Nursing and the School of Public Health, University of Illinois at Chicago. She earned her Ph.D. in Human Development at the University of Chicago. Her major research interest is women's health, especially the menstrual cycle. She was a founder of the Society for Menstrual Cycle Research. She is currently conducting research on physical activity, hormonal changes, and bone integrity in midlife women. She has edited several volumes of papers from conferences of the Society for Menstrual Cycle Research.

Sherwin Davidson is Assistant Dean of Continuing Education and Director of the Center for Adult Learning and Career Change at the University of Utah. She is also Adjunct Assistant Professor in the Department of Educational Psychology and Editor of the *Colleague*, a quarterly publication on lifelong learning. Her research interests include friendship among women and adult career exploration as a metaphor for personal change. Her current focus is on work as a central organizing principle in adult life.

Lucia Albino Gilbert is Professor of Educational Psychology at the University of Texas at Austin and teaches in the department's doctoral program in counseling psychology. She is author of the book *Men in Dual-Career Families: Current Realities and Future Prospects* and she edited a special issue of *The Counseling Psychologist* on the topic of dual-career families. She serves on the editorial boards of the *Journal of Counseling Psychology* and *Professional Psychology* and is Associate Editor of *Psychology of Women Quarterly*.

Norma Haan was a research psychologist who worked for some 25 years with the long-term longitudinal data supplied by the Oakland Growth and Guidance Studies at the Institute of Human Development, University of California, Berkeley. She was a recipient of Research Scientist Awards from the National Institute of Mental Health beginning in 1979. She is the author or coauthor of several books, including *Coping and Defending* and *On Moral Grounds*. She also was coeditor of *Present and Past in Midlife*, which presented comprehensive analyses of the Institute of Human Development's longitudinal work. Editor's note: Sadly, Dr. Haan died in July, 1988.

Julie Hakim-Larson received her Ph.D. in life-span developmental psychology from Wayne State University in 1984. Since then, she has served as Research Associate at Wayne State University on a project involving emotional regulation from adolescence through older adulthood. She is also Lecturer of Psychology at Eastern Michigan University. Her research interests include postformal cognitive development, emotional development in adulthood, and parent-child interaction.

Ski Hunter is Professor in the Graduate School of Social Work at the University of Texas at Arlington. She received her Ph.D. in Social Work from the Ohio State University in 1972. She has written a number of journal articles, the most recent of which focused on the results of a national study of the careers of social work educators. She teaches a course on adult development and her current research interest is in the area of midlife myths.

Gisela Labouvie-Vief was born in Germany and attended the University of Saarland from 1964 to 1968. She received her graduate training at West Virginia University, where she earned a Ph.D. in life-span development in 1972. Since 1976 she has been on the faculty of Wayne State University, where she is Professor of Psychology. Her research has focused on adaptive cognitive changes in adulthood. She has published major reviews and theoretical contributions on the topic of progressive transformation in adult thought.

Henry S. Maas, Ph.D., Professor Emeritus, University of British Columbia, was previously Professor, Social Welfare, University of California, Berkeley, and Associate Director, Institute of Human Development; Assistant Professor, Committee on Human Development, University of Chicago; and Research Associate, Washington School of Psychiatry. He is the author of *People and Contexts: Social Development from Birth to Old Age*, and *From Thirty to Seventy: A Forty-Year Longitudinal Study of Adult Life Styles and Personality* (with J. Kuypers).

Boyd C. Rollins is Professor of Sociology and Associate of the Family and Demographic Research Institute at Brigham Young University. He received his Ph.D. from Cornell University in Child Development, Family Relationships, and Sociology. For several years he served as director of the Interdepartmental Family Studies Ph.D. Program at Brigham Young University. His published research is primarily in the areas of marital quality and parent-child relationships.

Martin Sundel is the Roy E. Dulak Professor in the Graduate School of Social Work, the University of Texas at Arlington. He received his Ph.D. in Social Work and Psychology from the University of Michigan in 1968, and has published extensively on the application of behavioral science knowledge to the helping professions. He is coauthor of *Behavior Modification in the Human Services* and *Be Assertive*, and coeditor of *Assessing Health and Human Service Needs* and *Individual Change Through Small Groups* (second edition). He is currently interested in midlife issues involving helping professionals and their clients, and in the integration of research findings on midlife with the caregiving approaches and methodologies of health and human service providers.

Lois M. Tamir received her Ph.D. from the University of Michigan in Developmental Psychology. At the University of Michigan she worked as Research Fellow at the Institute for Social Research, analyzing national data on the family life cycle, men at middle age, and old age. Her book *Men in Their Forties* represents a portion of these national survey results. She currently is Clinical Assistant Professor of Psychiatry, Division of Psychology at the University of Texas Southwestern Medical Center, Dallas.

Lillian E. Troll is Professor Emeritus of Psychology, Rutgers University, and is currently affiliated with the University of California, San Francisco. She received her Ph.D. from the University of Chicago in Psychology and

Human Development. She is a Fellow of the Gerontological Society of America and is on the editorial boards of *Psychology and Aging* and *The Gerontologist*. Her major publications include *Early and Middle Adulthood*; *Looking Ahead: A Woman's Guide to the Problems and Joys of Growing Older* (with J. Israel and K. Israel); *Perspectives on Counseling Adults* (with N. Schlossberg and Z. Liebowitz); *Child Influences on Marital and Family Interactions*; *Families of Later Life* (with S. Miller and R. C. Atchley); *Continuations: Development after 20*; and *Family Issues in Current Gerontology*.

Ruth B. Weg is Professor of Gerontology (biology) and Research Associate at Andrus Gerontology Center, University of Southern California. She received her Ph.D. at the University of Southern California in Biology/Physiology. Her published work includes *Nutrition in the Later Years*; *An Invitation—to Total Health in the Mature Years*; *Sexuality in the Later Years: Roles and Behavior*; and a number of book chapters and journal articles.

Ann Weick is Dean of the School of Social Welfare, University of Kansas. She earned her Ph.D. at Brandeis University. Her publications include the edited book *Women, Power and Change* (with S. Vandiver), and articles and chapters on processes of individual and social change in the areas of human development, health care, and women's issues. Her work also includes publications on paradigm research and inquiry.

Sherry L. Willis received her Ph.D. in Educational Psychology from the University of Texas at Austin in 1972. She is currently Professor of Human Development in the College of Health and Human Development at Pennsylvania State University. Her research interests and publications focus on cognitive development across the life span. Recently, she has been studying issues related to professional obsolescence and updating with midcareer college faculty.